Editors
Martin Banham
James Gibbs
& Femi Osofisan

Guest Editor
David Kerr

Reviews Editor
Martin Banham
Emeritus Professor, University of Leeds

Associate Editors
Eckhard Breitinger
Forststr. 3, 95488 Eckersdorf, Germany

John Conteh-Morgan
Dept of French & Italian, Ohio State University, 248 Cunz Hall, 1841 Millikin Rd,
Columbus, Ohio 43210-1229, USA

Hansel Ndumbe Eyoh
PO Box 8222, University of Buea, Buea, Cameroon

Frances Harding
SOAS, Thornhaugh St, Russell Square, London WC1H OX9, UK

Masitha Hoeane
Wits Technikon, PO Box 1106, Aukland Park 2006, South Africa

David Kerr
Fine & Performing Arts Department, Chancellor College, University of Malawi, PO Box 290, Zomba, Malawi

Amandina Lihamba
Dept of Fine & Performing Arts, PO Box 35051, University of Dar es Salaam, Tanzania

Olu Obafemi
Student Affairs Unit, PMB 1515, University of Ilorin, Ilorin, Nigeria

Ian Steadman
Faculty of Arts, University of Witwatersrand, PO Wits 2050, Johannesburg, South Africa

Titles already published in the series:
African Theatre in Development
African Theatre: Playwrights & Politics
African Theatre: Women
African Theatre: Southern Africa

In production, a special issue of *African Theatre*
Soyinka: Blackout, Blowout & Beyond

Contributions are invited for the forthcoming title:
African Theatre: Young People & Performance

Articles not exceeding 5,000 words should be submitted preferably on disk and always accompanied by a double-spaced hard copy.

Format: either IBM or Apple, 3.5 inch floppy disks, preferably in Word for Windows, Word (DOS) 6, Word Perfect 5.1 for DOS or WordStar 5.5. If using Apple format please save all files as Word for Macintosh version 6.0.1 or lower if possible. Please label all files and disks clearly. Typewritten submissions may be considered in exceptional circumstances if they follow the standard double-spaced format.

Style: Preferably use UK rather than US spellings. Underline or italicise titles of books or plays. Use single inverted commas except for quotes within quotes. Type notes at the end of the text on a separate sheet. Do not justify the right hand-margins.

References should follow the style of this volume (Surname date: page number) in text. All references should then be listed at the end of article in full:
Surname, name, date, *title of work* (place of publication: name of publisher)
Surname, name, date, 'title of article' in surname, initial (eds) *title of work* (place of publication: publisher).
or Surname, name, date, 'title of article', *Journal*, vol., no: page number.

Reviewers should provide full bibliographic details, including the extent, ISBN and price.

Copyright: Please ensure, where appropriate, that clearance has been obtained from copyright holders of material used. Illustrations may also be submitted if appropriate and if accompanied by full captions and with reproduction rights clearly indicated. It is the responsibility of the contributors to clear all permissions.

All submissions should be accompanied by a brief biographical profile. The editors cannot undertake to return material submitted and contributors are advised to keep a copy of all material sent in case of loss in transit.

Editorial address
8 Victoria Square, Bristol BS8 4ET, UK • james.gibbs@uwe.ac.uk
Books for Review & Review articles
Jane Plastow, Reviews Editor, *African Theatre*, School of English,
University of Leeds, Leeds LS2 9JT, UK • plastow@english.novell.leeds.ac.uk

African Theatre
Southern Africa

Editors
Martin Banham
James Gibbs
& Femi Osofisan

Guest Editor
David Kerr

Reviews Editor
Martin Banham

James Currey
OXFORD

Africa World Press
TRENTON, NJ

David Philip
CAPE TOWN

First published in 2004 in the United Kingdom by
James Currey Ltd
73 Botley Road
Oxford OX2 0BS

and in North America by
Africa World Press
541 W. Ingham Avenue, Suite B
Trenton, NJ 08638

and in South Africa by
David Philip
an imprint of New Africa Books (Pty) Ltd
99 Garfield Road
Kenilworth, Cape Town

British Library Cataloguing in Publication Data
Southern Africa. - (African theatre)
    1. Theatre - Africa, Southern
    I. Banham, Martin   II. Gibbs, James   III. Osofisan, Femi
    IV. Kerr, David
    792'.0968

ISBN 0-85255-597-0 (James Currey paper)

Library of Congress Cataloging-in-Publication Data
A catalog record for this book is available from the Library of Congress.

Typeset in 10/11 pt Monotype Bembo by Long House, Cumbria, UK
Printed and bound in the United States

Contents

Playscript

Book Reviews

Notes on Contributors

Kennedy Chinyowa is a lecturer in African Drama at the University of Zimbabwe, currently completing his PhD at the Centre for Applied Theatre Research, Griffith University, Brisbane, Australia. His interests and publications centre round children's theatre/games, storytelling and indigenous ritual theatre.

Judy El Bushra has worked in the field of community development in Africa for twenty years, specialising most recently in research on gender and conflict and on development methodologies. Her interest in Theatre for Development led to a Masters dissertation for the University of Leeds, from which the material presented in this issue was prepared.

Athol Fugard is South Africa's most well-known, frequently performed and prolific playwright. Among his famous plays are *Bloodknot*, *Boesman and Lena*, *Hello and Goodbye* and *Master Harold and the Boys*. With John Kani and Winston Ntshona he created the classic works of anti-apartheid resistance theatre, *Sizwe Bansi Is Dead* and *The Island*.

Yvette Hutchison is a South African currently lecturing at King Alfred's College, University of Southampton. Since 1992 she has been the assistant editor of *Southern African Theatre Journal* and has co-edited books on African theatre with Kole Omotoso and Eckhard Breitinger. Her research interests include: the relationship between African theatre/performance and history/memory, intercultural theatre as defined by its ideological and social determinates, and the impact of orality on South African theatre.

David Kerr is a playwright, director, film-maker and poet, who has taught at several universities in Southern Africa, specialising in socially committed theatre/media. The author of *African Popular Theatre* and *Dance, Media Entertainment and Popular Theatre in South East Africa*, he is currently Professor of Drama at the University of Malawi.

Cont Mhlanga founded Amakhosi Theatre Productions in 1980, in Bulawayo. Since that time Amakhosi has become Zimbabwe's best known theatre company, touring extensively both in Zimbabwe and abroad. Mhlanga has been both director and playwright for the group, writing a string of award-winning plays including, *Children, Children* (1983), *Nansi le ndoda* (1986) and *Stisha!* (1990). His intention has always been primarily to serve the communities of the 'povo' (poor) and to make art which provokes thought and change.

Luís Mitras is a South African at present based in Lisbon. He has published on Lusophone literatures, and translated novels, short stories and poetry from Portuguese and Spanish. He is adjunct Associate Professor at the European Division of the University of Maryland.

Nomhle Nkonyeni is an actress, director and author with a vast experience of South African theatre, dating back to the Serpent Players in the late 1960s. She has performed ground-breaking roles in plays by Athol Fugard, Zakes Mda, Fatima Dike and many others. She is also well-known for her roles in South African soap operas, such as *Egoli* and *Generations*, as well as in such feature films as *Chikken Bizness*.

Dennis Walder, Professor of Literature at the Open University (U.K.), is the author of the first full-length study of Athol Fugard, whose plays he has also edited for Oxford University Press. His latest book on Fugard is published in the Writers and their Work Series for the British Council, and the 2nd edition of his *Literature in the Modern World* is forthcoming in 2003.

Terence Zeeman is a lecturer in Theatre Studies at the University of Ulster (Northern Ireland). He has been the executive director of the National Theatre of Namibia (1991–93), Head of Drama at the University of Namibia (1993–95). He is the editor of *Goats, Oranges and Skeletons* (New Namibia Books, 2000) and *New Namibia Plays*, Volumes 1 & 2, (2000–2002), and *Action: A Drama Manual for Namibian Students* (2003)

Obituary
Yaw Asare
1953–2002

JAMES GIBBS

The Ghanaian playwright, director and choreographer (Alphonse) Yaw Asare, who died in Accra on 1 August 2002 at the age of 48, was among the most versatile and accomplished of the moving spirits active in the Ghanaian theatre. He is probably best known for *Leopard's Choice*, the first major play presented at the National Theatre in Accra (1993), and for *Ananse in the Land of Idiots*, a production that delighted audiences and held the stage for several years in the mid-1990s. Asare enjoyed international renown as a result of *Secret of an Ancient Well* (1998), produced both in English and French, and *Desert Dreams*, which he co-directed with Fulbright Scholar Marlon Bailey (1999). Other international links included his choreography for Femi Osofisan's *Nkrumah ni ... Africa Ni* (1994), organising a workshop on Suzuki Training Techniques with Martinez Fernandes (1994), and being a resource person for the Workshop for Young Theatre Directors that was part of MASA (Abidjan) (1999).

Quite early in his career, Asare made a major contribution to young people's theatre in Ghana by leading the National Youth Theatrical Ensemble to North Korea (1989). He subsequently became a leading figure in popular theatre and in theatre for development in the country. He was called on as a specialist by numerous organisations, and his outstanding achievements as a scholar and writer were recognised by the Kwame Nkrumah Prize for Excellence in African Studies (1992) and the Arts Critics and Reviewers Association of Ghana (ACRAG) Playwright of the Year Award for 1997.

Born at Nkonya-Tayi in the Volta Region, Asare attended primary school there and middle school at Nkonya-Ahenkro, before moving to Nkonya Secondary School ('O' levels, 1971). Further education at St Francis Teacher Training College (TTC), Hohoe (1971–3, Certificate A, post-secondary) was followed by three years as a teacher in Pedeku-Ada and a Diploma in Theatre Arts, with dance as a major subject, at the School of Performing Arts (SPA), Legon. After another three years in teaching, split between Agogo TTC and Nkonya Secondary, Asare returned to Legon where he successfully undertook a degree in English and Theatre Arts (1982–6).

Always eager to be involved with education, Asare subsequently taught in the SPA, with a spell (1988–9) at the National Commission on Culture, before completing an M Phil in African Studies at Legon, specialising in African oral performance arts (1990–3). In 1994, I shared an office with him while we were both teaching at the SPA. Later that year, he moved to the National Theatre, and for five years was the artistic director of the resident drama company, Abibigromma. During that time his output included, in addition to plays already mentioned, *King Kokroko* (1994), *Bride of the Gods* (1996), *The Choice* (1996), and *Ananse and the Price of Greed* (TV 1996).

Asare returned to Legon in 1999, where he continued to write for newspapers, the stage, radio, television and video, and, in 2000, founded a campus-based experimental theatre company, Dawuro Africa. Before ill-health overtook him, Asare was full of plans for furthering his education by doing a PhD which would draw on his research into folklore and popular performance, and link up with the productions he was putting on. Indeed, he was due to travel to the University of California, Santa Barbara, on 18 August 2002 to begin his doctoral work as a Fulbright Scholar.

The foregoing attests to the energy, range, versatility and dedication that impressed all who knew Yaw Asare. He is sorely missed by his many friends, and by his grieving family. Members of the wider community of those concerned with the performing arts in Ghana mourn his untimely passing. Too young, Yaw has danced and joined his ancestors; too soon, his name has been added to the list of the illustrious departed who have enriched the Ghanaian theatre.

Introduction

DAVID KERR

My editorial brief for this issue was to publish material on Southern African theatre that did not solely reflect mainstream South African drama (about which so much has already been written) but beamed the spotlight on some of the geographical and methodological byways of the region. As expected, I received many submissions about South African theatre, most of which I had to refuse for the above reasons. The resulting collection is still not representative of Southern Africa (nothing from Botswana, Lesotho, Malawi, Mozambique or Zambia), but still does throw windows open to some areas of Southern African theatre hitherto very inaccessible to most readers. In addition, the Noticeboard section fills in some of the geographical gaps.

The presence of two articles about Angola addresses the almost total ignorance, among anglophone readers, of theatre from lusophone Africa. The presence of Mozambican groups such as Teatro Ola at recent Community Theatre Festivals run by the Market Theatre Laboratory in Johannesburg has at least given some exposure to Mozambican drama in the rest of the region. Angolan theatre, however, is virtually unknown. The two articles represent very different aspects of Angolan performance, perhaps reflective of their contrasting resource bases. Judy El Bushra's article deals with the relatively well-trodden field of Theatre for Development. However, the familiar issues (didacticism, NGO funding, a reluctance to engage in evaluation) do not disguise major differences, particularly the prominence of the army and the importance of churches in the training of actors and funding of productions.

One interesting contrast between El Bushra's account of community-based theatre and Mitras's analysis of a mainstream play by José Mena Abrantes is the question of outside influence. El Bushra describes a cultural milieu quite isolated from influence, both from the rest of Southern Africa and from other lusophone countries (such as Brazil). Mitras, by contrast, places *Sequeira, Luís Lopes ou o Mulato dos Prodígios* within an Atlantic lusophone cosmopolitan culture that ranges from Brazil through Portugal, Cape Verde and Guinea-Bissau to Angola. The Mena Abrantes play, with its postmodern questioning of historical truth, speaks to an urbane, multicultural, festival-oriented set of audiences. Mitras's article itself reflects the quizzical, ambiguous, non-committal nature of the play.

Kennedy Chinyowa's article on Shona storytelling is in stark contrast. In *Sequeira*, and Mitras's article about it, indigenous African culture is distanced through a historicising filter (seventeenth-century African kingdoms) and symbolism (the magic stone, which syncretises African and Catholic associations). In Chinyowa's article, on the other hand, precolonial African performance modes are foregrounded. He shows how cultural markers such as community participation and social control, present in indigenous Shona storytelling performance, have survived colonisation and urbanisation to find reinvigorated expression in Zimbabwean community and children's theatre. The Chinyowa emphasis flags up issues – such as educational drama, cultural continuity, performance exchange and globalisation – that no doubt will be explored in more detail in a later volume of *African Theatre* focusing on young people and performance.

Namibia, like Angola, is another geographical area about whose drama very little, until recently, has been published. Considering that literary drama as an inclusive activity has really only been popular since a little before Namibia's independence in 1980, its theatre has shown some extraordinary variety and experimentation. The play which Terence Zeeman highlights (Vickson Hangula's *The Show Isn't Over Until...*) is, like *Sequeira*, a postmodern fable centring on the rehearsal of a play and themes of creativity in the multiracial cast performing it. Where the Mena Abrantes play looks for contemporary meaning in the distant past, however, Hangula's examines up-to-the-minute Namibian issues such as racism, dictatorship and censorship. *The Show Isn't Over Until....* perhaps indicates a tradition in Southern African political theatre emerging in the 1990s that goes beyond the full-frontal, anti-apartheid radicalism of the 1970s and 1980s. Hangula's play gains much of its political bite from the irony the author is able to generate through tension between the actors' roles and their own characters, made more complex by the fact that the real actors are playing both 'actors' and 'characters'. Zeeman places that complexity within a broader theory of theatrical representation.

Dennis Walder's interview with Athol Fugard seems to be as mainstream an entry as we could possibly find. One reason for including it is that Athol Fugard assured Walder that this would be positively his (Fugard's) last interview – too good a scoop for *African Theatre* to lose, particularly as Walder has probed some of Fugard's less critically exposed, more recent productions. Perhaps having one mainstream contribution also helps orientate the other more 'marginal' articles.

The interview with Nomhle Nkonyeni provides a fascinating contrast to Fugard's, and continues a trend started with Adeline Ama Buabeng's interview in *African Theatre: Women*, in which actors and other practitioners are focused on, as well as playwrights. Nkonyeni's first acting break came with the Serpent Players, and she provides a fascinating alternative story to the standard history of those early years. Her highly politicised version of the Serpent Players and her later career adds a refreshingly subaltern voice, from a Pan-African Congress and Black Consciousness perspective, to the broader South African theatre narrative. She is particularly vivid in her reproduction of the difficult political choices faced before 1994, by professional black actors who were committed to the struggle against apartheid.

Yvette Hutchison's article on museum sites also moves in a direction that takes her far from mainstream South African theatre. Much recent post-modern experimental theatre in Europe and America takes the form of 'site-specific' performance, where the cultural, architectural, ecological or atmospheric associations of a space invest the performance with unique ambience. Hutchison shows how curators of historically significant museum sites in South Africa have attempted to bridge the gaps between tourism, 'truth and reconciliation' and public memory in order to create a performance mode which explores South Africa's recent violent and racially divided past for the understanding both of tourists, and more importantly, South Africa's post-1994 multicultural citizenry. Despite its postmodern credentials, such theatre also has its roots in African traditions of historical re-enactment (as found, for example, in spirit possession and heroic poetry) by creating a space where the dead can interact with the living for the continuity of community identity. As with Theatre for Development in the 1980s, this type of performance makes an uncomfortable and sometimes morally disturbing transgression of the line between 'reality' and representation.

The play text in this issue of *African Theatre* differs from those in earlier issues in that it is not very recent. It is, however, a key text for understanding Southern African theatre. Cont Mhlanga's *Workshop Negative*, which was published in a rather obscure and now out-of-print Zimbabwean version, was a 1986 *cause célèbre*. At that time theatre in Zimbabwe could be divided roughly into two major institutional groupings, those associated with the National Theatre Organisation (NTO), which had its origins in the conventional formal theatre tradition established by whites during the colonial period, and the anti-imperialist, socialist-oriented theatre associated with the Zimbabwean Association of Community Theatres (ZACT). Under the leadership of Susan Hains, the NTO tried to shake off its racist past. Mhlanga's earlier siNdebele play, *Nansi le ndoda* (Here is the Man) performed at the NTO festival, scandalised many white members of the audience, and caused some white theatre groups to drop out of the organisation in protest at the success of an African language play. *Workshop Negative*'s attack on white racism and on government neglect of industrial workers managed to alienate two powerful sectors of society, white business and the government. The latter was scandalised because the play's messages, a mixture of leftist solidarity and calls for racial reconciliation, made broad accusations that the government's own declared socialist policy was hypocritical. Powerful ZACT activists accused Mhlanga of oversimplification. *Workshop Negative* caused a huge national furore and extensive debate in the media. This pivotal play provides insights into the ambiguities and complexities thrown up by the process of decolonisation in Southern Africa.

As in previous volumes, this issue of *African Theatre* contains one of James Gibbs's fact-packed Noticeboard sections. This provides an indication of what is happening throughout the region, not just in the countries under focus in the main articles. Unfortunately, however, this will be the last issue to contain a Noticeboard section. The long gap between the gathering of the information and the final publication has tended to make the information somewhat out of date. Hopefully, information of recent productions will still be covered through play reviews. Potential critics are urged to send reviews not just of published play texts, but also of play or dance performances.

Staging Angola's Early History
Sequeira R. Luís Lopes or the Wondrous Mulatto by José Mena Abrantes (1993)

LUÍS MITRAS

The play *Sequeira R. Luís Lopes ou o Mulato dos Prodígios* (Sequeira, Luís Lopes, or The Wondrous Mulatto) was written by Angolan playwright and director José Mena Abrantes in 1991 and performed for the first time in 1993. *The Wondrous Mulatto*, the name by which we are going to refer to the play, is a good point of entry for those wishing to become more familiar with what has been happening in Angolan theatre in recent years. The play is well crafted and the theatrical performance reveals an intelligent handling of theatrical space; it is a play which 'translates' well into the theatre.

Another reason for the play's importance is the way it focuses on history and the representation of the historical. *The Wondrous Mulatto* centres on the real-life figure of Luís Lopes Sequeira, a seventeenth-century mulatto military officer who worked in the service of Portuguese colonial power in Angola. The story of his rise and fall is enacted on stage, but various events from his life are framed by discursive interludes in which the actors pose questions about aspects of his life that they either have acted out or intend to explore. The questions they ask turn on issues such as whether the past can ever be retrieved, or whether it can be free of the ideological complicity of the person who is telling the story. They wonder whether the figure of Luís Lopes, a person who has come down to us through the hagiographic portraits issued by successive generations of colonialist historians and ideologues, can ever be reclaimed as a forerunner of a national, non-tribal Angolan identity.

In the process of presenting and debating the life of this semi-legendary historical figure the actors exploit all the legendary elements that accrued to the portrait of Sequeira, and the result is a play full of fantastical elements. There are apparitions of the Virgin Mary, magical stones and even alien bird-men. But these are not gratuitous displays of the fantastical, for most of them are elements that have come down to us through historical accounts of the period and are integral to the story. All the same, they certainly contribute to making the performance of *The Wondrous Mulatto* richer and livelier, both as a play and as a visual spectacle.

1

I

The wondrous talent of José Mena Abrantes

José Mena Abrantes, the author and director of the first performances of *The Wondrous Mulatto*, is a prodigiously talented creator, but his name is probably known only to those who are already familiar with current developments in Angolan theatre.

In many ways Angolan theatre only 'came of age' in the period following independence in 1975, a circumstance not unrelated to the specific contribution that has been made by Mena Abrantes himself. This is not to say that theatrical forms did not exist in the period prior to that. Theatre of the Western kind – usually with the support of a written text – has been present in Angola since the seventeenth century. The oldest tradition is that of the *auto*, a play, usually the enactment of a Gospel scene, staged under the auspices of the Catholic Church. Performances were highly codified and they also served a quasi-liturgical function. In many ways they were not unlike the English medieval miracle and morality plays. This sort of play continued to be performed right until the eve of independence. Angola's first play written in a native language – in this case, Kimbundu – was a Christmas morality play: Domingos Van-Dúmen's *Auto de Natal* (Christmas Play), which was performed in Luanda in 1972. There were also the vaudeville performances, widely popular with settler audiences. By vaudeville I am referring to what the Portuguese call *teatro de revista* (literally 'revue'), which is a mixture of song, dance and farcical comic skits. Present-day Angolan theatre still owes much to this tradition of vaudeville. These theatrical genres provide an important part of the historical backdrop, although they have probably had little impact on the work of Mena Abrantes.

Theatre by native Angolans and with more topical (or political) themes began to make its appearance from the 1950s onwards. Many plays written in this period were never performed, and the work was often of low quality. There are many reasons why theatrical activity should have been stifled in the colonial period. The colonial state was a fascist dictatorship with an ever-vigilant security police that would ban any play that could be construed as questioning the legitimacy of the state; this made theatre a less than enticing vehicle for creative expression. There was also an unfamiliarity on the part of writers with the formal developments in modern theatre, which meant that what they produced often had an old-fashioned air about it. Allied to this was a generally poor handling of the mechanics of dramatic writing, so that much that was performed was often stilted and undramatic. Finally, many of the most talented writers in the period before independence were out of the country, either because they had joined the guerrillas or because they were in exile in Europe. This is true of José Mena Abrantes, who returned to Angola only in 1974, after a *coup d'état* by military officers in Portugal had put an end to the fascist régime. Mena Abrantes had a wide experience with theatre groups in Europe, an experience that would serve him well in revitalising theatre in Angola.

The son of settler parents, José Mena Abrantes was born in Malanje, a town in the interior of Angola, in 1945. He studied English and German at the University of Lisbon. It was during his student days that he first became involved in theatre work. He also took various courses in acting, directing and theatre craft, both in Portugal and in Belgium. In the early 1970s he took part in a German street theatre group (Faust) in Frankfurt. He also directed a Spanish student and workers' theatre group called La Busca, which was to perform at the first International Festival of Worker's Theatre' in 1973. That same year he was appointed assistant director to Augusto Fernandez, an Argentian director who at the time worked in the most important theatre house in Frankfurt, the Frankfurter Staedtische Buehne.

On his return from exile Mena Abrantes helped to found the Tchinganje theatre group, which has the honour of having performed the first play after independence, *O Poder Popular* (People's Power), in November 1975. In 1977 he co-founded Xilenga-Teatro company, whose first performance was a play based on a Chokwe folktale. Between 1985 and 1987 he directed a theatre group which operated under the auspices of the Faculty of Medicine in Luanda. This group was largely made up of former members of Xilenga-Teatro. In 1988 he founded Elinga-Teatro, which drew its members from the previous two groups. The first play it performed was Pepetela's *A Revolta da Casa dos Ídolos* (Revolt in the House of Idols), which also dealt with conflict between the Portuguese and the indigenous Kingdom of Kongo. Elinga-Teatro has toured Spain, Italy and Portugal. It has also performed many of the important plays written by Abrantes himself. One of these plays is *Ana, Zé e os Escravos* (Ana, José and the Slaves). Set during the period from the termination of the slave trade (1836) to the abolition of slavery itself (1878), it focuses on a woman slave trader (*Dona* Ana Joaquina) and her relationship with a social outcast who becomes a settler in Angola (José do Telhado). *Ana, Zé e os Escravos* was awarded the Sonangol literary award in 1986.

Mena Abrantes has worked as a journalist since 1975. At present he is also the media adviser to the Angolan president, José Eduardo dos Santos. A two-volume edition of Abrantes' plays was published in Portugal in 1999, a measure of his recognition in the wider Portuguese-speaking world.

The Mindelact Festival

The Wondrous Mulatto was first performed in 1993 by Elinga-Teatro in the Angolan capital of Luanda. But it was in 1997, at the Mindelact Festival, that the play was first performed before an international audience. Mindelact is an annual 'Lusophone' theatre festival. The festival takes its name from the fact that it is held in Mindelo, a city on the Cape Verdean island of São Vicente. An interesting feature of *The Wondrous Mulatto* as it was performed at the Mindelact Festival is that it was the result of a co-production between Elinga-Teatro and Cena Lusófona, a Portuguese theatre group. This followed a series of workshops which Rogério de Carvalho, an Angolan-born Cena Lusófona actor, ran in Luanda in 1995. The play was so well received that the Elinga-Teatro–Cena Lusófona co-production toured various Portuguese cities in June 1998, and, in September of that same year, went on a tour of Brazil. The repetition of these performances reveals, for one, the extent to which this play has been popular with audiences and critics (see Ferreira 1998; Cena Lusófona 1998).

The choice of Mindelo, a mid-Atlantic city roughly between Portugal, Angola and Brazil, as a host venue for theatre from the seven Portuguese-speaking countries makes geographical sense. But there is also something symbolic about the venue and why *The Wondrous Mulatto* should have been performed at this place. For centuries the port city of Mindelo was a refuelling station for the ships that criss-crossed the Atlantic in their triangular voyages between Portugal, Angola and Brazil with their cargoes of slaves, gold and sugar. This is especially true of the period between 1592, the date of the founding of Luanda, and 1822, when Brazil declared its independence from Portugal. In many ways Mindelo keeps alive the memory of a time when the destinies of Angola, Brazil and Portugal were closely linked.

The strange case of Luís Lopes Sequeira

The trans-Atlantic community that was Angola, Brazil and Portugal left lasting legacies on the cultures of these countries, particularly language and religion. Whether such influences were ultimately beneficial is an issue outside the scope of this article. What is undoubtedly true, however, is that this intercontinental community was built on foundations of savage cruelty, a fact which is quite evident in the story of Luís Lopes Sequeira, a man who conquered three African kingdoms in Angola in the seventeenth century. His exploits cannot be separated from the consequence that followed from his actions: the consolidation of colonial power and easier access to the captives who, ultimately, would be transported to Brazil.

Portuguese contacts with the Kongo kingdom at the mouth of the Congo River go back to the fifteenth century, but it was only in 1592, during the period when the Portuguese and Spanish crowns were united (1580–1640), that the Portuguese formalised their settlement in the area around Luanda. In 1641 the Dutch invaded and occupied Luanda. The Dutch had also occupied many coastal areas in Brazil but in the 1640s the Brazilians were able to drive them out. It was an armada from Brazil that in 1648 reconquered Angola for the Portuguese. Angola, of course, was an important extension of the Brazilian economy. Between 1580 and 1680 at least one million Angolans were transported as slaves to Brazil.

Luís Lopes Sequeira appears on the scene in 1665. That is when the battle of Ambuíla took place, when the Portuguese vanquished the kingdom of the Kongo. The governor at the time was André Vidal de Negreiros, a Brazilian who had fought the Dutch. Negreiros is credited with the order to build the 'Nazaré' (Nazareth) church. This baroque church is one of the architectural landmarks of Luanda. It is famous for the Italian marble altar and the glazed tiles depicting scenes from the battle of Ambuíla. I make mention of this church not only because of the Brazilian connection, but because the actors in the play talk about it in a reference any urban Angolan would immediately identify.

The exploits of Luís Lopes Sequeira did not end with this famous battle. In 1671 he vanquished the Ndongo nation and, in 1681, the Matamba kingdom. Three important kingdoms in Angola were thus defeated in his lifetime. He died in battle in what seems to have been a fit of folly. One of the questions the actors in the play frequently ask is whether his death was the result of negligence or if it was a kind of suicide. If his death was in some sense premeditated this would perhaps suggest guilt or shame, or at least an ambivalent attitude to his achievements. These questions, of course, cannot be answered: more than three hundred years later, we are not privy to what was going on in the mind of Luís Lopes. The play offers possibilities, tests them out by staging them, but leaves the question open.

II

I would now like to talk about the manner in which the play stages historical events, and the self-reflexive way it questions its own staging of the historical; at the same time I would like to tease out some of the scenic possibilities suggested by the various historical and self-reflexive scenes. This will involve re-telling much of the play, but this is probably necessary since both performance and the published text are likely to be unfamiliar to English-speaking readers.

The scenery and the actors

First of all, I would like to provide some information on the scenery and the actors. The stage notes to the play recommend that the stage should either be bare or that there should be a platform with a few wooden blocks. This suggests some austerity. Because the actors never leave the stage transitions are indicated by lighting and, sometimes, with the aid of music.

The cast is made up of five male and two female actors. The principal role they play is that of actors – they are playing themselves, in effect – who happen to be on stage and who ad-lib a debate about the figure of Luís Lopes and about the other roles that they will be playing. Each of these actors doubles up with another role. The actresses, for example, will have to play the roles of Luís Lopes Sequeira's black mother, the slave girl, the Virgin Mary and, maybe, even one of the bird-men that appear in the play.

The actors and actresses wear everyday clothes, although they wear period costumes for historical characters. The period in question, the mid-seventeenth century, is also the colourful baroque age. The constant contrast between the modern everyday clothes and the flamboyant seventeenth-century costumes shows that this is not a naturalistic representation of the past and, it consequently foregrounds the illusory nature of any artistic re-appropriation of the past.

The costumes of the more 'fantastical' beings are left to the discretion of the director. The use of costume to designate the Virgin Mary is essentially unproblematic, since there is an entire tradition of Christian iconography behind the portrayal of such a figure (the woman in blue or in a blue gown or mantle). Costumes for the bird-men depend on how they are interpreted, whether as aliens, modern-day mercenaries, rapacious capitalists or imperialist war-dogs. In the Lisbon production the bird-men wore wings that made them look like sinister angels.

The play

The first scene of the play introduces the audience to the pivotal question: why did Luís Lopes allow himself to be killed? This happens also to be the opening line of the play. One of the actors asks one of the actresses: 'And what about you, do you think it was negligence or was it suicide?' (p. 35).[1] The actors sound out various possibilities. One of these is the suggestion that Luís Lopes's death was a kind of self-immolation, when he realised that he was fighting for the wrong cause. This idea is quickly rebuffed by another actor who, in turn, suggests that the others have been watching too many cowboy films on TV. One actor even suggests the Aristotelian idea of a 'tragic flaw' as the reason for his downfall. As a way of making sense of all these contradictory ideas, the actors decide amongst themselves that they are going to act out three vignettes from his life. It is made quite clear to the audience that the actors are rehearsing their ideas about Luís Lopes, even though they make constant reference to the historical accounts that they have consulted.

The first vignette presents us with two Portuguese military officers talking about Luís Lopes's life and his fantastic deeds in Ambuíla. The actors not participating in this exchange are visible behind, but half-hidden in the darkness. The two officers also mention the magic stone, which his mother has given him. This leads to the next (but chronologically earlier) scene where Luís Lopes's mother presents him with a magic stone. She says the stone will help him in life, adding, 'When you look at it and see that it is shining, it is because I am also looking at you' (p. 39). The magic stone is the thread that links the three mini-scenes. The third vignette enacts a scene from Luís Lopes's school-days when he refuses to reveal to his Jesuit priest teacher what he is hiding – the magic stone – and is punished for it.

Acted out, these scenes have also indirectly introduced the next set of questions to be taken up by the actors: was it because his father was a Portuguese military officer, or was it because of the severity and strictness of the Ignatian discipline that he became so tough? The actors then act out a short scene where the young Luís Lopes asks his father if he can follow a military career. At first the father objects because his mulatto son is not likely to have any chance of promotion:

Luís Lopes ... I would much rather follow the same career as you, father.
Father With that colour of a brown monkey? Only if it's to clean the
pots ... (p. 42)

Only when Luís Lopes explains that under Jesuit influence he has learnt to
withstand much suffering does his father give reluctant consent.

In the next scene the actors discuss the battle of Ambuíla, the accounts from
the period, and the strangeness of it all. One of the actors says: 'We've started
with magic stones, next thing we'll end up with flying saucers ...' (p. 44). The
line is significant enough to be repeated later. But another actor responds: 'And
why not? There are accounts from the time of extraordinary prodigies that had
never been seen before.' The discussion is followed by a monologue by Luís
Lopes before the battle. He holds the magic stone, talks to it, and asks how he is
likely to recognise a sign. The scene is interrupted by the entrance of a
subaltern who says the men have been dismayed by the sound of a terrible noise
and by the appearance of black birds that hover in the air. Luís Lopes interprets
this as a sign that they are going to win. He says he will advance at the front of
his men. They beg him not to, but the lights go down and there is an apparition
of what they suppose is the Virgin Mary. Luís Lopes comes back holding the
decapitated head of the King of Kongo. The actors then discuss the fate of this
head. It is explained that the head was put inside the walls of the Nazaré church
because of a promise made to the Virgin by the governor at the time of the
battle. This leads to a discussion of the role of the Virgin Mary in the historical
accounts. One of the actors says, 'For them the Virgin seemed to be everywhere. She was like a Rambo with skirts' (p. 49). Because they cannot make
any sense of this, the actors decide to devise another scene in which two
officers discuss Luís Lopes' rapid ascendancy and their fear that he will soon
eliminate them.

The fifth vignette is a love scene. The actors discuss whether they should act
out something to show that Luís Lopes was aware of the racial contradictions of
the time and felt something of an outsider on account of his skin colour. This
leads to a monologue in which Luís Lopes, in an appeal to his absent mother,
wails against the petty jealousies and hatred all around him. When this is
concluded the actors discuss whether it would be appropriate to *invent* a love
affair for him. The actors discuss various possibilities: whether his lover should
be a black woman, someone who is white or, better still, someone of mixed
race like himself. The fictionality of the scene is made quite evident. They opt,
as the love of his life, for one of his father's black slave girls. A scene is acted out
where Luís Lopes tells the slave girl that he will defend her from his father's
wrath. While the two are making love in the shadows one of the actors turns to
the others and says: 'So! Are you happy with the love scene?' (p. 54). The other
replies: 'It's all too shocking. Having a mother who's a slave, going out with his
father's own slave girl.... All that's very incestuous' (p. 55). And a little later
another actor adds: 'If we continue this way we'll end by making a soap opera'
(p. 55). The actors consider whether they should delete the love scene. They
agree to let the lovers finish it. This is also the end of Act I.

The first scene of Act II presents us with a scene between Luís Lopes and his mother. She asks why he never looked at the stone again. He says he did, but she never appeared again. He later admits that he lost the stone. She then gives him the stone back – we are led to believe that it is the same stone. She also invites him to travel with her in time. Luís Lopes realises he is in the theatre and that an audience is watching the events from his life – and also his death. He asks his mother if he is dead already and she explains to him that he will eventually die. The lights dim and the actors repeat word-for-word the discussion in the first scene of the play, the one beginning with the words: 'And what about you, do you think it was negligence or was it suicide?' (p. 60). Luís Lopes overhears this and is naturally quite confused by these voices that speak about him. How is it possible for them to be telling his story if he is present on the scene? His mother asks, 'Are you sure they're telling our story? More than three hundred years later ... How could they possibly know what really happened?' (p. 61). This questions leads directly back to the discussion between the actors. It is here that the line about the magic stones and the flying saucers is repeated (p. 62). Luís Lopes asks his mother about the stone and she tells him that it comes from Mpungu-a-Ndongo, her place of birth. The place is significant since it is also the site of one of the battles.

In the scene that follows the actors suggest that it is time to talk about the other two kingdoms that Luís Lopes helped to destroy, the Ndongo and the Matamba. They basically agree that giving the audience too much historical information would probably be rather boring. They consider another love scene, possibly even a gay scene.

They opt to have him stare at the magic stone and address his mother. This he does; he tells her that preparations are afoot for an assault against the Ndongo and that he has been chosen to lead it. He concludes his monologue with the words: 'I can't fight against the people from the land where you were born!' (p. 65). There is something too pat about his words because this is precisely what the actors had been suggesting earlier. The focus moves to a dialogue between military officers who fear that if he wins the battle no one will be able to stop him; he will be too powerful. The actors then discuss the battle and how they should represent it. One of the actresses suggests that maybe they should include a song or a dance. While they are talking about this, fearsome drums begin to sound and one of the actors gives a long speech about the adjectives and phrases which had been used to describe Luís Lopes in the accounts from the period: 'egregious', 'the terror of the heathens', 'an Atlas of conquests'. There is something particularly dramatic about these grandiloquent and archaic phrases, taken from original historical accounts, being declaimed to the sound of drums.

The next scene is called 'The Winged Beings'. Here Luís Lopes finds himself confronted by two human-like but winged creatures. He asks them if they were the black birds in Ambuíla. They tell him they are not birds, but that they were the ones who created the whole confusion with fire and light, which made it possible for him to get to the king and cut off his head. He asks them about the Virgin and the magic stone, and they scoff at him. Finally, he shows them the stone. His mother quickly appears and reprimands him; he had promised never to show anyone the stone. She says that these flying men had long suspected that such stones existed in Mpungu-a-Ndongo and that in the future many more of them would come to oppress the people. Once again the actors discuss his career and the 'tragic flaw'. One of them mentions that if they are to be consistent they should speak of the Virgin. This leads directly to a scene where Luís Lopes has a vision of the Virgin. She says that it was she who cast the light, although not the fire, and the reason she did this was because there was something disproportionate about the battle scene against the 'pagans'. He was also someone with a clean heart, and she felt he was worthy of her protection. She adds that as a sign of her presence she would leave her footprints on the rocks. As in precolonial mythology in many parts of Africa, there may be some legend associated with this.

The finale is the death scene. It begins with a discussion by the actors. One of them says: 'I think we've run out of special effects ... Should we finish the play or not? The spectators will begin to think this is all a mystical bore' (p. 76). But they still have to resolve the fundamental question: did he or did he not kill himself, or was he just killed in battle? The vignette that follows has Luís Lopes speaking at length to a prisoner. We are later informed the prisoner was eventually able to escape and the actors suggest that Luís Lopes died of shame. They discuss all the various reasons again. One of the actors makes a longish speech, which is derided by some of the others, but which is important, nevertheless, since it provides the reason why a modern-day Angolan audience would find some value and interest in the figure of Luís Lopes Sequeira, and is the reason also for the staging such a play:

> ... For me at the least the guy destroyed in less than 20 years the three main kingdoms in Angola because he could foresee that if they existed separately they would weaken Angolans and that would prevent them from constituting a single nation. He was a visionary, one of those appears only once every few centuries.... (p. 81)

The final scene has Luís Lopes running across the stage in slow motion as though he were driven with arrows. He falls on the ground, dead. The mother, the bird-men and the Virgin then appear on stage. The Virgin revives him. He looks at the bird-men and asks how is it possible that the demons are here with them. The Virgin replies that now everyone is the same, the magic stone has united them all. The mother then tells him that the magic stone never actually existed. When Luís Lopes asks what would explain the wondrous happenings of his life, his mother replies:

> The only wonder, my son, the only one which really exists and which makes us exist, both me and you and all them ... that wonder is ... the THEATRE. (p. 83)

The suggestion is that more prodigious than the fantastical deeds of the real-life and long-dead Luís Lopes Sequeira is the theatrical performance itself. For it is the performance that can momentarily make Luís Lopes come alive for a modern-day audience, and it is precisely by framing his theatrical 'life' within the discourse of metafiction or self-reflexiveness that the various possibilities offered by his life can be tested, sounded out, acted. In doing so, the ambiguous figure of Luís Lopes – for he was in many ways what we would now call a 'sell-out'– acquires moral and patriotic value for a contemporary audience. It is through this sort of metafictional theatre that Luís Lopes Sequeira can be reclaimed, provisionally perhaps, as one of Angola's national heroes.

NOTES

1   All quotations from the text are my translations.

REFERENCES

Abrantes, José Mena (1999) *Teatro*, 2 volumes, Coimbra: Cena Lusófona.
Cena Lusófona (1998) 'O Mulato dos Prodígios.' < http://www.cenalusofona.pt/mem1998/ mulato.htm> (2 February 2002)
Ferreira, J. Alberto (1998) 'A Pedra Mágica do Elinga-Teatro', < http://www.ciberkiosk.pt/ arquivo/ciberkiosk3/espectaculos/prodigios.html> (2 February 2002)

FURTHER READING

Abrantes, José Mena (1995) 'Breve Olhar sobre o Teatro Angolano', *Setepalcos*, 0 (1995): 32–41.
Mindelact (1998) 'A Associação de Teatro em Cabo Verde.' < http://www.portugal-linha.pt/ mindelact/> (17 November 2001).

Community Theatre in Angola

JUDY EL BUSHRA

Reflecting the country's general cultural isolation, Angolan theatre is relatively unfamiliar to anglophone audiences in Southern Africa. While language differences clearly play a role here, Angola's strong links with metropolitan Portugal add to its isolation within both anglophone and lusophone environments.

This article[1] outlines the historical, political and cultural context in which community theatre[2] has evolved in Angola, and describes the roles played by two international organisations, the United Nations Children's Fund (UNICEF) and the Agency for Cooperation and Research in Development (ACORD), which have provided different types of support to local non-government organisations (NGOs) that use drama as an adjunct to their developmental programmes. It concludes that the relatively didactic style of community theatre in Angola has been shaped by the country's history as well as by the policies and approaches of external agencies; and that these agencies could play a more proactive role in reducing Angola's isolation from its Southern African neighbours.

Country background

Angola was under Portuguese colonial rule for almost five centuries, from 1482 until 1975. Until the nineteenth century, the colonial presence was mainly concentrated in coastal enclaves, from which an intensive trade in slaves from the interior was carried out. With the official abolition of slavery, however, Portugal sought new sources of revenue and, over the next century, developed a larger-scale industrial and agricultural economy aimed at exploiting Angola's natural resources.

During the 1960s and early 1970s investment in mining, manufacturing and commercial agriculture intensified with the importation of skilled labour from Portugal, comprising almost one twelfth of the total population. The colonial regime practised a policy of 'divide and rule' towards the native population, distinguishing both in law and in practice between *assimilados* (Angolans, mainly of mixed descent, who had adopted Portuguese lifestyle and language and who thus qualified for educational, economic and administrative privileges) and the remainder, who served the Portuguese as unskilled labour and whom the colonists, describing them officially as 'uncivilised', maintained in a state of semi-slavery. The sudden departure of colonial personnel in the mid-1970s left Angolans with no substantial class of skilled or managerial labour to run the vacated enterprises, and many fell into disuse and disarray.

Angola's three liberation movements – the National Front for the Liberation of Angola, (FNLA), the Popular Movement for the Liberation of Angola (MPLA) and the National Union for the Total Independence of Angola (UNITA) – all emerged during the early 1960s, employing guerrilla war tactics against Portuguese economic and military interests. Portugal's response was intensive military intervention. In 1974, however, a military coup against the Salazar regime in Portugal led to the sudden withdrawal of Portuguese troops and other personnel from Angola (Elkaney 1976) and the consequent establishment of an interim government made up of the three movements.

Disagreements between the three, however, were exacerbated by the intervention of other powers (USA, South Africa, Zaïre, the USSR and Cuba) who were prepared to provide financial and military backing to their proxies in the hope of gaining access to Angola's mineral wealth and its position as a strategic political and military foothold. Thus began a devastating cycle of conflict which continues to this day and is still fuelled by the involvement of outside interests.

When in 1975 the MPLA captured the capital city of Luanda it gained the military advantage and established itself as the single governing party, a position it has held ever since. Although the war which raged for the best part of the ensuing 20 years ended formally in 1991, with the Bicesse Accord and elections that saw the victory of MPLA, UNITA failed to observe the agreement and in 1993 reopened hostilities. A stalemate continued until early 2002,[3] with UNITA occupying sufficient territory in the diamond-rich enclave of Kabinda to finance its increasingly isolated resistance and with neither side making serious commitments to peace talks.

During nearly three decades since independence, dominated by MPLA rule, the country has experienced two main periods in terms of political orientation. The first, coloured by MPLA's long-standing alignment with the Eastern Bloc, was characterised by one-party rule and a centrally planned economy aimed at maximising the role of the state in production and social reproduction. The substitution of ration cards for public sector salaries, the decline in commercial agricultural production, and the nationalisation of state farms and enterprises led to ordinary people relying for survival on subsistence farming and non-monetary forms of exchange. The nationalist agenda led the state to fund social services and to promote the development of national consciousness through cultural activities. The state encouraged people's participation in mass development activities such as literacy movements. Party membership conferred privileged access to facilities such as good housing and overseas scholarships; political repression and control of security was high, in both the government-held and UNITA-held areas.

The second period, following the Bicesse Accord in 1991, has been characterised by the establishment of multi-party elections and a transition to a market-oriented economy. While this has paved the way for a freer civil society and a more open and accountable bureaucracy, the country continues to be weakened by insecurity, high military expenditure, high inflation and a combination of massive internal displacement and rural–urban migration, resulting in levels of poverty amongst the highest in the world. The decline of agriculture (due to insecurity, soil exhaustion and the collapse of internal distribution networks) renders a largely proletarianised population dependent mainly on informal sector employment. Angola currently experiences the worst of all worlds – it has lost the safety nets of subsistence production on the one hand and state-supported services on the other, while market liberalisation is insufficiently advanced to create significant new opportunities. Links with Portugal (itself peripheral and relatively 'underdeveloped' within Europe) still dominate economic and cultural life.

Theatre in Angola

Despite Portuguese attempts to marginalise indigenous culture and privilege Portuguese lifestyle and language, a number of Angolan theatre groups and writers did emerge in the preindependence period, in the main as part of the anti-colonial resistance. When the MPLA government came to power, it developed a cultural policy that supported cultural performance within the overall context of its nationalistic drive. It brought together previously disparate ministries and institutes concerned with culture under one depart-ment in the Ministry of Education. In 1976 it sponsored the establishment, by a group of actors who had been sent on government scholarships to study theatre in Portugal in the 1970s, of the National Theatre and Dance School, using instructors and directors from Portugal, Brazil and Cuba. From this school the first amateur theatre groups soon emerged.

The National Council for Culture launched a mass cultural movement promoting cultural activities in schools, factories and military units all over the country, and a number of national and local theatre groups evolved during the 1980s. In 1989 the first National Culture Festival was held, with the participation of 18 groups representing 14 provinces. Theatre groups were both supported and in effect managed by government (Colombo, 1999). Informants speculated that the government may have seen this as a way of controlling the theatre movement in case it became a vehicle for criticism.

The newly elected government of 1993 established a separate Ministry of Culture, which has continued to provide state support to the emergence of theatre groups. This period has witnessed Angola's participation in inter-national theatre events, and a flowering of interest in theatre in the country generally. While interest in drama is growing, it is nevertheless perceived to involve skills which come less naturally than dancing and singing and which have to be acquired through training. Theatre groups (combining drama with other forms of performance) that have emerged since independence tend to concentrate their activities in the capital and in the main towns, offering entertainment to audiences from the small but growing middle class.

Training in theatre arts is now provided by state cultural institutions and by foreign cultural missions such as the Alliance Française. A strong youth movement is developing in Angola, supported by international institutions such as churches (both Protestant and Catholic) and the Scouts, and interest in theatre is high among youth groups, many of whom credit the Catholic Church as having provided them with basic acting skills, and most community theatre groups in Angola have been influenced by or have some connection with church activities. For young people, there are few other channels for self-expression or for reflecting the situation in which they live. Indeed, since the early 1990s there have been strong associations between theatre groups and movements of conscience, with commercial plays being produced on, for example, AIDS or environmental concerns.

The education system has also been instrumental in developing drama skills. Teachers have been encouraged to use drama in schools from independence onwards. This has included using role play as a strategy for solving behaviour and discipline problems, such as cheating in examinations, by asking the children to act out the issues as they saw them.

Community theatre

Community theatre began to attract interest in the early 1990s.[4] The particular impetus for this was the intervention of UNICEF in the late 1980s: however, this intervention built on traditions of longer duration, including the state-sponsored 'classical' theatre referred to above. The Catholic Church has offered widespread experience of formal theatre to church youth groups; many current practitioners learned their basic acting skills through them, and most community theatre groups in Angola have probably been influenced by or have some connection with church activities.

UNICEF became involved in community theatre when in 1989 the communications officer at that time, who had expertise in community theatre, identified a number of groups to support. Of these, the only one to survive their 1989 funding was Juventud y Luz (Youth and Light), otherwise known as JULU, which started in 1992 around the time of the elections with the aim of promoting civic and electoral education. UNICEF provided JULU with trainers from Israel, Zimbabwe and Brazil, and arranged for JULU to make exchange visits and attend conferences. In 1993 UNICEF contracted JULU to promote its goals of children's rights in Angola, especially in relation to health, education and landmine protection, by carrying out development communications activities around these main aims and by training other theatre groups in the same techniques. JULU thus built an informal network of community theatre groups across the country (in, for example, Malanje, Bengom, Muxico, Luanda, Uige, Kuito and Lubango, and including the public health authority in Benguela). These groups provide support to various NGOs and UN agencies by transmitting messages for campaigns on human rights, AIDS, environmental health and so on. JULU is in the process of consolidating its experience of training by publishing a community theatre manual (again funded by UNICEF) for the use of theatre companies and NGOs. The image of community theatre in Angola today is decisively shaped by the JULU initiative, itself heavily influenced not only by its church and governmental origins but also by the orientation and training provided by UNICEF.

With UNICEF's continued support, JULU is now changing its legal status from a commercial theatre group into an NGO, giving it a wider view and broader remit, and increased access to opportunities for collaboration with other development agencies (some of which have been constrained in collaborating with JULU by its commercial status). UNICEF's hope is that the impact of community theatre can be scaled up through, for example, the creation of a formal network of community theatre NGOs across the country, and the increased use of broadcast media to disseminate plays more widely. UNICEF aims to use any means at its disposal to advocate and mobilise for behaviour change around children's rights to health; it therefore works with all population groups including community leaders and opinion formers.

The process of developing a community theatre performance, as described by JULU, follows a number of steps. First, the theatre group is commissioned to prepare a play relating to a specific need, identified by the commissioning agency, in a specific community. It then carries out research in and about the community: topics include the causes of the problem identified, customs, folklore and ethnic origins. It identifies the issues arising, and devises the play. Both research and playmaking are usually a collective effort by the team. The play is a reflection of the research; sometimes the characters in the play are drawn from observation of people met in the community. The Artistic Director (Lourenço Mateus) does the casting and organises rehearsals, assisted by the choreographer and music assistant, and the performance is advertised in the community. Two weeks after the performance, the theatre group returns for a follow-up meeting with the community and local authorities to assess the play's impact on people's awareness and comprehension.

This is the basic pattern that tends to be followed with variations by organisations that have been trained by JULU. For example, ADMA (see Box 1) devises plays on the JULU model but based on the observations of human rights monitors resident in individual communities. Different approaches are sometimes used, however, as in the case of ADCP discussed in Box 1.

Theatre initiatives supported by ACORD

ACORD began working in Angola in 1986, eventually establishing three programmes based in Luanda and Lubango. The Luanda programme operates in peri-urban squatter settlements where environmental conditions are over-crowded and unsanitary, with the aim of strengthening community organising capacities around improving the urban environment. Of the Lubango

Box 1: Organizations supported by ACORD

JICS (Jovenes Incansáveles Contra SIDA – Youth Indefatigable Against AIDS), Luanda. JICS members are all ex-trainees from an artisan training project organised by ACORD who formed themselves into a youth group in September 2000. Following a training workshop on HIV/AIDS issues organised by ACORD, the group changed its name and decided to focus its attention exclusively on AIDS. The group's main motivation is to provide information to members of their community about the dangers of HIV/AIDS. Theatre is a major part of the JICS programme; plays are usually performed at weekends and take place in whatever dry open spaces can be found. Group members have received no drama training, although some have been involved in other theatre groups and they hope to receive training from JULU. To date the group has developed one play, *Mario and Francesca*, based on the true story of a couple used as a case study in the HIV/AIDS training workshop. In the play the very promiscuous male partner becomes ill with AIDS, infects both his wife and their child, and eventually dies (see Box 2 for a description of a performance of this play).

HIV/AIDS activists of the Angolan armed forces and police, Lubango. The work of this group, formed in September 2000, is particularly sensitive because the armed forces and police are reluctant to acknowledge HIV and AIDS as an issue for their personnel. Group members include both health and non-health personnel, and although the military authorities support the group's activities, members work in their spare time. The group sees drama as a particularly dynamic method of awareness raising, and in April 2001 began developing a play giving information about HIV testing and urging tolerance of infected people.

Prazedora ('Pleasure and pain'), Lubango. Prazedora started three years ago as an AIDS organisation (developing ways of 'keeping the pleasure but not the pain') and has been using theatre since late 2000, with the aim of teaching people the dangers of HIV. It normally works in schools, discos, markets and villages, taking a different theme each time according to the context. For example, work in schools often focuses on attitudes towards people with AIDS, whereas in villages the subject is likely to be use of condoms. A new play is developed every time, sometimes involving members of the community themselves, especially if – as in the case of teachers for example – they have particular information to impart). The performances are followed by discussion. *Prazedora* keeps records of enquiries made to its information and advice service; it has found that the volume of enquiries usually increases after a performance, and that the enquiries tend to concern the subject of the play performed.

Olongende ('Travellers'), Lubango. This drama group of several years' standing works in community theatre, entertainment theatre and radio plays broadcast to the general public on local radio stations. They are students and act in their spare time, performing twice a month. They also work with organisations such as ADMA and Prazedora to whom they provide training and support. The current manager acquired his acting skills in 1995 in a church group in Luanda, and also with Alliance Française, and taught his friends; they have also received training from JULU. Olongende usually develops plays for community theatre on request from the commissioning NGO, carrying out research in the community which sometimes involves community members doing role plays to illustrate a point. Radio plays are mostly about youth issues such as drugs and HIV.

International Committee of the Red Cross, Lubango. ICRC has an HIV sub-group which started in mid-2000 and uses theatre in its community work. Two or three group members go to a community to identify problems and develop a play on that subject, based on their experience. About 15 storylines have been developed so far. One, for example, concerns a person with many partners who contracts HIV but who seeks treatment from a doctor only in the last stages of illness, after having first wasted time visiting a herbalist because of ignorance. The team discusses the performance afterwards, but there is no community discussion.

ADMA (Associação para o desenvolvimento da mulher – Women's Development Association), Lubango. ADMA promotes women's and girls' rights through the work of human rights monitors resident in individual communities, who also serve as rights educators. It is their reports and observations which form the basis of the plays which ADMA devises and tours.

ADCP (Associação para o Desenvolvimento Cominitário Participative no Sul de Angola – Association for Participatory Community Development in the South of Angola, Lubango. ADCP operates a project for street children in which the children are encouraged to develop their own plays based on their lived experience. This is partly seen as a form of therapy for the children, many of whom are severely traumatised; in addition, the children also perform the plays in schools, hospitals and other institutions to raise awareness of the children's situation and to advocate recognition of their rights.

Box 2: A performance of *Mario and Francesca*

By around 9.30 am when the audience starts gathering, the stage has been set up in an open space in Marcal (one of Luanda's squatter settlements) where ACORD has built a drainage pit, and which is therefore dry even though the streets nearby are flooded with rainwater. Across one side of the square a stage has been made from breeze blocks (supplied for constructing pit latrines) for the floor, covered with a piece of carpet, and flattened cardboard boxes for the backdrop (decorated with a welcome sign and AIDS posters). A bright orange strip of satin cloth forms the main exit from the stage. In the audience space, about 20 plastic chairs have been arranged under a sunshade: to their left is the concrete housing for the drain cover, with around 30 children aged up to ten sitting on it. The chairs are for the ACORD visitors and for JICS members, though most of the latter. Other members stand around, boys getting the sound system ready, girls chatting. Many are wearing T-shirts with 'Choose Life not AIDS' (in Portuguese) printed on the front.

First, a dance group called *Bota Fogo* (Kimbundo for 'throw the fire'), a frequent JICS collaborator from the same community, comes on and performs two dances: *ku duro* ('tight buttocks'), a type of hip-hop based on an Angolan rhythm, followed by *dombolo* a Congolese rhythm, both very popular with young audiences across Angola. Though the rhythms are local, the dance style is high-energy disco. The dancers, three girls and three boys, have carefully choreographed and practised their performance. By this time the audience has swelled to around 200. Most of these are young men and women, standing behind the seated children, plus a handful of curious older adults (mostly men). It being Sunday morning, most of the adults are in church.

At around 10 am the JICS president introduces the play using the microphone, and it starts, lasting around 45 minutes. In the first scenes, Francesca and Mario have been engaged for six years and Mario has still not produced bridewealth satisfactory to Francesca's parents, a matter which angers Francesca as Mario does not seem serious about their marriage. Frustrated, Mario runs after other women but ignores his friends' advice to use condoms. Neighbours observe his behaviour and he becomes the subject of much gossiping, to the audience's delight.

After Francesca and Mario get married, Mario's behaviour continues to be reprehensible: even on his wedding day he is running after women. One day when Francesca is in the last stages of pregnancy, Mario goes out, pretending to be at work. By the time he comes back, drunk, she has gone into labour and has been taken to hospital by a neighbour. Mario complains about his wife's absence but calms down when she returns, accompanied by the neighbour, with a baby.

In the next scenes Mario is sick with a cough and diarrhoea and is very thin. His friends take him to hospital. The neighbours discuss his situation and we learn that Francesca's baby is dead and that she herself is sick. Suspecting that Mario is the cause of this misfortune, the neighbours reject him. Meanwhile Mario reads a hospital report which has been sent him and is distraught to read that he is HIV+. His friends, though pointing out to him that he has ignored their advice to use condoms, support him and persuade the neighbours to do the same, explaining that neighbourliness does not lead to infection. In the last scene, Mario's friends and Francesca gather round Mario as he lies dying. The audience, though looking terrified, are in stitches of laughter and clap wildly. The cast freezes around Mario's deathbed, holding out packets of condoms. The audience is clearly moved and delighted by the performance.

The energetic and fast-moving acting style has contributed to the audience's delight. Actors use the space of the stage fully, and move round it using gestures of exaggerated realism to make the storyline clear and to highlight the emotional content of the scenes. The satin curtain and cardboard sheets are used as exits and entrances, enabling one scene to be shown at a time and players to change costume unnoticed. Costumes contribute another layer of meaning to the action – the neighbourhood gossips wear traditional clothes, while Mario's other love interest wears a short skirt and cropped shirt, Francesca appears with a padded stomach in the pregnancy scene. Props are kept to an absolute minimum.

After the play is over, the JICS president presents a commentary on HIV rates in Angola and urges the audience to think about their families. The dance group performs a second set. Older members of the audience drift off at this point, but some stay to take part in the discussion session which follows. The audience is invited to make comments or raise questions. A man of about 35 says he had learned that sexually active people must use condoms. Another man aged about 30 asks if AIDS can be contracted through mosquito bites. A girl of about 16 asks how long it takes for a person to get ill from AIDS. All these questions are answered with factual information by the president or by ACORD staff. Finally, a man of about 30 comments enigmatically, before walking off, that he has enjoyed the play, but that there were some mistakes that need to be improved.

When I talk to the group after the performance, they say they are keen to receive drama training so as to develop their skills. Discussing the impact of the performance is difficult: the performers have no clear answer as to why the audience laughed at Mario's death, nor do they have a strategy for assessing their performance. But belief in the power of drama to convey information about HIV transmission is strong, and they are committed to continuing activism through drama.

programmes, one offers organisational support to about 27 emergent Angolan NGOs based in the three provinces of Huila, Kunene and Namibe. The other is implemented jointly by ACORD and ADRA (*Associação para o Desenvolvimento Rural e Ambiente* or Association for Rural and Environmental Development), an Angolan national development agency. The programme supports community initiatives carried out by the Mungambwe and Muakahona, two highly marginalised pastoralist communities in the Gambos, an isolated area in the south of Huila province.

All three programmes apply a Freirean methodology developed jointly by ACORD Angola and ADRA, and involving a continuous process of analysis carried out together between partners. ACORD sees its role as being primarily one of organisational support, rather than a source of expert knowledge on the particular areas of work of each group. By bringing partners together to discuss their experience, ACORD aims to facilitate mutual learning between the partners.

The Gambos communities, faced with encroachment by wider Angolan and global cultures, are keen on retaining indigenous performance arts of singing and dancing as means of communicating with others, and ACORD is supporting this process. In contrast, the Luanda and Lubango programmes work with partner organisations that currently include seven Angolan NGOs and community groups using community theatre in their work as activists (see Box 1). While some are specialist theatre groups, the majority use drama to campaign around issues such as AIDS, street children or women's rights. Most have been established within the last two years for only a few months or have been involved in theatre work for a similarly short time. Donor encouragement of the use of theatre for rights–based activities, especially from the United States Agency for International Development (USAID) and its partners such as World Learning, partly explains this sudden growth.

ACORD sees its role as being primarily one of providing organisational support, rather than a source of expert knowledge on the particular areas of work of each group. The type of support it provides includes training workshops and seminars on issues of common concern such as management approaches and skills, fundraising, or report writing. A core group of organisations also acts as the advisory board for the ACORD programme in Lubanga. In this way ACORD aims to provide and receive intellectual resources with which it and its partners can become stronger organisationally. Since the partners work on a variety of different issues, however, ACORD does not attempt to provide expertise in the substantive areas in which they work.

Conclusions

While observations based on a short visit must be provisional, some indicative conclusions can be drawn. Firstly, community theatre in Angola seems to be strongly influenced by one particular methodological approach; while elements of community participation are incorporated to varying degrees, the approach is predominantly didactic in nature. Storylines tend to promote modernising social values, such as the backwardness of traditional healers or the importance of sending children to school. Though some elements of participation are incorporated into the process (for example, researching the cultural context in preparation for developing the play), and while the style of some performances (such as *Mario and Francesca*) is clearly oriented sharply towards the targeted audience, this is largely to ensure the audience's interest and acceptance of the 'message' being promoted.

Several factors may be contributing to this. First, informants speculated that Angola's experience of bureaucratic authority has been heavy-handed, so that didactic forms of communication are what is expected. Second, agencies feel they have sound reasons for promoting messages, especially when these concern health imperatives such as limiting HIV transmission or promoting vaccination against children's diseases. UNICEF, currently the major sponsor of community theatre, is understandably more concerned with driving its children's health messages home through all possible means, than with applying a process-oriented, participatory development methodology. Third, Angola's strong links with Portugal and its cultural and economic isolation mean that there has been limited networking with practitioners of other methods, even in neighbouring Southern African countries. Portugal takes precedence over other Portuguese-speaking countries, so that the work of, for example, Brazilian theatre pioneers such as Augusto Boal is not widely known in Angola. A final factor is that training opportunities appear to be largely informal, and in any case community theatre is expanding more rapidly than training can be provided.

A second observation is that theatre for HIV/AIDS activism is a particularly noticeable growth area in Angola (as it is in many countries most severely affected). Given the sensitive nature of this subject, and given the notorious difficulties of monitoring the immediate and longer-term impact of theatre performances generally, there is room for debate about the risks involved in such a strategy. This may be particularly pertinent in a country where experience in theatre for development is relatively new, and where knowledge, skills and expectations remain to be consolidated. Much of the growth of HIV/AIDS work in Angola is attributable to a desire to spread knowledge of the disease widely at the grassroots level: however, without a well-established system of training, monitoring and evaluation, this very grassroots focus may carry the risk of knowledge and skills being watered down. And where unreliable information about the disease (for example, about HIV testing procedures) is combined with the emotive impact of drama performances, the lack of monitoring methods or indicators could have serious consequences.

Finally, as in other countries, there are questions to be asked about the role of the international community in promoting participatory community theatre. Is it addressing long-term structural issues relating to poverty, exclusion and conflict, or has it largely restricted its focus to emergency responses? As the holder of the purse strings, is it using its influence to promote a bottom-up, or a modernising concept of development? At present it seems as though the community theatre movement in Angola is being driven forward by theatre professionals and social activists whose talent, enthusiasm and commitment are prodigious but who are constrained by the lack of opportunity to share ideas with others working within different frameworks. This suggests that there may be a role for agencies concerned with development communications in the broad sense, working alongside UNICEF and others who already have experience of the context, to open up such opportunities and to encourage the development of an expanded range of methods and approaches, as well as a broader debate about the meaning and methodologies of development.

Notes

1 Material for this article was gathered on a short visit to Angola during April and May 2001, under the auspices of ACORD Angola, to whom many thanks are due. ACORD is an international development agency operating at community level in 17 African countries. I am also grateful to Henda Ducados for her information, insights and support.
2 'Theatre' in this context is used inclusively to describe the general context of performance, in contrast to 'drama' which refers to formal acting of plays. 'Community theatre' involves performances which are based on research and discussion about community issues rather than on formal texts: this is the way the term is generally applied in Angola.
3 The death in battle of Jonas Savimbi, leader of UNITA, paved the way for a peace agreement signed in April 2002, the outcome of which is unclear at the time of writing.
4 Information for this section was provided by Lourenco Mateus, Artistic Director, JULU, and by Celso Malavoloneke, Social Mobilisation Officer, UNICEF, in April and May 2001.

References

Colombo, D. (1999) 'The Status of Theatre in Angola', in Renato Matusse (ed.), *Past Roles and Development of Theatre Arts in SADC*, SACIS Series no. 1, Gaborone: SACIS.
Elkaney, N. (1976) 'Angola: Post-mortem of a conflict', *Présence Africaine* 98, 2.
Vines, A. (2000) 'History and Human Costs of the Conflict', London: Human Rights Watch.

Confronting the Mask
Some contemporary Namibian contexts of protest

TERENCE ZEEMAN

This article links two commentaries: one examines conventional expectations of the actor in the role of satirist or protester-by-proxy and the other explores the recent emergence of protesting performers featured alongside their characters in contemporary Namibian protest drama and poetry. A particular focus will be Vickson Hangula's play, *The Show Isn't Over Until...* in which actors protest against the neglect of Namibian performing artists in state-sponsored post-independence reconstruction initiatives alongside scenes in which they portray members of other sectors of the economy enjoying, unjustly, the rewards and spoils of independence. Shortly after its first run in 1998 and following a tour to neighbouring Botswana, the play was called an 'embarrassment' to the ruling SWAPO party and the Namibian government. Despite earlier attempts to curtail the play's tours, *The Show Isn't Over Until...* continues to be performed with much success within Namibia and beyond its borders. The State Theatre of South Africa chose to produce the play with a South African cast and director as part of celebrations marking the launch of the African Union in Johannesburg in July 2002.

Some readers may not be familiar with Namibia or the state of its contemporary play-making. Its modern history begins during the 'scramble for Africa', when in the 1880s Germany colonised (as German South West Africa) what was later to be known as Namibia. After the First World War, the League of Nations granted the territory known as South West Africa to South Africa as a mandate, a 'sacred trust of civilisation' where peoples 'not yet able to stand by themselves' were to be placed 'under the tutelage of advanced nations' – a mandate that was annulled by the UN in 1966. Despite many international calls for withdrawal (UN Resolution 435:1978 being the most insistent), apartheid South Africa continued to occupy Namibia as an aggressive colonist, ruling Namibia as its fifth province and using the northern territories as a convenient staging post from which to wage war against the 'Communists' in Angola, Zambia and Zimbabwe. Namibia became independent in 1990 and SWAPO (the South West African People's Organisation) became the ruling party.

Before independence, the arts establishment in 'South West Africa' was sadly, and with woefully few exceptions, caught up in the exclusive presentation of

European 'high culture' and seemed inclined, as local theatre director Gerrit Schoonhoven noted, 'not to promote the arts but to stifle them' (*The Namibian*, 17 March 1989). Heavily subsidised by the state, the South West Africa Performing Arts Council, in a purpose-built, 472-seat theatre in the centre of Windhoek, the capital city, provided its white (predominantly German and Afrikaans-speaking) public with expensive imported European and South African productions. In addition, a South West African government depart-ment, the notorious 'Administration for Whites', funded a prestigious and expensive Conservatoire, also located in the capital's centre, that offered opportunities (again heavily subsidised) for white children and teenagers to study classical music, ballet, the visual arts and drama. This state-sponsored investment, while racist in its application, nonetheless allowed a few privileged white students to be trained in the arts to such levels that international awards were not uncommon.

As independence approached, disadvantaged black artists expected these state-sponsored arts institutions to be transformed radically by refocusing their Eurocentric pedagogical and production biases. They expected post-independence reparation to take the form of continued, generous state sub-sidies, redirected in transparent and accessible ways to the constituency that had contributed to the struggle most vigorously. In a 1989 interview marking the return from exile of SWAPO's cultural troupe Ndilimani, Nguno Wakolele, social and cultural adviser to Hage Geingob, then SWAPO's Election Director and later Namibia's Prime Minister, reassured black artists (and of course potential voters):

> the Namibian people have a golden opportunity to form a national culture ... the aim is to encourage Namibians to start making their own music, their own drama ... once SWAPO is in power, the government will continue to allocate resources to arts and culture ... there will be a fair distribution of resources ... an independent Namibia can definitely afford to allocate certain funds to culture. ('Moving towards a National Culture', *The Namibian*, 4 August 1989)

Augmenting the efforts of Ndilimani (which included in its repertoire numerous dramas and songs designed specifically to maintain morale and confi-dence in the struggle), youth groups in exile regularly staged dramas that brought attention to the dismal social conditions which spurred the Namibian masses to overthrow apartheid. Within the country, protest drama had incubated within schools, youth groups and at the university. Frederick B. Philander's Serpent Players (later the Windhoek Players and then Committed Artists of Namibia) regularly produced provocative theatre pieces for both township and city audiences including *The Curse* (formerly known as *Katutura 59*), a play dealing with forced removals under the segregation laws of workers from the 'old location' in Windhoek in 1959 (performed from 1987 on). His group initiated what is arguably the most influential showcase in Namibia today, the annual Youth Drama Festival (started in 1985, now in its eighteenth year) through which many of those working in Namibian theatre today received their first exposure to wider audiences. The University of Namibia's

Drama Department contributed a range of innovative and often biting satires featuring chorus and actors including Dorian Haarhoff's *Orange* (1988), *Skeleton* (1989) and *Guerrilla Goatherd* (1990). The Bricks Collective, with André Strauss and Leon Beukes, also produced a number of community drama works from their People's Centre in the heart of the black township, Katutura, concentrating on community mobilisation and development. After independence, the new National Theatre of Namibia (NTN) started to realign its activities, employing for the first time a permanent company of Namibian actors who toured the country with their *Stories and Legends of Namibia*. Having established the first permanent black theatre company in Namibia, the NTN followed its inaugural production with *Fast Norman and his Girlfriends*, featuring Norman Job, formerly a fighter with PLAN (People's Liberation Army of Namibia, SWAPO's military wing) and a student of Freddie Philander's. The production played to an estimated 20,000 people in the Caprivi region alone.

At the time of independence, the arts scene in Namibia's capital city Windhoek was abuzz with activity, facilitated by a peaceful national transition to liberation and a tentative, and ultimately successful, period of reconciliation. Newspaper headlines (1989–91) are representative of the excitement and aspiration in the arts community around the time of independence:

> Moving towards a National Culture; Bricks [a community organisation] Prepares for a Cultural Revival; Community Drama Takes Off; New Arts Council on the Way; Namibian Culture – No Longer a Quaint Tourist Sideshow; Power of Drama Recognised; NTN Establishes Permanent Cast; African Theatre on the Airwaves; Cultural Education for All; Cultural Revolution Here!; Namibia's Storytellers Set the Record Straight; New Life into Namibian Theatre.

By Namibia's second independence anniversary, the momentum was well established:

> NTN's *Forcible Love* [featuring former Ndilimani member and ex-PLAN fighter Ueshitile Banana Shekupe] puts the company fairly and squarely on the cultural map and justifies its claim to the title 'national theatre'. (*The Namibian*, 25 March 1991)

But, in spite of all the new-found public enthusiasm for the theatre and the arts generally, concerns about the new government's commitment to the arts were already evident. Writing in 1990, Philander notes: 'People's theatre started in this country as a reaction to the so-called conventional or colonial theatre which aided and abetted the colonial regime ... and it should be nurtured so that it can take its rightful place in the promotion of a genuine national culture' (Philander 1990). Under the headline 'Why Keep Arts on Backburner?', drama critic Kate Burling wrote in the year of Namibia's independence:

> In the absence of a strong lead from the government, organisations are left to do their best ... tagged onto the end of a Ministry already responsible for Education and Sport, culture does not seem a very likely candidate for serious attention. ... [N]ot to have made good use of the performing and visual arts to illuminate difficult concepts such as national reconciliation and nation-building will have been a waste of extremely valuable resources ... [H]ow can the arts hope to play necessary social and educational roles in Namibia without official promotion? (Burling 1990)

By 1998, Vickson Hangula's *The Show Isn't Over Until…* echoed increasingly strident calls for adequate government support for the arts:

> The Ministry of Basic Education and Culture doesn't give a shit. They'd rather spend the money on expensive hotel bills, as the so-called Culture Officers jet from one stupid cultural conference to another … we as local artists have a right to be part of this society. Like [government-sponsored] soccer, hockey and athletics. (Hangula, 2000: 26)

Soon, the play's call had resonated into a crescendo of condemnation. Again, the newspaper headlines (1998–2002) are representative:

> Artists on Zero Tolerance; Namibia Lacks Arts, Culture Co-ordination; Artists Urged to Get Their Act Together; Artists Union Holds Meeting; Rights of Performers take Centre Stage; Playwrights Throw Down the Gauntlet; Do Not Forget the Artists; Show Us the Money, Say Artists; Calling All Artists to Action; Youth Speak out on Arts and Culture Development; The Arts Get a Raw Deal; Call [to cultural officers] to Step Down; Artists Not Second-Class Citizens; Working

---

Box 1   Press coverage of protests by Namibian artists

'Most of those in charge of government arts and culture institutions are out of touch with the real cultural needs of Namibians. Our [the artists'] efforts are hardly ever acknowledged.' – Vickson Hangula quoted in 'Bureaucracy Frustrates Arts Efforts', *The Namibian*, 19 May 2001.

'In Namibia, culture and politics are inseparably part of our existence. Proof of this is the fact that some artists working for the government get paid to shut up and toe the line, a very unhealthy situation.' – Yellow Solo, quoted in 'Bureaucracy Frustrates Arts Efforts', *The Namibian*, 19 May 2001.

'The non-payment of [arts] workers in the Ministry of Basic Education's Arts Extension programme is to my mind the worst case of bureaucratic harassment against people who play a pivotal role in the human resource development of the Namibian nation…. Among those artists negatively affected are respected people who have contributed considerably to the cultural emancipation of the Namibian people in the dark days of the liberation struggle and should be respected as such.' – Freddie Philander, 'Personally Speaking', *The Namibian*, 9 February 2001.

'[S]elf-taught artists with practical skills should be allowed to be working as full time teachers in schools; courses and the format of lecturing at the College of the Arts should also be changed to suit the needs to aspiring artists and academic qualifications should not be the sole criteria for artists to develop their skills at government institutions.' – Snobia Kaputu, as reported in 'Youth Speak out on Arts and Culture Development', *The Namibian*, 5 May 2000.

Artists Woes; Own Ministry of Arts the Solution; Bureaucracy Frustrates Arts Efforts; Stand Up for Your Rights, Shekupe Urges Artists.

Frustrated by more than a decade of protest and disappointment that the mechanisms used to articulate cultural activity in Namibia remained hidden and bound in the bureaucracy of the state, almost ten years to the day after Namibia's liberation from apartheid South Africa, Namibia's artists called for a protest march through the capital city to State House to 'agitate for a better deal'. Prominent choreographer, musician, activist and former freedom fighter Banana Shekupe called for more government support: 'Arts played a big role in our liberation struggle. It opened the eyes of the international community to the plight of Namibians. President Nujoma was always at the forefront of the arts then, and it was hoped that he would support the arts industry in an independent Namibia.' The administrative secretary of the Namibia Arts Union quoted from the petition intended for the President: 'For a long time, [those engaged in] the arts industry and arts in Namibia have not been regarded as serious entrepreneurs whose industry needs the kind of incentives accorded to other professions' ('Artists to Agitate for a Better Deal', *The Namibian*, 31 March 2000).

By February 2002, government delays in implementing an effective policy to support the arts culminated in an open rejection by artists on a national television programme, *Talk of the Nation*. As commentator Patience Smith reported:

> The artists have reason to be frustrated as the [proposed Government] policy is definitely not inclusive of all. These [grassroots] artists are not arts and culture *activists* anymore, they are arts and culture *combatants* now as they have been insulted for far too long ... stop working for the artists and start working with them. ('Artists Reject Arts and Culture Policy', *The Namibian*, 22 February 2002)

The Show Isn't Over Until...

Vickson Hangula is now one of Namibia's most respected film-makers and impresarios. He graduated from the UNESCO/Zimbabwe Film and Television Training School in 1997, and has won numerous national and international awards for his films. He has also directed and acted in many local theatre productions and his company, Homebrewed Productions, is at the time of writing, probably the most successful theatre and film venture to have emerged in Namibia. His first successful play, *The Show Isn't Over Until...* , has enjoyed a series of revivals after its first two-night run at the College of the Arts in Windhoek in October 1998 was acclaimed by critics and audiences.

In the same month, the playwright won the National Theatre of Namibia's Golden Pen award for Best Play. Following this success, the play was scheduled by the National Theatre for two more nights at the 200-seat Warehouse Theatre in Windhoek as part of the annual independence festivities in late March 1999. Again it played to full houses and enthusiastic notices:

a great play by great actors, the best local production on a burning contemporary issue ... a play that does not pull any punches in exposing the deteriorating *status quo*, politics and many artificial problems Namibian actors are still facing almost a decade after independence. (*The Namibian*, 19 March 1999)

Meanwhile, the Arts Directorate in the Ministry of Basic Education and Culture had recommended the play's inclusion in the Southern African Maitisong Festival in Gaborone, Botswana (19–27 March 1999) and sponsored its transport costs. Again it played for two nights to large houses, but this time the official response was less than favourable. The Namibian High Commissioner was in the audience and wrote to the Namibian President and the Minister of Basic Education and Culture, concerned about the play's content and the artists' conduct. The production was refused funding to enable participation in the Market Theatre Laboratory Community Theatre Festival (Johannesburg) a few months later in May 1999: there had been an investigation and both the playwright and *The Namibian* reported an increase in state surveillance of the cast's activities. For the first time ever in Namibia, a play featured as the headline story: 'Play Ban Anger: Govt's "Theatre of the Absurd" Smacks of Apartheid' (*The Namibian*, 19 May 1999). The newspaper commented that this 'act of censorship reminiscent of the apartheid era ... is akin to that of Nazi Germany ... The Arts fraternity has reacted with outrage [and some of its members] describe government action as "disgusting"'. According to the report, even the government driver on the Botswana trip was interrogated.

In a subsequent interview, the playwright explained that at the time of the Maitisong Festival, Namibia was embroiled in a dispute with Botswana over territory in its Caprivi region and a new opposition party, the Congress of Democrats, had announced its formation in Windhoek. While the playwright has no association with this party, nevertheless

word went out that people where looking for me ... that my name was being mentioned in State House ... people were threatened with dismissal ... I had strange cars parked outside my house at night ... I got it from reliable sources that it [the controversy] was quite a scene at State House and at SWAPO headquarters. (Interview with the playwright, Windhoek, 31 July 2002)

Tangeni Amupadhi, *The Namibian*'s arts correspondent, quoted a letter from the Permanent Secretary, Ministry of Basic Education and Culture, explaining why touring costs for the Market Theatre festival were refused:

Based on various reports received from sources that have seen the performance of *The Show Isn't Over, Until...* at the Maitisong Festival in Botswana ... the allegations of nepotism, sexual harassment, inefficiency in government and sexual abuse during the liberation struggle are in our view domestic issues and problems that are not suitable for a foreign audience. The performance of a political satire in Botswana has therefore caused embarrassment to Namibia as it spread anti-SWAPO and anti-government propaganda in a foreign country ... the Ministry cannot continue sponsoring a body that is spreading anti-government sentiments. (Quoted in *The Namibian*, 21 May 1999)

In spite of the government's withdrawal of support for transport and increased state surveillance, the players, with donations offered on condition of anonymity, slipped through the net that had been placed around them and travelled to South Africa using an alternative route. Their attendance at the Festival in Johannesburg was only announced after the cast had left Namibia for fear that they would be prohibited from performing. The refusal of support for this tour resulted in national media coverage and an extended debate on artistic freedom in Namibia. The play was also staged in Durban at the Ninth International Anti-Corruption Conference in October 1999 (the invitation had come from Amnesty International, whose representative had seen the play in Botswana). Although the Durban performance was a setback (reports circulated that some of the cast were too drunk to perform adequately), at its last performance with a Namibian cast at Johannesburg's Market Theatre in April 2001, the play had another triumph. In a report that speaks of 'standing ovations, capacity houses, glowing press reviews and an invitation for an extended run', Eddie Mokoena of *The Sowetan* concluded that: 'This simple, unconventional, uncompromising but highly entertaining play is definitely a political lesson to South Africans and a fresh breeze for protest theatre in this country' ('Namibian Play Conquers The Market', *The Namibian*, 27 April 2001). In July 2002 it was staged by the South African State Theatre on the occasion of the launch of the African Union in Johannesburg, an impressive honour for a protest play. Eighteen members of the Namibian embassy were invited, and according to the State Theatre press office, the play was 'well received'.

The play's stages

Vickson Hangula's *The Show Isn't Over Until...* is not a realist play — that is, it does not present a cohesive story or plot in which characters and 'their world', rather than the actors and their circumstances, are seen to be the focus. Rather, it is about four actors and their director who are rehearsing such a conventional play. As the initial stage directions note:

> A group of actors have the most brilliant play that they are putting on. They are all seasoned actors and have travelled this road many times before, but will their professional differences allow them to 'live it up' in the play? Especially when they know that it is going to be a rather controversial play.

We are offered bits of the 'play-in-rehearsal' as the actors and their director choose to deal with last-minute problems; more importantly, the work shows actors engaged in the process of dealing with the problems that the content of the 'play' they are rehearsing presents. So the audience moves between layers of (re)presentation: on the one hand, the content of the play-in-rehearsal which deals provocatively with corruption in government circles and, on the other hand, the conflicts of the actors themselves as they prepare the 'rather controversial play' that will be presented 'tomorrow night'. Indeed, when the production opened, some members of the audience enquired of the playwright when all of the 'actual play' was to be produced, disappointed that they had attended only a rehearsal. In short, the (real) play is actually the rehearsal of the play-within-the play.

The matter or the subject of the rehearsal (the play-within-the-play) is not the primary focus of this discussion: suffice it to say that the scenes rehearsed include a brutal and satirical attack on nepotism and tribalism in determining government contracts and the assimilation of former freedom fighters into a modern economy. The actors stop the rehearsal in fear; in part they are afraid that the more successfully they deliver the 'truth' of their performance, the greater the risk that they themselves will be mistaken for the parts they perform. They try to change the script. The director refuses.

The rehearsal does not proceed smoothly. It is the day before 'opening night' and tensions are running high. Steve, an actor, stumbles when delivering a particularly difficult line – a contentious anti-government retort, his character's warning that civil war is imminent if the government does not start employing former combatants. Steve breaks up the rehearsal to ask the director, 'Should I really say that?' The director explains: 'Say the bloody lines. It is not you saying that, it is the character you are playing. Say it, loud. Action!' Karin, another of the actors assembled for rehearsal, likewise cannot get 'into character'. She too has a problem with the subject matter and is clearly intimidated by the vituperative outbursts she is to deliver – her character accuses the 'bloody SWAPO government' of employing 'illiterate "memes" [rural women]' and abandoning the 'poor AK-47 wielding fools ... now so poor and hungry in their liberated motherland'. It seems that for the actors the dialogue is too overtly critical of the government:

> **Director:** 'What is this? Where is your professionalism? You are an ACTOR!!' Do you think all those white people who portray white trash – Ku Klux Klan, psychos and murders – are like that in real life? Those are respected actors like Woody Harrelson, Robert de Niro, James Woods, Sharon Stone, the super bitch Julia Roberts and the others. And why do people love them so much? Because they do justice to their characters! Now, ACTION!
>
> **Karin:** But honestly, right now is not an ideal time to come up with such characters. Maybe in another ten years. You know the political set up in this country. If Peter Tshirumbu's Men in Black [intelligence agency operatives] are in the audience, they will not differentiate between my character and me! Those bunch of assholes will soon start following me wherever I go!
>
> **Director:** Bunch of assholes, right? I like that. Now, take the same anger and energy and just put it into your character. Pick up where you have ended – Action!

Karin's dilemma is acute. For an actor, the job of play-making convention-ally involves tricking the audience into an experience of constructing from the actor's efforts that fiction called 'character'. The director wishes the performer's protesting self to be subjugated to such a degree that the self-deceiving audience sees the character's action only – as opposed to the actor's uncertain attitude towards this action. As Karin, the actor, achieves the blurring of the boundaries between her self and the 'fake' self she constructs as character, she fulfils the Director's requirements of her: 'Put yourself into your character,' says the Director to Steve. 'Put yourself deeper into your character ... you are supposed to be the character, not yourself', says the Director to Judy, too. Judy, like Karin, is 'only' an actor, but she is another who fears her own complicity. And, confronted with the readiness of the agents of the state to clamp down on resistance (particularly given the play's first performances before a crucial election) she, is acutely aware that the actor's success in fabricating fictions that masquerade as truth (in other words playing the part convincingly) could potentially remove the protection of the conventions theatre employs – that the aesthetic distance between her production of the character and the force and effect of her character's utterances might narrow and fuse, so exposing the actor's 'self' as the source of political agitation and therefore grounds for complicity in subversion.

Actors rehearsing plays (and the playwrights who 'wright' them) are aware that playscripts are prompts for future ephemeral events. These texts, appearing to be complete and 'already happened', are dormant potentials – awaiting the actor to release and realise them only in or at the moment of performance. The text in the script is not a rigid template an actor learns, then recites in a parroted execution of the printed 'record' of events 'to-be-repeated'. Nor is the dialogue a residue of what has already 'actually' happened in the imagination of the playwright sometime before. Actors who subscribe to such a convention (which is akin to the casual interpretation of Stanislavski's 'Method' used by Hangula's Director character) will view the process of rehearsal as an opportunity faithfully to 'replay' and 're-present' these presumed 'past events' in order to derive a set of given circumstances that would render a plausible society in the delivery of the play in performance.

The text instead offers a *proposition* or a *prediction* by the playwright in the form of lines that *seem* to be a record of words *already* 'spoken'. The text, or script, is really a leap of the imagination, or a medium or a conveyance to the occasion of the proposed performance – an accurate prediction (can we say *prediction*?) of what *might* be uttered if humans in the roles assigned were placed in 'similar', 'real' situations. A play's text requires an actor to embody and produce symbolic efforts (which we call words) which will later defer or provoke conflict in the moment of performance. Text therefore engages the body of the actor directly in the form of human language and action.

In the context of Hangula's play and its reception, it is important to consider *whose* body? Surely not the body of the character – which exists only as a fiction? The hesitation the actors experience in the rehearsal of *The Show Isn't Over Until...* is related to the precept that the text can be seen to encode (*pre*-'scribe' or *pre*-'dict') conditions for the actor's body. As the actor's body (re)produces the required sounds and efforts at language constructed by the playwright, so the responsive body of the actor fleshes character by producing the precursors to these efforts: a systemic inhalation of the play's pretexts or 'thought'. It is therefore dangerous for Karin (as an actor afraid of the state's confusion as to 'actor' and 'character') to invite the text to incubate in her own body the illusion (literally 'playing into') of a character whose politics are incompatible with her own.

The actors instead disrupt the rehearsal, seeking reassurances that the conventions governing the artist's right to 'interpret life as artistically as we can' are still intact. The actors cannot be convinced and, as Steve says at the end of the rehearsal, 'If people attack me for the character I played, I will always refer them to the Director.' Karin likewise, after being congratulated by the Director on her performance, says: 'You must be prepared to be my bodyguard once Siirumbu's [sic] Men in Black start following me around.' The Director replies: 'Don't worry. I will personally write a letter in Oshiwambo [the President's mother tongue] to State House explaining that we are *only* doing a play.'

Fronting the mask

Those of us who worked at the National Theatre of Namibia in the early 1990s suspected that the Windhoek Theatre was haunted. The then stage manager, who was often required to work very late at night, was particularly convinced. After midnight, when no one else was in the building, lights would switch on, toilets would flush and the tinkle of the piano upstairs in the rehearsal room could be heard. We may never know whether the Windhoek Theatre was in fact visited by ghosts, but it is the case that many theatres in the world are considered haunted by the ghosts of 'characters' that actors had once brought to 'life' on stage and later abandoned in the theatre after the play had closed. It is said that the disembodied 'characters' remain in the charged atmosphere of the dark theatre, reduced to the substance of memories waiting for the next performer's body to reincarnate them. For what is a character but an entity created by an actor – a 'something' that 'appears' to be like a person in action and seemingly representative of 'us', the assembled audiences? An ephemeron? Yet, so compelling is the 'presence' of character that it is quite common to speak of characters *as if* they are human and to discuss and analyse 'their' conflicts and 'their' circumstances *as if* they were present in the world outside the theatre.

This is arguably, even certainly, an oversimplification, but most people who regularly go to the theatre would, if asked, agree that an actor at work on stage in a play is not actually (really) the same person as the character being portrayed. Conversely, most audiences would agree that their enjoyment of 'conventional' drama (realism) is enhanced if they are able to regard the actor as the character – that their pleasure in going to the theatre involves a certain degree of 'let's pretend'. This may be especially true of television soap operas where audiences, week in and week out, follow the doings of the character (in what is called the plot or the story) with little thought for the craft of the actor or medium through which the character is produced (this is especially so in long-running American soap operas where several actors can play the same character). In such 'conventional' dramas, the audience expects the actor to keep up the mask of character and not let it slip. Only after the play is done can the actor remove the mask of character and become 'herself' again.

In this dramatic realism, the temporary society assembled as audience participates in an entertaining and pleasurable deception: an agreement to view the events of the stage as if they were, plausibly and reliably, the products of actual lives lived – as if the characters portrayed were representative of [standing in the place of] general or particular society. In such dramas, the expectation of the actor's work is to offer a pretence – a 'playing out' – that is 'lifelike' and 'real' and to construct a persona or mask of character that eclipses the actor's own self in performance. In terms of the Director's coaching of the actors in Hangula's play, the 'good' actor is one who convinces her audience that, for the duration of the play at least, she is the person she is playing, aware, again in terms of the Director's instructions to his actors, of an audience whose expectation, experience and enjoyment of the theatre and the drama it presents fall loosely or exclusively within the bounds of 'plausibility' – whether the play is presented as realism or departs from it. If this sort of drama is to be regarded as usual or 'conventional', then most of the scripted and published drama presented in Namibia today follows the convention – that of requiring the skilful actor to 'pretend' to be someone else, to put on the mask of character in the performance, to represent the character 'truthfully'. In this conventional view the story (and the characters within the story) portrayed by the actors is more important than the opportunity afforded to observe the actor's own production of it.

And for good reason. If the situation and story of the drama concerns itself with pressing and serious social matters (as the protest or 'issues-based' play does), all the more reason for the actor to make sure the play is not marred by a performance that draws attention away from the (illusion of) reality presented and the appearance of truth in the message that the play proposes. For protest to be effective, conventional reception requires the mask of 'character' to remain in place. The published protest or 'issues-based' drama of Namibia offers many such conventional roles: The 'old location' woman (Handjievol) and her struggle against the white brute of a policeman (Lombaard) in Freddie Philander's *The Curse*; Kubbe Rispel's crazy president (the Leader) who is obsessed with the cleanliness of his throne in *Die Stoel*; the tribal chief (Chief Lewanika) who faces resistance from his wives protesting against a tribal polygamous patriarchy in *Gods of Women* by Sifso Nyathi; Norman Job's *Mai Jekketti*, which explores issues of inheritance; the Mother's bloody revenge against the Father's abuse of their child in Laurinda Olivier-Sampson's *A Moment in Our Lives*; and the sad tale of the Luderitz fisherman caught up in illegal diamond smuggling in *Onele yo Kawe* by Kay Cowley and Tanya Terblanche.

All the plays listed (and they may be considered a representative selection of the script-based, published drama of post-independence Namibia) require the actor to work in such a way that the audience constructs the illusion of lives lived in a 'society' that is recognisably resonant with their own. Persuaded by the events on stage, the audience might be moved to protest or, at least, moved to greater sensitivity to the issues presented. The actor's working is part of this process, encouraging the illusion by remaining 'hidden' behind the mask and in subjugation to the role. In such a system:

> The artist shall remain a puzzle
> Not the Who, but the Why.
> (Christi Werner, 'Battered Paintings for Sale', in Kgobetsi (ed.) 2000: 54)

The willingness of audiences to participate in the *as if* (let's pretend) premise of the theatre (an almost magical tricking of the complicit audience's collective 'mind'), invites, even tempts, the researcher to regard the theatre as capable of rendering, in microcosm, the dramas of 'real' life. The many metaphors and analogies linking theatre with actual human experience further encourage the association:

> Give me a poem that can
> Lift the eyelid and open the ear-curtain
> A poem i can engrave on stone
> Act out on stage
> ...
> Madame Poet in me
> Select and arrange
> Words of my range
> Words that move my mind
> Closer to scenes seen or unseen
> (Siballi E. I. Kgobetsi, 'Give me a poem' in Kgobetsi (ed.) 2000: 13)

Actors (in a play) take on roles only for the brief time they are on stage. After the performance, the 'characters' are no more. They become ephemeral 'blips' in the consciousness of the audience that participated in the transitory performance. Likewise, the ephemeral qualities of the theatre (here today, gone tomorrow) are often evoked as analogous to the human situation. Jacques in Shakespeare's *As You Like It* makes the analogy obvious:

> All the world's a stage
> And all the men and women merely players:
> They have their exits and their entrances;
> And one man in his time plays many parts....

Antonio's quip in *The Merchant of Venice* is even clearer:

> I hold the world but as the world, Gratiano;
> A stage where every man must play a part....

In everyday conversation we refer to events happening *behind the scenes*, long for a *change of scene*, or attempt to *set the scene for notable occasions*. If the world (the collective bustle of human traffic we call 'our world' or 'our society') is likened to the ephemera of the theatrical performance (the momentary embodying of the conflict of the human will that is the engine of drama), so too the theatrical performance and the drama it produces can be easily confused with, or substituted for, its twin or mirror: 'life'. It might be tempting then, to view the theatre as a useful laboratory in which the sociologist is able to investigate conflicts presented by characters *as if* they were representative (accurate and real) members of a real community and to use their 'experience' as reliable testimony within which and against which activists for change might rail. I say 'tempting' though, because a performance is more than the character's journey. The 'ephemerons' which produce drama are actors, not characters; and it is here, at this point of partial eclipse, that the agitating 'pulse' of the theatre can be taken more accurately by examining what the artists say about themselves more closely than what their characters say in the dramas they produce.

Confronting the mask

Bertolt Brecht is unequivocal in his rejection of the assimilation of character and the stance of the performer ('the tasteless rehearsing of empty visual or spiritual palliatives'), accusing the conventional theatre 'of having degenerated into branches of the bourgeois narcotics business' (Brecht in Willet 1964: 189). And his complaint is resonant with Hangula's play: 'Our representations of human social life are designed for … upturners of society, whom we invite into our theatres and beg not to forget their cheerful [proletarian] occupations while we hand the world over to their minds and hearts, for them to change as they see fit' (ibid: 185). But such overt performance confuses the actor trained in the conventional realism espoused by Hangula's Director, for in such plays actors produce 'societies' that are fictions – are ephemeral – and do not really 'exist' at any time – even in the play's performance. If they seem to exist, they do so as mere false memories imprinted in the audience's imagination. The 'world of the play', then, only exists as 'a dream of passion' and 'a fiction', and the producers of these impressions, the actors, are 'shadows' or 'ciphers'. Within this context, the world of conflict observed and re-presented by the playwright can be dismissed as *literally* immaterial to the material facts of a [real] society's contradictions: the 'truth', however well presented on the stage, cannot be equated with the 'facts' of real life. If play and players are ephemeral, 'shadows', 'dreams of passion' or 'fictions', the claim can be made that they ought to present no 'real' threat to the state, that 'characters' cannot be activists and certainly not agitators – hence, in Hangula's play, the Director's letter of explanation to the President explaining that 'we are only doing a play'.

The Director's assertion that the cast are *only* doing a play (rather than something tangibly overt and 'real'), and the Director's assumption that this particular form of non-threatening activity would need to be *explained* to State House, might, on the one hand, be a facetious dismissal of a government so unsophisticated as to require tuition in the conventions of theatre in order to avoid confusing the mask with its bearer. But, given the anxiety that the actors' work and utterances are under state scrutiny and surveillance, the gist of the explanation is to reassure the state that the performers are not 'really' agitating for change – just simply narrating, at a remove, the fiction of that agitation, which is actually *only* play-acting and idle dabbling. As the actors attempt to unravel the contradictions between representation and being, the problem of 'acting for' the state while under the conventional cover of character, and taking action against the state, forces the actor to both front and confront the mask of character. To question, to unsettle and destabilise the authority of the 'conventional' mask exposes the actor as 'imperfect' and 'out of character', therefore debilitating the cogency of authentic voices of protest that appear outside the fictional world of the play masquerading (and accepted by the audience) as 'truth'.

But it is precisely this problem that the actors in *The Show Isn't Over Until...* want to overcome when telling their *own* stories. They want to be seen, noted, taken seriously – not just for the characters they present as artists, but as artists that have their own tale to tell. They would greatly prefer not to be dismissed as ephemera and shadows. For to the actor, playing is work. They complain from the stage, and from within the context of their drama, that 'everybody is taking us for granted. Look, now we have to eat brown bread and chips everyday. We have been on the same diet ever since the community theatre days before independence.' They point out that performing arts funding from the private sector is spent on shows that 'appeal mostly to white, rich audiences' and that 'black artists are really marginalised. Actors, Directors, Visual Artists, and the lot.' And, as they become more strident: 'Most African governments don't think theatre is as important as any other sorts of development ... we as local artists have a right to be part of this society. And we expect the same support that they give elsewhere in society. Like to soccer, hockey and athletics.'

Hangula is not alone in Namibia in allowing the performer to act beside the mask. To refer briefly to another play, Keamogetsi Joseph Molapong's *The Horizon Is Calling* presents four persons in its cast list but the names of Boetietjie Kavandje, Anna Louw, Donovan Isaacks and Karl Pietersen are not the names of characters – they are names of the actors themselves, appearing as themselves and as characters. From the stage, Anna and Karl offer affidavits of their own experiences, then interweave these monologues with scenes in which they appear as themselves and as other characters, reminiscent of elements in the work of Augusto Boal. Here, the most essential medium of the theatre (the actor's own body on stage) is used by performers as a means of protesting the eclipsing of the artist in national reconstruction. For the theatre, and the drama it presents – for all its transitory and ephemeral nature, peopled by 'ciphers', 'shadows' and ghosts – nevertheless is concrete in one way: the theatre must have an audience and so gathers a group of people ready to be persuaded by the propositions of the stage which can accommodate both characters operating with the viscosity of thought and actors *re-minding*, in unmasked performances, the collective audience. It is in this latter moment that the theatre is perhaps at its most powerful through its ability to impress (to make a mark, to imprint with imagination's stylus) a call to action in the minds of a collection of real people.

When the actor in a play or on the world's stage is engaged in politicisation, the theatre rediscovers the reasons why societies invented/needed the mimetic arts in the first place (the need to test the effects of action). A decade after independence it should not be surprising that plots are more complex. Namibian playwrights are less inclined now to stage, in caricature, the apartheid drama (the black and white 'us' and 'them'). The struggle now has moved on. Yet anxieties remain – albeit, perhaps, more intricately coded in the texts represented. As the artists begin to rehearse their protest, they begin to script themselves (their own selves) into the *dramatis personae* of their theatre productions, so exposing the performer as a legitimate agent, agitator and 'actor'. The performers do this by projecting their own protesting selves in experiments with theatrical form as opposed to puppeting this protest through the produced 'character' of conventional drama.

Hence the direct call to artists by Namibian poet Keamogetsi Joseph Molapong in 'Let's go to Parliament'

Let's invade Parliament
Exhibit our interests
Perform our hunger to them
Let's sing to them of our thirst
And do the poverty dance

Let's screen for them the movies
Depicting our [the artists'] honest suffering
With detailed pain and curse

Let's recite poetry of a failure
To appreciate visual art
Understanding performing art
Let's colonise Parliament

Let's persist with our art
Speak through our poems
Draw with our sweat
On the canvases of our skin

Let's move the Parliament
To new grounds, space, time
Cultured foundations of strength
Influenced by innovative art.

Keamogetsi J. Molapong, 'Let's go to Parliament', Kgobetsi (ed.) 2000: 56.

NOTES

1 This article draws on some material first presented in the preface to *New Namibian Plays Volume One*. The article also reworks material submitted for a sociology reader for Namibian students to be published by the University of Namibia.

BIBLIOGRAPHY

Brecht, Bertolt (1964) 'A Short Organum for the Theatre', in John Willet (ed.), *Brecht on Theatre: The Development of an Aesthetic*, London: Methuen.

Burling, Kate (1990) 'Why Keep Arts on the Backburner?' in *The Namibian*, 15 May.

Haarhoff, Dorian (2000) *Goats, Oranges and Skeletons, A Trilogy of Namibian Independence Plays*, Windhoek: Gamsberg Macmillan/New Namibia Books.

Hangula, Vickson (2000) *The Show Isn't Over Until...*, in Terence Zeeman (ed.), *New Namibian Plays Volume One*, Windhoek: Gamsberg Macmillan/New Namibia Books.

Philander, Frederick (1990a) *The Curse*, Braamfontein: Skotaville Publishers.

Philander, Frederick (1990b) 'Cultural Education for All: People's Theatre in Namibia', in *The Namibian*, 27 July.

Kgobetsi, Siballi E. I. (ed.) (2000) *Poetically Speaking*, Windhoek: Gamsberg Macmillan.

Shona Storytelling & the Contemporary Performing Arts in Zimbabwe

KENNEDY C. CHINYOWA

Apart from the various anthropological compilations of different types of folktales (see Fortune 1974; Kileff 1983; Pongweni 2001), the study of indigenous storytelling in Zimbabwe has hitherto been carried out within the context of oral literature, also known by a variety of terms such as orality, orature, oracy, folklore or folk literature (Okpewho 1992:3). Oral literature itself encompasses a broad range of artistic genres from myths, legends, epics and tales to proverbs, idioms, poems, riddles, music and song. Knowledge of storytelling has been overshadowed by a compulsive tendency to see it as part of the whole oral 'literary' canon. The aesthetic elements of storytelling as narrative performance have not been fully appreciated.

This article explores the art of storytelling among the Shona-speaking peoples of Zimbabwe. It examines the role of the *sarungano* (storyteller), the context within which she composes and transforms her narratives into exciting theatrical performances, and the aesthetic strategies employed by the *sarungano* to engage with her participating audience. As far as possible, the focus will be on the continuity between the indigenous storytelling tradition and contemporary Zimbabwean theatre. As Chinua Achebe says through one of his central characters in *Anthills of the Savanna,* 'the story is our escort; without it, we are blind, ... it is the story that owns us and directs us.' (1987: 124).

The article will finally examine existing attempts being made to adapt Shona storytelling to the contemporary Zimbabwean theatre context. It will be argued that traditional Shona storytelling still lives on but in modified forms such as community-based theatre, children's performing arts and other theatrical modes. Zimbabwean theatre practitioners are transforming indigenous Shona narratives into popular theatre modes that enable them to address the problems currently affecting society. To an extent, the practitioners are still grappling with the transition from tradition to modernity. Hence, Shona storytelling aesthetics continue to provide a powerful source of inspiration.

The context of performance

In the traditional Shona context, the *sarungano* was usually a woman. *Sarungano* means 'owner of the tale', implying that the composition, delivery and impact of the story largely depended on the artistic ability of the storyteller. The story took its character from the way the *sarungano* told it and from the response of her participating audience. She stood at the centre of tradition as the chronicler of the community's beliefs. Through the medium of animal or human metaphor, she erected the ethical principles that ultimately defined the moral consciousness of the time. As grandmother or aunt, she was regarded as a reservoir of the cultural wisdom and knowledge that was to be imparted to succeeding generations. (see Chinyowa 2001a).

The *sarungano's* stories were mostly performed around the evening fire, especially in the village hut. The winter season was regarded as more convenient for storytelling since people were no longer occupied in the fields. The Shona people believed that narrating stories during daytime was taboo. This was intended to discourage people from telling stories when they should be doing other work. Evening was the time when people could relax. At the beginning of the storytelling session, as the *sarungano* sat by the fireplace, her mostly young audience would bring some firewood and even maize cobs as token 'payments' for the story.

Both the time and place setting were suggestive of the story. The darkness of the evening and its accompanying sounds were conducive to the creation of an atmosphere of mystery and fantasy in which the animal characters of the story could 'prowl' around behaving like humans. The grim shadows and silhouettes produced by the flickering flames of the fire played on the *sarungano's* hands and face to instil a sense of the marvellous into her actions. The whole atmosphere enabled the *sarungano* to lure her audience, making them more receptive to the presentation and consumption of the story. In short, the context of performance was such that it created a heightened sense of wonder, excitement and reverence for the words, images and symbols released during the storytelling.

The *Sarungano* and audience relationship

Ropo Sekoni (1990:139), whose work is mainly based on the Yoruba people of Nigeria, argues that storytelling should be viewed as a performative social discourse between narrator and audience designed to explore and communicate the dominant concerns of the community. As a communicative act, the story calls for a closer examination of its artistic composition, delivery and the aesthetic engagement of the audience. There is a dialectical interplay between the medium and its reception and interpretation. In the process of engaging the audience's imagination and feelings, the *sarungano* gives them new insights into themselves and their environment. The close link between the art form and its consumption can be observed in the harmonious relationship that prevails between the *sarungano* and her audience.

As she delivers her story, the *sarungano* receives constant feedback from the audience to create a close dialogic relationship. She will open her story with the formulaic utterance, '*Paivepo* ...' (Once upon a time ...) to which her audience respond by saying, '*Dzepfunde* ....' (Proceed). Later she closes the narration with the formulaic ending, '*Ndipo pakafira sarungano*' (That is where the story-teller died) or '*Ndipo pakaperera sarungano*' (That is where the storyteller ended). The opening informs the audience that a performance is about to begin. It also suggests that they need to prepare for an imaginative journey in which the exigencies of time, space and place are trivial. Instead, the limitations of reality are suspended in order to transport the audience into the realm of the fantastic. Although the *sarungano* brings her own personal imprint into the narration, she does not own the story. It remains the property of the community. This is why she has to die a symbolic 'death' at the end of her performance. She 'dies' in order to allow others to tell the story in their own way. Such 'death' is usually enacted through a variation of verbal utterance and ritual gesture. She can either proclaim the usual formulaic ending or she lies down as if in a trance, then 'awakens' to the beginning of yet another story. It is not uncommon for a storyteller from among the audience to immediately come forward to fill up gaps in the previous story or to follow it up with a different story (see Chinyowa, 2001a).

As the *sarungano* proceeds with the story, her audience picks up the rhythm of the narration, turning the story into a collective performance. It is through their active involvement in the performance that the participating audience comes to learn the art of storytelling. As an aesthetic experience, audience participation may be viewed from two related angles. First, the *sarungano* takes advantage of the call–and–response technique in order to involve her audience. She displays her aesthetic skill by her ability to influence and move the audience, leading them to think, act and feel with her. Through her use of language, body movement, expressive voice, animation of character, dramatic pause, mime and gesture, she evokes feelings of tension, anxiety, suspense and delight thereby intensifying audience response to the performance. In the words of Okpewho, a talented oral artist should be able to create, 'a complete aesthetic experience' (1992: 224) through a histrionic manipulation of the audience's sensations comparable to the rhythmic effect of a musical performance. The call–and–response technique functionalises the African concept of community through its harmonious integration of performer and audience. Malaika Mutere (1997) likens the call–and–response strategy to a transaction between life's creative forces 'dancing' to the tune of a narrative composition. The narrative performance becomes a kind of verbally inscribed 'rite of passage' mediating the audience's lived experience. It makes storytelling an essentially communal participatory experience. This probably explains why storytelling plays such a pivotal role in the education and socialisation of the young.

The *sarungano* also aims to retain audience involvement through the manner in which she manipulates the core images of the story. Sekoni (1990:141) points out that the patterning of images of the story is one of the most important factors in the attainment of aesthetic harmony, and the emotive and cognitive satisfaction of the audience. Such images become the units of behaviour externalised through the portrayal of characters within the story.

Pellowski has described the dynamism with which a Yoruba storyteller conveys the images of her animal characters in these words:

> To the Rabbit, of course, (s)he gave a wee voice, to the Elephant, (s)he gave a deep bass, to the Buffalo, a hollow mooing. When (s)he attempted the Lion, the veins of (her) temple and neck were dreadfully distended, but when (s)he mimicked the Jackal, one almost expected a terrier-like dog to trot up to the fire(place), so perfect was (her) yaup yaup. (1977: 111)

The impact of the story is heightened by the manner in which the *sarungano* acts 'in character' rather than 'out of character', giving detail and dimension to each of her characters. She personifies the different characters in accordance with their nature and function. In a way, she *becomes* the characters by virtue of her immediacy of delivery, thereby concretising her characters' actions in such a way that they remain a memorable experience in the minds of the audience.

Storytelling is meant for entertainment and enjoyment. Through the celebratory medium of narrative performance, the *sarungano* takes her audience along a comic journey in which their emotions are aroused, heightened and purged. Either actively or vicariously, she enables her participating audience to 'act out' their joys and sorrows, hopes and dreams, trials and tribulations. For instance, during the performance of an animal trickster tale, the mere entry of the trickster into the performance usually heralds the beginning of a comic odyssey. The audience begins to witness the ironic spectacle of a dimunitive figure endowed with feats of disguise, deception, pretence, treachery and escape. The repeated 'fooling' of strong and powerful characters like lion, leopard and elephant, at the hands of seemingly insignificant characters like Hare, Tortoise and Spider provokes feelings of surprise, excitement and bewilderment. In the end, the audience feels a sense of comic relief when the trickster is finally outwitted at his own game.

The performance of Shona stories may also include choric song, music and dance. The audience gets involved in creating a joyous atmosphere in which they help in 'telling' the story by complementing it with other performative genres in a mutually supportive, enriching and interdependent manner. In the process, a situation of inter-textuality, or what Joseph Mbele calls 'inter-orality' (1999: 137) emerges that gives different layers of meaning to the story. The music and song not only helps to vary the narrative action but also serves to boost audience participation in the performance. The fusion of storytelling with other genres can thus be regarded as a more holistic means of rendering the story.

Variability and adaptability

The potential of Shona storytelling to adapt to changing circumstances really begins with the *sarungano's* tendency towards variability. The situational nature of each narrative performance implies the production of a 'text' that cannot be reproduced. This means that almost all the elements of the story are susceptible to change. These would include the performer herself, her audience, and the composition and delivery of the story. Variability becomes part and parcel of the whole constitutive process, if not the very source of creativity. Whether performed by the same storyteller or not, each narrative performance is liable to vary and adapt to the needs of the occasion and the interests of the particular audience. (Agatucci, 1998).

For example, in Shona storytelling, variability may be discerned at different levels of performance. It is manifest at the beginning and ending of the story. Apart from '*Paivepo* ...' (Once upon a time), the *sarungano* may vary her formulaic opening with other utterances such as '*Ndokunge paine* ...' (There was once ...), or '*Kare kare kwazvo* ...' (A long time ago ...). Similarly, there are Shona tales in which the trickster character has been known to vary from the usual Kalulu, the Hare to Kamba, the Tortoise (Kileff, 1983). This is also typical of trickster figures in other parts of Africa: Ananse, the Spider in Ghana; Chakijana, the Mongoose in South Africa, and Mpungushe, the Jackal in Kenya (Canonici, 1996). In order to create the appropriate tone, mood and atmosphere for her target audience, the *sarungano* varies each performance. In short, variability testifies to the adaptive capacity of Shona storytelling.

In the contemporary Zimbabwean context, the undying presence of indigenous storytelling became most pronounced after the attainment of national political independence from Britain in April 1980. In order to legitimate settler hegemony, successive colonial regimes had suppressed indigenous forms of cultural expression. The rise of African nationalism, which culminated in the protracted liberation struggle (1966–79), witnessed a strong revival of indigenous theatre modes. In the words of Stephen Chifunyise:

> The dynamic use of the diverse and popular forms of indigenous performing arts, for instance ... ritual dances, poetic recitation, chants, songs and storytelling enabled the combatants to mobilise ... the peasants' solidarity with the liberation struggle. (1994: 55)

This rather new form of theatre that emerged at the war front became popularly known as *pungwe* (all night celebration). Apart from being a carry-over from pre-colonial performing arts, *pungwe* theatre became an effective way of telling the story of colonial injustice and nationalist resistance. It may also be viewed as a nascent form of agit-prop theatre because of the manner in which it dramatised the people's response to colonial oppression. It made use of such storytelling aesthetic techniques as role play, audience participation, mime, gesture and movement. The audience had so much control over the whole process that Ross Kidd describes the *pungwe* as 'a theatre-with-the-people experience' (1983: 12).

According to Owen Seda (2001: 39), the roots of post-independence Zimbabwean theatre, which is largely community-based, are to be found in the pre-colonial and colonial periods. Community-based theatre aims not only to entertain, inform and instruct, but also to address the people's problems, hopes and aspirations. It was born out of the new black government's policy of cultural regeneration that had started with the liberation struggle. Soon after independence, several township theatre groups began to emerge in the new nation state. This led to the formation of an umbrella theatre organisation, the Zimbabwe Association of Community Theatre (ZACT) on 15 February 1986. The establishment of ZACT was meant to coordinate the activities of the township theatre groups. As a popular theatre movement, ZACT also aimed at articulating the cultural nationalist sentiments of the newly liberated Zimbabwe.

Community-based theatre relies heavily on indigenous expressive modes, particularly storytelling. Usually there is no individual authorship for the performance script, but collective improvisation and experimentation. The 'final' performance is part of an ongoing process that could be 'edited' by an interactive audience. Ogah Abah (in Breitinger 1994: 87) points out that the community theatre script is a rehearsal for action, loosely structured to allow spontaneity, debate and change. The idea of collective authorship in the production of the performance 'text' has been borrowed from the narrative performance.

Community theatre-based participation also typifies the narrative performance in terms of actor–audience dynamics by allowing room for audience involvement during and after the performance. The audience may spontaneously interject, heckle or applaud a performance in the process of unfolding. Such responses may create considerable variations to the 'final' performance. This often happens when one of the actors steps forward to play the double role of being both performer and narrator at the same time. To illustrate this point, a typical narrative sequence for a community-based theatre for development (TfD) workshop on HIV/AIDS runs as follows:

- Ben dies from a mysterious disease.
- Village elders meet to decide who will inherit his widow.
- Nyasha, Ben's widow, refuses to be inherited.
- She is warned that her refusal will bring an ancestral curse. The whole village will be wiped out. She will be haunted by her husband's spirit.
- Nyasha accepts the wishes of the community out of fear.
- She is inherited by Tendai, her late husband's young brother.
- After a while, Nyasha and Tendai suffer from the same mysterious disease.
- The performance freezes at this point.
- The narrator steps forward to ask the audience, 'Do you think we should continue with this practice of widow inheritance?'
- Possible responses: both widow and inheritor should have an HIV/AIDS test; widow should be left free to live her own life; continue with the practice but no sexual contact; inheritor should use condoms.
- A heated debate ensues on the use of condoms.
- Performers capitalise on the 'new tension' and improvise a play-within-a-play based on condom usage.
- Chamu, a promiscuous sales executive, is married to Tsitsi, a faithful housewife.
- Chamu has several sexual encounters with different types of women.

- The narrator steps forward to pose another question, 'How can Tsitsi be protected from her husband?'
- Possible responses: Chamu should change his job; Tsitsi should divorce Chamu; Chamu should use condoms in his extra-marital affairs.
- Performers then continue the last episode of the first performance (that is, the episode before the 'condom' play-within-the-play)
- An elderly grandmother takes care of over 20 grandchildren left by her three sons and their wives who recently died from HIV/AIDS.
- Her tragic circumstances are enough to make the audience empathise with her.
- The narrator finally steps forward to hear the audience's final conclusions.

The narrator's relationship with a participating audience closely parallels that of the *sarungano*. Apart from changes in purpose and context, the TfD narrator ensures that there is reciprocity and dialogue between performers and audience. He/she draws upon shared knowledge and values by allowing the audience to intervene in the happening. The audience, in turn, readily participates by offering suggestions which may or may not be viable. The remaining gaps will be filled by the performance itself. To a large extent, therefore, the above community-based theatre piece demonstrates the adaptability of Shona storytelling within the contemporary context.

Shona storytelling, especially the trickster narrative, has been much adopted and adapted in the area of children's theatre. Most of this activity is being undertaken by the Children's Performing Arts Workshop (CHIPAWO), a theatre group for children and young people whose ages range from three to eighteen years. CHIPAWO was formed in 1989 in response to a felt need expressed by concerned parents based in Harare. They wanted their children to be exposed to the cultural performance heritage of their people. While being an acronym for the name of the organisation, *chipawo* is also a Shona word which means 'please share with others'. Thus CHIPAWO's major objective is to enable children to create, contribute, participate and share with others within the framework of the performing arts.

Children are actively engaged in performances that are rooted in their own cultural traditions apart from being exposed to new performance modes from within and outside the country. Robert McLaren, one of the founders of CHIPAWO, says the organisation subscribes to a pedagogy that regards the performing arts as 'a liberating approach to the educational development of the child' (2001: 1). Through their participation in storytelling, music, song, mime and dance, children are empowered to develop the necessary cultural competence that the formal school system has tended to ignore. In a way, CHIPAWO should be viewed as a modern substitute for the *sarungano* as it helps to socialise children into the collective philosophy of their society through the joyous experience of dramatising, singing, miming and dancing.

As regards storytelling in particular, CHIPAWO has tried to reclaim and preserve Shona folktales in an age where such traditional performance practices would have been viewed as anachronistic, especially by the young generation.

Plays like *Vana Vanotamba* (The children are playing), *Mutongi Gava* (Jackal the judge) and *Jari Mukaranga* (Jari, the most favoured wife) are adapted versions of past narrative performances. *Vana Vanotamba*, for instance, is based on a trickster narrative entitled, *Tsuro naGudo* (The Hare and Baboon). In the play, children aged three to five act out roles as Hare and family make fools out of Baboon's family in order to eat all the food prepared at a feast. *Jari Mukaranga* is a dramatisation of the domestic intrigue that ensues in a polygamous marriage where the youngest wife usually becomes the most favoured of them all. In *Mutongi Gava*, ten-to-twelve-year-olds perform the story of Leopard whose greed, betrayal and ingratitude make others regret ever having come to his rescue. It is only when Jackal arrives on the scene that the misunderstanding is resolved.

CHIPAWO performed *Mutongi Gava* at the World Festival of Children's Theatre held in Hvidore, Denmark, in 1997. An examination of a video-tape of the play reveals performance elements that reflect very close parallels with its folktale model. The narrator introduces the performance with the usual formulaic utterance, '*Once upon a time …*' This is then followed by plot sequences that comply with the original tale. For example :

(i) Leopard falls into a trap and cannot free himself.
(ii) Leopard asks Man passing by to help him out.
(iii) Man is afraid that Leopard might turn against him afterwards.
(iv) Leopard reassures Man that he will be the best of friends.
(v) Man agrees to free Leopard.
(vi) Leopard wants to eat Man.
(vii) Man pleads with Leopard that they seek the opinion of other 'creatures'.
(viii) Man asks Tree to mediate in the dispute.
(ix) Tree supports Leopard because Man always cuts him down.
(x) Man then asks Cattle to intervene.
(xi) Cattle supports Leopard because Man overburdens him with work.
(xii) Jackal comes along and hears the story.
(xiii) Jackal orders both Leopard and Man to take their original positions.
(xiv) Leopard tries to resist but later goes back into the trap.
(xv) Man also goes back to where he was.
(xvi) Jackal orders Man to go his way.
(xvii) 'What about me?' asks Leopard from inside the trap.
(xviii) 'Never bite the hand that feeds you,' replies Jackal the Judge.

CHIPAWO's rendition of *Mutongi Gava* shows more similarities with the original folktale than differences. The usual fireplace setting of the past has now been transformed into a conventional theatre stage. The *sarungano's* multiple roles have been replaced by individual actors standing for different characters of the story. The introduction of a new character like Tree, in place of the original Antelope, is meant to instil a sense of environmental awareness in the audience. Perhaps in order to retain the interactive audience factor, the various sequences of action are punctuated by occasional interludes of song and dance. Man's continuous insistence on having other 'creatures' mediate in his dispute with Jackal brings in the idea of repetition as the key structural device, what Harold Scheub calls, 'an expansible image'. (1970: 119) The device also enables the action to move forward through a cumulative framework of confrontations towards the final resolution. As in the original folktale, repetition becomes the core cliché responsible for advancing the various functions of plot. In terms of content and form, *Mutongi Gava* shows that Shona storytelling remains a potent source of inspiration for children's performing arts. As Mbye Cham (1990: 267) has noted, modern African artists have, with varying degrees of success, consistently tapped the resources of their narrative traditions at all levels – structure, style, character and theme.

Mutongi Gava is a fitting statement on Shona moral justice, cultural identity and communal values. Leopard personifies what the society considers as vice and folly. His actions are contrary to the Shona proverbial dictum: *Rega kutsindira mwena unobuda neshwa* (Do not destroy the anthole that gives forth the delicious flying 'termites'). This is because Leopard decides to turn against the very person who has just rescued him. The community sees him as a character who wants to satisfy his selfishness and greed on an unsuspecting good Samaritan. In a way, Leopard behaves in the typical mould of a trickster through his duplicity, dishonesty, cheating and callousness. All these are moral depravities that society regards as unacceptable. Such unbecoming characters threaten the otherwise harmonious spirit of the community.

Jackal's judgement on Leopard demonstrates how Shona society alienates those who decide to go against the social norm. The proclamation, 'Do not bite the hand that feeds you,' echoed by all the other 'creatures', is a stark reminder to those who may find their double in the character of Leopard. The community celebrates the punishment of Leopard because he has acted against the common good. For CHIPAWO children, *Mutongi Gava* warns them to be wary of confidence tricksters who put on the mask of friendship and innocence when in reality they want to capitalise on privilege and opportunity. The animal characters are just a distancing device, an allegorical way of criticising or affirming human behaviour in an oblique way. In acting out *Mutongi Gava*, the children have taken over the *sarungano's* role. They are revealing their own culture's moral philosophy, the virtues that are esteemed, the vices that are condemned and the follies that are ridiculed.

From an early age, children are connected to the past that helps to inform their present and possibly future moral outlook. They gain insights on moral justice, personal greed and ambition, excessive individualism and covetous behaviour. These motifs are as relevant today as they were in the distant past from which the performances have been derived. However, some of CHIPAWO's productions are modern adaptations of different types of narrative performances. An example is the popular play, *Dhongi raSabhuku Mangwende* (Mr Mangwende's Donkey), which has been adapted from an animal fable. Mr Mangwende, who happens to be the head of his village, and his callous wife, over-work, ill-treat and under-feed their only donkey. The 'community', made up of villagers and their domestic animals, begins to sympathise with the way Donkey is made to suffer by his masters. The domestic animals of the 'community' decide to come to Donkey's rescue. They advise him either to refuse to work or to leave the Mangwende family for greener pastures.

For countless generations, storytelling has been a storehouse of the African people's knowledge and wisdom. As an adaptation of an animal fable, *Dhongi raSabhuku Mangwende* is an attempt to externalise the people's awareness of their lived experience. It can therefore be interpreted at different levels. At one level, it may be viewed as a metaphorical statement on the causes and effects of contemporary mental trauma, emotional depression and physical stress symbolised by the donkey. At another level, the play alludes to the current political conflict and socio-economic turmoil engulfing the country. While the immediate post-independence period was characterised by much euphoric celebration arising from the ordinary people's high expectations of freedom from colonialism, their hopes have since turned into frustration, anger and despair (Chinyowa, 2001b: 96–8). Those in positions of power and privilege have tended to ignore the interests and aspirations of the masses for the sake of political expediency and personal economic gain. Under such unfavourable circumstances, the Fanonian 'wretched of the earth' simply exist on the margins of history. Like Mr Mangwende's donkey, their continued subjection to manipulation, repression and corruption has created a culture of violence and fear that has forced them to internalise the perpetual condition of victim.

Future issues and prospects

Is there any future for Shona storytelling in contemporary Zimbabwean theatre? Although one should not lose sight of all the hurdles to be surmounted, the direction in which community-based theatre and children's performing arts are going seems to give a ray of hope for the future of storytelling. The fact that community-based theatre continues to depend on the use of indigenous storytelling techniques will enable the narrative genre to remain a source of inspiration and creativity.

As a form of grassroots theatre, community-based theatre has also given rise to the theatre for development movement. Today, TfD has become a popular communicative tool for identifying development problems, searching for solutions and coming up with collective strategies for the community's well-being (Chifunyise, 1994: 66). As we have seen, storytelling still offers techniques for collective play-making that are crucial to the success of TfD workshops. The infusion of dramatised storytelling with other indigenous performance modes like music, song and dance makes it even more appealing to a wide spectrum of Zimbabwean society.

The future of children's theatre based on the CHIPAWO model cannot be in doubt. By drawing on the narrative traditions of the past, the organisation is making children grow up with pride in who they are. Once children develop confidence in their identity, they can relate to other peoples of the world from the vantage point of their own cultural diversity. Difference becomes, not a liability, but a source of enrichment for global cultures. This has been amply demonstrated by several narrative-based performances that CHIPAWO has presented at regional and international theatre festivals that include:

- 1994 – *Chipo and the Bird*, Harvest of Plays Festival, Nairobi, Kenya.
- 1996 – *Vana Vanotamba*, (The children are playing), Images of Africa Festival, Velje, Denmark.
- 1997 – *Mutongi Gava*, (Jackal the judge), World Festival of Children's Theatre, Hvidore, Denmark.
- 1998 – *Jari Mukaranga*, (Jari, the most favoured wife), World Festival of Children's Theatre, Lingen, Germany.
- 2000 – *Dhongi raSabhuku Mangwende*, (Mr Mangwende's donkey), World Festival of Children's Theatre, Toyama, Japan.

The fact that these performances are deeply rooted in the narrative poetics of the children's culture means they are reimagining and revitalizing it in the process of sharing their worldview with the outside world. As Thomas Riccio says, 'Those that take also give back' (in Seeds 1996: 33). CHIPAWO's performances abroad could be seen as a form of cultural exchange. On their return, the children will bring back valuable insights from other cultures. However, one should take cognisance of the possible negative effects of globalisation on the children. If their travels abroad are taken as a form of cultural voyeurism, they may fall victim to the hegemony of global cultural politics and become alienated from their culture. A more reciprocal cultural exchange would regard these children as the future of the global village. Their cross-cultural interaction through theatre is likely to play an important role in the shaping of that future.

Conclusion

This article has demonstrated that Shona storytelling has survived the ravages of time and continues to be a source of creative inspiration for posterity. The shadow of the *sarungano* remains as much a legacy of traditional artistry as a model for the contemporary performing arts in Zimbabwe. Through the use of such narrative performance techniques as call-and-response, animation of character, audience interaction, repetition and inter-textuality, Shona story-telling has been shown to provide useful frames of reference for Zimbabwean theatre today.

The variability and adaptability of the Shona narrative performance has also proved to be an invaluable asset for the development of the modern performing arts. Theatre practitioners in the country continue to take advantage of the staying power of the indigenous narrative tradition. Thus post-independence Zimbabwean theatre has emerged as a dynamic site for the reappropriation of a narrative idiom that readily combines with other indigenous expressive modes to create a vibrant culture of community-based theatre and children's performances.

REFERENCES

Achebe, C., 1987, *Anthills of the Savanna*, London: Heinemann.

Agatucci, C., 1998, 'African Storytelling: Oral Traditions', in *Cultures and Literatures of Africa* (http://www.cocc.edu/cagatucci/classes/hum211/afrstory.htm)

Awoonor, K., 1974, 'Tradition and Continuity in African Literature', *Dalhousie Review*, vol. 53, 4: 655–67.

Breitinger, Eckhard, (ed.), 1994, *Theatre and Performance in Africa*, Bayreuth: Bayreuth African Studies.

Canonici, N.N., 1996, *Zulu Oral Traditions*, Durban: University of Natal Press.

Cham, M.B., 1990, 'Structural and Thematic Parallels in Oral Narrative and Film: Mandabi and Two African Oral Narratives', in I. Okpewho (ed.), *The Oral Performance in Africa*, Ibadan: Spectrum Books.

Chifunyise, S., 1994, 'Trends in Zimbabwean Theatre since 1980', in L. Gunner (ed.), *Politics and Performance: Theatre, Poetry and Song in Southern Africa*, Johannesburg: University of Witwatersrand Press.

Chinyowa, K.C., 2001a, 'The Sarungano and Shona Storytelling', in *Studies in Theatre and Performance*, 21, 1: 18–31.

Chinyowa, K.C., 2001b, 'Shona Literature of Independence in Zimbabwe', in M.T. Vambe (ed.), *Orality and Cultural Identities in Zimbabwe*, Gweru: Mambo Press.

Fortune, G., 1974, *Ngano*, vol. 2, Harare: Mercury Press.

Jordan, A.C., 1973, *Tales from Southern Africa*, Los Angeles: University of California Press.

Kidd, R., 1983, *From People's Theatre for Revolution to Popular Theatre for Reconstruction: Diary of a Zimbabwean Workshop*, The Hague: CESO.

Kileff, C., 1983, (ed.), *Shona Folktales*, Gweru: Mambo Press.

Mbele, J.L., 1999, *Matengo Folktales*, Bryn Mawr: Buybooks.

McLaren, R.M, 2001, 'Tried and Tested', CHIPAWO Arts Educator's Manual, (unpublished).

Mutere, M., 1997, 'African Oral Aesthetics', in African Odyssey InterActive (http://artsedge. kennedy-center.org/aoi/html/ae-guide.html)

Okpewho, I., 1992, *African Oral Literature: Backgrounds, Character and Continuity*, Bloomington: Indiana University Press.

Okpewho, I., 1990, (ed.), *The Oral Performance in Africa*, Ibadan: Spectrum Books.

Pellowski, A., 1977, *The World of Storytelling*, New York: R. R. Bowker.

Pongweni, A., 2001, 'A Responsive Audience: Texture, Text and Context in Shona Folklore', in R.H. Kaschula (ed.), *African Oral Literature: Functions in Contemporary Contexts*, Claremont, South Africa: New Africa Books.

Scheub, H., (1970) 'The Technique of the Expansible Image in Xhosa Ntsomi Performances', *Research in African Literatures*, vol. 1, 2: 119–27.

Seda, O., 2001, 'Towards an Alternative Theatre in Post-Independence Zimbabwe', in M.T. Vambe (ed.), *Orality and Cultural Identities in Zimbabwe*, Gweru: Mambo Press.

Seeds, D.E., 1996, 'Trickster by trade: Thomas Riccio on indigenous theatre', *The Drama Review*, winter, vol. 40, 4: 118–35.

Sekoni, R., 1990, 'The Narrator, Narrative Pattern and Audience Experience of Oral Narrative Performance', in I. Okpewho (ed.), *The Oral Performance in Africa*, Ibadan: Spectrum Books.

Memory & Desire
in South Africa
The Museum as space
for performing cultural identity?

YVETTE HUTCHISON

In recent years both academic and popular discourses have focused sharply on memory and alternative visions/practices of history. The great interest shown in redefining exhibition and museum spaces in many parts of the world has even been referred to as a thriving 'memory market'. David Coplan argues that this 'memory market' is important insofar as many of the emergent issues in the South African context require 'the centering of the arts and sciences in memory and testimony, of self-recognition and representation in popular genres' (2000: 124). I would like to extend this argument further, to suggest that such initiatives, particularly in the arts, are not only tracing memories in relation to history; they also move into performance. I propose that the Robben Island and District Six Museums offer performance platforms through which individuals can explore contemporary memory and desire in South Africa.

I have chosen to write this article from a personal perspective, based on my own experiences in these museum spaces from 1999. I propose to look at the place of theatre in these discourses. I ask how both the personal and collective narratives stand in relation to historic and cultural encoding; how much is actual memory, and how much desire, and whether the distinction is important. I also ask to what extent this may facilitate or inhibit social and personal transformation. I use the term 'theatre' beyond the conventional notion of a scripted performance by actors for an audience, which is usually passive, to include aspects of participatory, improvised theatre where the division between audience and performers is blurred, often until there is little or no separation between them. I thus argue that theatrical elements such as set, costume, characterisation and scripted lines are evident in these performative contexts in the way people are represented or project themselves, and the ways in which the spaces themselves are conceived. In the context of the more improvised interaction, aspects of personal narrative and role play become essential in negotiating and defining the moment of transition between the personal and collective memory.

Historic and cultural encoding occurs primarily in two ways: either linguistically, through narrative, both written and oral; or spatially, through images of our environment and ourselves. The latter is most evident in art as cultural artefacts, architecture, gardens, museums and exhibitions. These processes can be informal and individual, or a formal national reconstruction of memory. In the latter case, the state sets up structures to 'remember' for a nation.[1] The most obvious linguistic version is in the written histories of nations. These are presented as verifiable, factual and reliable. They may include commemorative days and archives, which reflect and support the dominant sense of the inscribed 'history', and often tell one more about the time in which they are constructed than about the period to which they are referring.

The second form of historic and cultural encoding is more complex, and involves the processes of formulating images of public memory. These processes often become clearer when old monuments of a fallen system are deconstructed and replaced by new monuments and commemorative days.[2] One of the important issues in this process is the place of marginalised people, for whose experience there is no formal 'national' commemoration. The lack of commemorative acknowledgement, together with their marginal position, forces them to shift the focus of memory from the exact outlines of history (public memory) to that of the private world where private symbols of an atemporal, often dream-based world dominate. In a postcolonial context, the bleaker the present seems, the more glowing the sense of the 'lost paradise' of the past tends to be.[3] This becomes particularly significant when such memories are reclaimed in a new context.

Both processes require participants to construct or reconstruct perception and experience, often by means of a creative form. The process includes shifting from the personal to public 'meaning' by ordering and interpreting experience; this, in turn, shapes our understanding of ourselves and our world. Museums play a large role in this creation of public meaning, and are significant because they are part of the cultural ideological state apparatus (Althusser 1993: 15–22), elements of which 'represent the ruling class ideology, and are unified by political and class identity' (Meltzer 1981: 115). Museums visually standard-ise and fix a narrative or image of the dominant group, and thereby often interpret and marginalise 'others' outside this dominant narrative. Thus in recent years museums have been criticised for being 'mausoleums' in need of deconstruction and redefinition (see Van Tonder 1994).

Understanding the traditional role and place of museums is important when proposing that such spaces may be used for more negotiated, communal, frag-mented remembering, because both the curators and visitors to the spaces bring with them assumptions about the function and construction of exhibitions. South Africa has a long history of commemoration of the dominant European, primarily Afrikaner, hegemony in monuments like the Voortrekker Monu-ment in Pretoria and the Taalmonument (Language) in Paarl; in museums like the South African Museum in Cape Town, the former Africana Museum in Johannesburg, Pietermaritzburg's Natal and Voortrekker Museums, Durban's Killie Campbell Local and Natural History Museums, to a name a few; as well as in the art and film industry. When attempting to redefine the place of museums, both aspects of this legacy – the history of the space and the assump-tions of visitors – need to be overtly acknowledged and addressed.[4]

In the last decade South Africa has undergone major socio-political change, which has necessitated a reflection on and transformation of the country's history to reflect the new context.[5] I would argue, however, that even prior to 1994, theatre had articulated alternative narratives of South African memory and desire. If history may be defined as the dominant narrative of a country and its rulers, theatre in South Africa has been an important agency for narrating plural counter-memories to those histories, both during the apartheid era and now in the post-apartheid period of reconstructing identity and communities. South African theatre has long told the stories of silenced people from different communities and perspectives – like Athol Fugard's *Boesman and Lena*, Mbongeni Ngema, Percy Mtwa and Barney Simon's *Woza Albert!*, and Gcina Mhlope's collaborative play, *Have you Seen Zandile?*[6]

However, theatre as counter-memory has moved beyond traditional theatrical spaces to include the Truth and Reconciliation Commission (TRC), a national forum where individual stories intersected with South African history to offer new histories and communal memories.[7] From 1996 to 1998 South Africa heard individual testimonies of remembered experience under apartheid in both open and closed sessions. It was theatrical in the sense that it facilitated the public telling of individual, often complex and contradictory stories. However, the theatrical frame was tenuous and complicated. While providing a frame in which the experiences of people who had been silenced and marginalised for decades could be acknowledged, it was not a fictional space, nor one in which people were being represented by performers. At other, simultaneous levels it was also a forum for national confession and group therapy, and a forum of justice, with the related discourses of accusation and defence. These competing frames made the survivors who gave testimonies vulnerable: exposing them to being denied or attracting personal criticism. It tended to frame survivors as victims, despite the resistance to this role by many when testifying. Also, in practical terms, no single accused who refused to testify before the Commission or apply for amnesty has been prosecuted, and no compensation has been paid out to victims to date.

Another limitation was the lack of direct access to the wider audience. This meant that these narratives and the public response to them could not really form the basis for a 'social dialogue' of negotiation.[8] And finally, despite the opening out to accommodate multiple voices of South Africa, as a state initiative, these pluralised narratives could not remain at the centre. The Commission was part of the restructuring of a new national memory and needed to formulate the past coherently.

Yet Coplan argues that the TRC was a 'thumping success' because 'the narrative of the TRC is its own most important product' which has created 'a single moral and political story out of this unruly multivocality' (2000: 138). He goes on to argue that in many African cultures there

> is deep historical precedent for consensualising discourses, in local political tradition and its form of cultural memory. ...[T]he ideal of Basotho and Batswana court and moot, for example, might be that all should be listened to, in the end only a single

account should be heard, lest the polity imitate the famous malapropism and jump on its horse and ride off in all directions' (2000: 139).

In this sense, the TRC moved from the theatrically individual stories back into the realm of the historic initiative of creating a coherent, national narrative.

The theatrical potential of the TRC, bound up in exploring contradiction and conflict, was extended in the formal plays relating to the Commission that appeared from 1996. These include Paul Herzberg's *The Dead Wait*, the Khulumani Support Group's *The Story I'm About to Tell* and The Handspring Puppet Company's *Ubu and the Truth Commission*. These plays have reflected on both the processes and outcomes of the programme. However, the question that follows is how this breaking of the silence can be extended beyond conventional theatre to sustain the performance of complex, multi-faceted, individual and communal memories in non-traditional yet public spaces. Primarily, I want to look at how cultural and socio-political transformation may be facilitated through performative interaction in commemorative spaces.

Performing memory in museums

Traditionally museums have given material form to authorised versions of the past, in turn institutionalising these as public memory. I believe, however, that potentially museums are significant spaces from which ordinary people can (1) actively recover and collate memory; and (2) negotiate stories and identities for themselves – outside the formalised historic narratives of nation building, or the divides of their historically and geographically segregated communities.

I explore these possibilities for performing memory by comparing two commemorative spaces in Cape Town: the Robben Island Museum (RIM), opened as a South African National Monument on 24 September 1997, and the District Six Museum, which opened on 10 December 1994. I shall outline the specific narrative and spatial possibilities of each, and then compare these to suggest some of the issues that could influence the social and communal transformation made possible by encouraging the performance of memory and identity in such spaces.

Robben Island

When writing about Robben Island, one first has to acknowledge its significance as an internationally recognised commemorative site.[9] The Island has become symbolic of both the struggle and liberation in South Africa. The museum's vision statement summarises the thinking behind the project:

> While we will not forget the brutality of Apartheid we will not want Robben Island to be a monument of our hardship and suffering. We would want it to be a triumph of the human spirit against the forces of evil: a triumph of wisdom and largeness of spirit against the small minds and pettiness; a triumph of courage and determination over human frailty and weakness. (Ahmed Kathrada – ex-Robben Island prisoner, member of Parliament 1994–99, and now chairman of the RIM Council and the Ex-Political Prisoner's Committee.)

In this statement we see a clear seed of the emergent master narrative of reconciliation, similar to that of the TRC, as the struggle is remembered very much in black male terms. Although female activists were never imprisoned on Robben Island, their roles in the liberation struggle were recalled in the original South African Museum–Mayibuye Centre collaboration, *Esiqithini: the Robben Island Exhibition*; and both female and white dissidents are acknowledged in passing in the RIM narrative. However, Harriet Deacon argues that

> In opposition to attempts to naturalize the island's past, a group of ex-Robben island prisoners have brokered a reinterpretation of the island's meaning, as the university of the struggle and the crucible of change in South Africa. Through the recorded memories of Mandela and others, the prisoners' liberation within the prison and from the island has become a symbol of national liberation, moral modernity, and ethical maturity. This interpretation has also been important in underlining for a western audience the fitness of the new power brokers – the urban black middle class – to take the reins of the 'rainbow nation' in the context of the failure of other African states to maintain democracy after independence. (1998: 173–4)

There are a number of important national concerns suggested in this 'remembering' of Robben Island. These include legitimising contemporary power to the wider world, defining the importance of Robben Island as a centre of the struggle and the place of education both for the past and present South Africa.

The focus on education is clearly evidenced in the various tours and training programmes the Robben Island Museum offers. Apart from the standard tour, it has school tours, youth camps, a spring school and a travelling exhibition. These programmes are openly committed to raising heritage awareness and consciousness among young people regarding issues of 'nation building such as: racism, xenophobia, education and training, sustainable development, sexism and gangsterism' (http://www.robben-island.org.za). They have a training programme, a postgraduate diploma in museum and heritage studies, and short courses in heritage-related areas. All of this places this project within the more traditional museum-as-mausoleum state apparatus framework where there is a predetermined agenda and fixed narrative that limits the possibilities for more open, improvised and individual performative experiences.

The latter aspiration is perhaps most evident, and best evaluated, however, in the performative aspects of the Museum's public tours. The tours leave Cape Town by ferry to the island every hour from 9 am to 3 pm each day. Groups are bussed from the harbour around the island, where the scripted tour begins and visitors learn how the island has been a place of banishment since the Portuguese first left convicts there in 1525. The first political dissidents were Muslim leaders from Asia left on the island by the Portuguese and Dutch from 1667. When Britain took over the Cape, the island became a prison for local Xhosa dissidents, and in the nineteenth century a place of banishment for mentally-ill people (termed 'lunatics'), lepers, prostitutes and people with chronic illnesses or venereal diseases (Deacon 1994, 1998). It was controlled by the South African Defence Force during the Second World War, but was handed over to the South African Prison Services in 1960, when it was transformed into the political prison for which it is most infamous.

At the prison ex-wardens or ex-prisoners give the group a guided tour. This tour is a conscious performance of the national narrative of reconciliation. Nan Hamilton and Stephanie Marie-Curiel have described the guides both in museum and performance terms as being the 'primary "objects" on display' (1999: 4) and as 'performing transformation' (1999: 5). This is because they are the primary resource, beyond the space itself. Yet, paradoxically, they consciously edit out all that is personal, complex and contradictory in their narratives because, the guides insist, they do 'not want to say anything that will upset people' (1999: 3).

The ex-prisoner assumes a persona and moves from the lived experience to a scripted role, performing transformation for the tourist audience. The pressure on the guides is towards homogenising conventions of resolution rather than tackling the issues related to reconciliation, which would bring in the personal stories and experiences of difference and conflict. Each time I have been on the tour (1999, 2000, 2001) the guides have avoided personal questions. Instead they speak of the general experiences of fighting for and getting letters, banned books and, ultimately, education. They highlight how young many of the prisoners were, and focus on the experiences of those on the maximum security block. All of these focuses correspond to Harriet Deacon's analysis of how the 'prisoners have brokered a reinterpretation of the island's meaning'.

The profound commitment to projecting a narrative of hope and 'the overcoming of evil' makes this as much a performance of desire as it does of memory. This is illustrated most obviously in a mural at the end of the corridor of the maximum security block, painted after the prison was made into the museum (see photo 3). Nobody could tell me when it had been painted or why it was there. But the guide in 1999 told me ironically that they were trying to 'beautify' the place, and that it had 'never been like that'. The image suggests a Disney-like, Edenic garden – projecting desire in the midst of harsh memories, perhaps. Yet one wonders how much transformation is possible without negotiating and admitting the complexities and realities of the individually lived histories.

In 1999 Nan Hamilton and Stephanie Marlin-Curiel made an exciting proposal for a Participatory Museum Tour where, in Vivian Patraka's terms, the museum becomes an environment 'where we are asked to change from spectator/bystander to witness, where we are asked to make our specific memory into historical memory' (Patraka, quoted in Hamilton and Marlin-Curiel 1999:10). They suggested moving this process of engaging visitors in an experience of participation from weekend workshops into the public RIM tour. This would mean that each visitor would have to engage personally with her/his own and South Africa's memories and history.

However, although I think the idea exciting, I believe that moving this project beyond the traditional museum experience into a more engaged participatory experience would be difficult; the proposal highlights both the possibilities and limitations of theatre in a commemorative context. Within the theatre paradigm presented at the beginning of this article, this would involve visitors seeing themselves as more than passive recipients of knowledge, as in

1 The cave at the lime mine where men like Nelson Mandela worked, discussing ideas and issues with one another out of the sun's heat and glare. Sometimes referred to as the 'informal university' by guides (Photo: Yvette Hutchison)

2 Corridor of Robben Island prison, where a photo of prisoners has been put against the far wall. It is an example of how memory that seems personal is literally 'inscribed' on the physical building to create general meaning (Photo: Yvette Hutchison)

3 *Mural painted at the end of the corridor of the former maximum security block, Robben Island Museum. The guide had no idea when or why it had been painted, by whom or with what purpose.*
(Photo: Yvette Hutchison)

the more conventional museum context, to being at the least paying members of an audience, and at best, participants in an interactive, improvisational, performative experience. The difficulty lies both in the larger national agenda vested in the site, discussed earlier; and in the general constitution of the groups. Foreign visitors tend to dominate tour groups, with a few South Africans making up a minority of most groups. The primary reason for this is cost. The tour costs R150 (about US$25) for adults and R50 (US$12.50) for children, a day or two days' wages for the majority of South Africans who might have an interest in or even have experienced life in the prison.[10] The tourists tend not to have any real sense of the conflicts and history. Thus the tour becomes a performance of interest, but not necessarily of personal engagement, and the group perforce a more passive paying audience.

The commercial pressure on RIM also imposes severe time constraints on the tour. Market forces are evidenced in the daily number of tourists wanting to visit the island, often exceeding the official limit of 265 people per day (Davison 1998: 157). This rules out any possibility of the Boalian interaction proposed by Hamilton, which requires trust in role-play situations such as 'warden and prisoner'. There is time neither to establish sufficient trust for engagement in personal and potentially dangerous interaction, nor to develop significant transformational experience. Thus, the national narrative and economic pressures on this project render the interactive, open, performative proposal well nigh impossible.

These pressures are highlighted in the spatial trajectory of the tour, which moves swiftly through many areas and ends at the Museum Shop. Here memory is commodified in mouse-mats, posters, bottles of wine and T-shirts with Mandela's prisoner cell number printed on them. Arguing a theatrical model, I would propose that there is much pressure on this project to respond to economic factors and thus move from the marginal, engaged activity of improvising dialogue for personal and social transformation to function as mainstream theatre, where the performance is scripted and performed for an audience. In this sense it serves the discourse of traditional history – using a negotiated memory to project a communal desire, as the new master narrative of reconciliation – rather than exploring the deep-lying processes by which I believe this country is still attempting to negotiate transformation and complex, multiple identities.

I turn now to comparing this project to one on the mainland, the District Six Museum, situated at the foot of Table Mountain, near the city centre and harbour.

District Six Museum

District Six's history stretches back to 1867 when Cape Town was divided into six districts and Kanaldorp officially became known as District Six. It was a cosmopolitan community with people from all races, religions and parts of the world living together. This mixed community bred a consciousness that was politically subversive regarding the state narrative (separate development along race lines), rich in ideas and activities. In 1901 bubonic plague broke out and District Six experienced its first forced removals. Thousands of African people were forced out and two thousand homes were demolished and rebuilt. As the population in District Six grew, landlord and municipality interest in the area waned. Water and refuse facilities were inadequate and the roads deteriorated. The government used this neglect to designate the area a slum and so justify the proposed removals. In 1950 the Group Areas Act declared it illegal for people of different races to live in the same area. In 1966 District Six was declared a 'whites only' area, and between 1966 and 1980 sixty thousand people were forced to move, while their homes and shops were bulldozed to the ground. Only a few buildings, churches and mosques of the original suburb are left. Families and friends were separated according to race and most moved to the Cape Flats, stripped of a sense of community and the extended family. The government added to the insult by naming the streets and blocks of flats in the new areas by the old street names of District Six. So one sees Hanover Park, Tyne Court, Lavender Hill all over the Flats. The former District Six was designated a white area, but ironically no-one ever moved into it, and it remained a scar on in Cape Town's heartland.

4 *District Six Museum*
(Photo: James Gibbs)

5 *Mosaic floor in
the 'memory room',
District Six Museum*
(Photo: Yvette Hutchison)

6 *Floor sheet map of the former District Six*
(Photo: Yvette Hutchison)

7 *Former residents reinscribe themselves into the map*
(Photo: Yvette Hutchison)

Wider interest in District Six became focused in the 1980s, particularly through the dramatisation of Richard Rive's novel *Buckingham Palace: District Six* in David Kramer and Taliep Petersen's American-style show *District Six – the Musical*. Kramer's Afrikaans-Jewish cultural background combined with Taliep Petersen's experience and knowledge as a coloured[11] musician and writer from the Cape Flats produced a series of 'Cape' works over the years, including *Fairyland* and *Kat and the King*. These productions present diverse and popular perspectives on Cape Town and its communities. They were written for the white and coloured liberal audiences of Cape Town and abroad. But the plays are sentimental and don't really speak to or for the actual people who made up this community.

The District Six Museum was established as a project in 1989 to commemorate the area and honour the people who lost their homes and community in the forced removals. The Methodist Church in Buitekant Street was chosen as the venue because for 120 years it has been involved in issues of social justice. During the site's restoration, the exhibitions were housed in the Moravian and Congregational Churches in the heart of District Six. On 10 December 1994 the District Six Museum opened with its first exhibition entitled *Streets – Retracing the Past*. The title came from the original street signs which a resident had collected before the bulldozers came, preserved, and donated to the museum when the call went out for memorabilia in 1989. This donation was a typical response to the invitation that hangs on a flag in the museum:

> This exhibition is part of the project 'District Six and beyond' in which former residents from displaced communities in the Peninsula are invited to fill gaps in the story told in the District Six Museum by bringing their memories, stories, photographs and memorabilia and marking relevant spots in the museum spaces.

The logic for this is made explicit in this reference from the local author Achmat Dangor's novel *Kafka's Curse,* which hangs in the main exhibition space: 'It struck me that our history is contained in the homes we live in, that we are shaped by the ability of these simple structures to resist being defiled.' For me the museum's significance lies in its counter-narratives of memory and identity, which challenge a formal, linear narrative; and in its fundamental conception as an interactive space, in the sense of participatory theatre. This is the kind of memory referred to earlier, which emerges from groups of marginalised people whose memories are not centrally included in the formal state narrative. The coloured community in South Africa stood between black and white during apartheid, and still struggles with this place in the post-apartheid era.

From 1992 people donated photographs, documents, pass books, letters, personal stories and shared experiences of lost communities and the forced removals to the museum. The large pinboards and sheets made available for individuals to arrange or inscribe comments, poems, responses, memorabilia or even stories related to the area and their experiences in it become sets for the performance of memory in this space. Many of these sheets are later embroidered by women in prisons, and rehung in the museum. Individuals and groups have created tapestries to represent themselves and their memories. Flags representing the diverse religious affiliations of the people are prominently displayed. Pictures of artists, writers and other significant figures from District Six hang over the sides of the upper balcony into the museum's central room, thus framing the present with figures of communal pride from the past. Behind this room is a 'memory room', which has a mosaic floor made with tiles upon which former residents of the area were invited to draw or write poems or prose related to District Six. This is the space in which creative workshops around storytelling, art and cultural artefacts are run for people of all ages, and especially for school children.

One of the most powerful scenic elements of the museum is the floor sheet that maps the former District Six. Here former residents and their families are invited to reinscribe themselves into the map by standing where their homes once stood. In the course of their visits and activities they recreate a community that was literally blotted out.[12] In the years I have visited the museum, one of the most powerful moments came in August 2000 when a group of elderly people from Mannenburg, former residents of District Six, visited the museum for the afternoon. On arrival, their first response was to locate themselves on the map. They then began showing one another, and me, where they had lived, even walking along the tiny lines for roads. What followed were the stories – everyday life, jokes, and experiences. Upstairs there are recreated barber shops, hairdressers, a parlour for music. Old residents sat in the chairs and told me of their first important dance; uninitiated European visitors 'played' in the spaces, imagining themselves in the community. It was a performative, alive, creative experience. This particular afternoon the museum had invited a well-known and respected Cape Town tenor to sing old songs with the group. Music was central to the community of District Six; and on a badly tuned piano the people spent the rest of the afternoon re-enacting the past – for themselves and whoever wandered into the museum. They invited me to sing along, despite my not knowing the words. In this way I was able to move across both the history and geographies of apartheid, across the anger (one woman told me how she had wanted to bomb her old house when she returned and saw other people living in it, and then recounted her journey towards forgiveness), lack of understanding and shared experience; to hear the stories and meet the people, even to be welcomed into their space and memories.

It is experiences such as this that have convinced me that the District Six Museum practises participatory theatre, focusing on the individual and communal stories, and what they can achieve. In the same way that theatre is ephemeral, temporal, belonging to *an* evening, with *a particular* audience, so I was seeing lived community theatre. Its effect was multiple. For that group it was affirmative, restorative, healing – women in the group spoke of anger, pain and forgiveness, many cried. They were both constructing themselves and becoming involved in the process of personal mythologising through which any performance moves away from the actor towards the character. In moving back to a lost past they were performing parts of themselves that had been denied or marginalised. Perhaps some of those participants will continue to reclaim some of the lost forms or stories. Those of us who do not belong to

District Six were an audience: by witnessing their experiences we engaged with what is gone, and so were part of breaking national silences. Old residents thanked us just for being there and listening, for being, in effect, an interested audience/participant.

There is a sense beyond listening, however, in which we all have to take our places in the narrative. On one visit I was with three English-speaking white South African children, aged eleven, eight, and five, who were very disturbed by the stories of forced removals. Noor Ibrahim, a compelling storyteller and facilitator, showed them artefacts found on site and asked them where they had lived, what they had already left behind them in various moves, and the reason for the moves (mostly economic). In this way he made them part of the narrative, and he helped them to move beyond guilt to understanding. This is a space in which people from different, even opposing sides of South Africa can meet, listen, share and bridge historic and geographic segregation.

The Museum aspires to having no centre of control, no formal director, no entrance fee, only people to facilitate and make it a safe space in which to explore difficult issues and memories. The curators, Noor Ibrahim and Linda Fortune, answer questions, share and facilitate stories as former residents of the community. I particularly noted how they facilitate the stories of *all* visitors, from really young children to nervous elderly ladies. These performances of memory, however, are primarily by and for this community, and therein lies its strength.

While facilitating individual and communal stories, the museum is also trying to build from the present moment into the future by means of their sound archive. In 1997 the museum received a grant from the Swedish International Development Agency (SIDA) to enable individuals, communities, journalists, scholars and others to store music, stories and memories relevant to the area in a 'memory booth'. The project was started in June 1997 and was opened in June 1999. They have worked with a dance band and jazz musician Jimmy Adams to document and trace the life and growth of Cape jazz. Some of these sound recordings will be integrated into the resident and travelling exhibitions as part of the museum's commitment to 'a living archive, a living museum' (*Newsletter*, June 1998, p. 2).

This signals the role finance plays in such endeavours. The District Six Museum can remain open, negotiating many narratives, because it is not state-funded, and thus does not have to respond to the imperatives of a coherent narrative that supports the wider history. Such a project is as much defined by its space as by its funding. It is also focused on a liminal group of people whose (racial) identity was perceived by some as not 'white enough' under apartheid, and perhaps 'too white' now to be subsumed into the master narrative. In some ways it is also evolving a myth of 'coloured' history and identity, which never-theless is still sufficiently pluralised and marginal to challenge the emergent master narrative. And perhaps it is the performative aspect that has made this challenge possible.

Homi Bhabha has argued that transformation can be achieved by going 'beyond yourself in order to return, in a spirit of revision and reconstruction ...

as a mix of different times' and, I would argue, additional perceptions (1994: 3). If we can meet and interact with a variety of different people, performing memory and desire in safe spaces, perhaps highly conflictual histories and memories may be mediated to facilitate personal and social transformation. Thus museums *can* move from being mausoleums to being dynamic meeting places from which the people of South Africa, and perhaps other such contexts, can bridge the histories and geographies of separation. In this way we may be able to move towards both communicating memory and desire and transforming these memories and desires of reconciliation into lived realities.

NOTES

1 For recent publications on memorials see, for example, Hartman 1993; Hass 1998; Linenthal 1995; Lowenthal 1997; Schofield 1998; La Capra 1998; Milton and Nowinski 1992; Winter 1995; Young 1993.

2 This is particularly evident when looking at the former Soviet Union or South Africa. For example, 16 December was a day on which South Africans commemorated what was termed the Battle of Blood River, in which a Boer laager was attacked by vastly superior numbers of Zulu warriors. The Boers vowed that if God gave them victory they would keep that day sacred as the Day of the Vow or Covenant. So many Zulu men died that day that the river was said to have run red with blood, hence the name of the battle. Instead of the day being removed from South Africa's calendar of annual holidays in the post-apartheid era, it has been kept, and renamed the Day of Reconciliation, thus powerfully redefining South Africa's history and people.

3 See Naomi Greene 1996 on the effects of France's refusal to acknowledge or commemorate the war in Algeria for the French colonists (*pied-noirs*) returning. This process of creating mythic symbols commemorating a lost world is also evident in the way the District Six Museum has evolved.

4 For discussion of problems related to the reclamation and redefinition of the Africana Museum, now Museum Africa in Johannesburg, see Hamilton 1994. For discussion of the controversial attempt to challenge past representations of the San people by Pippa Skotnes in 1996, see Jackson and Robins 1999; also Davison 1998 and Hall 1998 on 'recasting memory'.

5 See for example the Arts and Culture white paper, 1993 and the 1992 Wits History Workshop conference on Myths, Monuments, Museums: New Perspectives on Initiatives for Transformation. Published papers include Sideris 1986; Wright and Mazel 1991; Hamilton 1994, Van Tonder 1994, Jackson and Robins 1999; Coplan 2000; Brown *et al.* 1991.

6 See Walder 1992, and Hauptfleisch 1997:115–56 on notions of playwrights as 'bearing witness' to silenced peoples during apartheid.

7 A complete transcription of the hearings is available in seven volumes, and extracts from the final report were also published in five supplements by seven newspapers and the Institute for Democracy in South Africa. Author Anje Krog's *Country of my Skull* (1998) relates much of the history and many of the stories that emerged from the TRC less formally than the official documentation.

8 See Bakhtin on the 'dialogic consequence' required of an audience, where a theatrical utterance provokes and interacts with audience response and thus both become active in 'social dialogue' (1981: 276).

9 For discussion on how it was conceptualised and the significance of this see Davison 1998, Hamilton and Marlin-Curiel 1999. Deacon (1998) traces the strong contestation for this site and what it could come to mean, from holiday haven to national memorial.

10 Special arrangements can be made for community groups to tour at no cost, or at a subsidised price for pensioners (R60) and R30 per head to disadvantaged schools (see website for details). This, however, is not the general make-up of the RIM tours.

11 I use the term coloured to refer to South Africans of mixed racial background, usually Malay and European, although many people are African-Europeans. There is much debate about this definition of racial identity. Erasmus and Pieterse (1999) and Erasmus (2001) argue that not all assertions of coloured identity are racist. They trace the evolution of the term, and discuss how the term is contested to serve different purposes. Although it is used in a politically conservative way in the apartheid sense of defining racial difference, it can also be a politically radical self-description.

12 See notes on Joseph Beuys's concept of the use of the social sculpture in Sacks (1997), and Alex Mavrocordatos relating social sculpture to mapping and Participatory Learning in Action.

REFERENCES

Althusser, Louis (1993) 'Ideology and Ideological State Apparatuses (Notes towards an Investigation)', in *Essays on Ideology*, London and New York: Verso, pp. 1–60.

Bakhtin, M. M. (1981) *The Dialogic Imagination: Four Essays*, translated by C. Emerson and M. Holquist, (ed.) M. Holquist, Austin: University of Texas Press.

Bhabha, Homi (1994) *The Location of Culture*, London: Routledge.

Brown, Joshua *et al.* (1991) *History from South Africa: Alternative Visions and Practices*, Philadelphia: Temple University Press.

Coplan, David (2000) 'Popular History: Cultural Memory', *Critical Arts*, 14, 2: 122–44.

Dangor, Achmat (1997) *Kafka's Curse*, Johannesburg: Kwela Books.

Davison, Patricia (1998) 'Museums and the Reshaping of Memory', in S. Nuttall and C. Coetzee (eds.), *Negotiating the Past – the Making of Memory in South Africa*, Cape Town: Oxford University Press.

Deacon, Harriet (1994), 'Leprosy and Racism at Robben Island', in E. van Heyningen (ed.), *Studies in the History of Cape Town*, Cape Town: UCT Press.

Deacon, Harriet (1998) 'Remembering Tragedy, Constructing Modernity: Robben Island as a National Monument', in S. Nuttall and C. Coetzee (eds), *Negotiating the Past – The Making of Memory in South Africa*, Cape Town: Oxford University Press.

Erasmus, Zimitri and Pieterse, E (1999) 'Conceptualising Coloured Identity in the Western Cape Province of South Africa', in M. Palmberg (ed.), *National identity as Democracy in Africa*, HSRC, Mayibuye Centre, University of the Western Cape, and Nordic African Institute, Sweden.

Erasmus, Zimitri (ed.) (2001) *Coloured by History, Shaped by Place: New Perspectives on Coloured Identities in Cape Town*, Roggebaai: Kwela Books and South African History Online.

Green, Naomi (1996) 'Empire as Myth and Memory', in *Cinema, Colonialism, Postcolonialism: Perspectives from the French and Francophone World*, Austin: University of Texas.

Götze, Adriani (1979) *Joseph Beuys*, London: Barrons Educational.

Hall, Martin (1998) 'Earth and Stone: Archaeology as Memory', in S. Nuttall and C. Coetzee (eds), *Negotiating the Past – the Making of Memory in South Africa*, Cape Town: Oxford University Press.

Hamilton, Carolyn (1994) 'Against the Museum as Chameleon', *South African Historical Journal*, 31 (November): 184–90.

Hamilton, Nan and Stephanie Mariel-Curiel (1999) 'Participatory Museum Tour: a Model for Performance Research in a Changing Society', unpublished SASTR conference paper, September.

Hartman, G. H. (ed.) (1993) *Remembrance: the Shapes of Memory*, Cambridge: Blackwell Publishers.

Hass, Kristin Ann (1998) *Carried to the Wall: American Memory and the Vietnam Veterans Memorial*, Berkeley: University of California Press.

Hauptfleisch, Temple (1997) *Theatre and Society in South Africa: Reflections in a fractured mirror*, Pretoria: Van Schaik.

Jackson, Shannon and Steven Robins, (1999) 'Miscast: the Place of Negotiating the Bushman Past and Present', *Critical Arts*, 13, 1: 69–101.

Kramer, D. and Petersen, T. (1987) *District Six: The Musical*, unpublished script, Baxter Theatre, Cape Town.

Krog, A. (1998) *Country of my Skull*, Johannesburg: Random House.

La Capra, Dominick (1998) *History and Memory after Auschwitz*, New York: Cornell University Press.

Linenthal, Edward T. (1995) *Preserving Memory: the Struggle to Create America's Holocaust Museum*, New York: Viking Press.

Lowenthal, David (1997) *The Past is a Foreign Country*, Cambridge: Cambridge University Press.

Meltzer, David J. (1981) 'Ideology and Material Culture', in R.A. Gould and M.B. Schiffer (eds), *Modern Material Culture: the Archeology of Us*, New York: Academic Press.

Milton, Sybil and Ira Nowinski (1992) *In Fitting Memory: the Art and Politics of Holocaust Memorials*, Detroit: Wayne State University Press.

Nuttall, Sara and Carli Coetzee (1998) *Negotiating the Past – the Making of Memory in South Africa*, Cape Town: Oxford University Press.

Patraka, Vivian (1999) *Spectacular Suffering: Theatre, Fascism, and the Holocaust*, Bloomington: Indiana University Press.

Rive, Richard (1986) *Buckingham Palace: District Six. A Novel of Cape Town*, New York: Ballantine.

Sacks, Shelley (ed.) (1997) *Social Sculpture*, Glasgow: Goethe Institute.

Schofield, J. (ed.) (1998) *Monuments of War: the Evaluation, Reading and Management of Twentieth-century Military Sites*, London: English Heritage.

Sideris, Tina (1986) 'Recording Living Memory in South Africa – the Need for Oral History in South Africa', *Critical Arts*, 4, 2: 41–53.

Thompson, John B. (1984) *Studies in the Theory of Ideology*, Cambridge: Polity.

Van Heyningen, Elizabeth (ed.) (1994) *Studies in the History of Cape Town*, Cape Town: University of Cape Town Press.

Van Tonder, Deon (1994) 'From Mausoleum to Museum: Revisiting Public History at the Inauguration of Museum Africa, Newtown', *South African Historical Journal*, 31 (November): 165–83.

Walder, Dennis (1992) 'Resituating Fugard: South African Drama as Witness', *New Theatre Quarterly*, 8, 32: 343–61.

Winter, Jay (1995) *Sites of Memory, Sites of Mourning*, Cambridge: Cambridge University Press.

Wright, John and Aron Mazel (1991) 'Controlling the Past in the Museums of Natal and KwaZulu', *Critical Arts*, 5, 3: 59–77.

Young, James E. (1994) *The Texture of Memory: Holocaust Memorials and Meaning*, New Haven and London: Yale University Press.

http://www.robben-island.org.za

http://districtsix.co.za

http://www.cdcarts.org/ppp

'On the Threshold of the Future?'
Interview with Athol Fugard

London 24 March 2002

DENNIS WALDER

Athol Fugard's plays – now numbering nearly thirty – continue to command audiences worldwide. He has transformed the lives of the Eastern Cape people he knows best into dramatic images of profound significance. His collaborative work with performers across racial divisions during the apartheid years helped legitimate black experience as a form of cultural expression, and he has remained a powerful influence upon all South African dramatists. His commitment to the theatre is total; his moral concern undeniable. His first play after the 1994 elections was *My Life*, an orchestration of the voices of five young women. His next, *Valley Song*, set in the small Karoo town of Nieuw Bethesda, premiered at the Market Theatre, Johannesburg, in August 1995, before successful runs abroad (including one adventurous production by Scotland's 7:84 Company in 1998). *The Captain's Tiger*, premiered at the McCarter Theatre, Princeton, in May 1998, before successful runs in South Africa and the UK, was a portrait of the artist as a young deckhand.

   Sorrows and Rejoicings, which premiered at the McCarter on 4 May 2001, followed by the Baxter Theatre, Cape Town, on 28 August 2001, had its UK premiere with the South African cast at The Tricycle Theatre, Kilburn, London, on 20 March 2002. The sorrows of the title are those of exile; the rejoicings are what is hoped for in the 'new South Africa'. Set in the semi-desert Karoo, the play shows two women of different racial and cultural backgrounds (Allison and Marta) struggling to reconcile themselves to the secrets and betrayals of the past, haunted by the exiled poet (Dawid) whose funeral they have just attended, and challenged by Rebecca, Dawid and Marta's illegitimate coloured daughter. The following interview was conducted during the play's London run. Before the interview, the playwright remarked that he had vowed to end all public speaking and interviews after his 70th birthday in June.

DW I wanted to ask you first of all, Athol, who are the three 'sisters' to whom *Sorrows and Rejoicings* is dedicated – Mary, Katrina and Dudu?

AF Katrina is my model for the Marta figure. She came into my life when we bought our first house in Nieuw Bethesda. This little 18-year-old girl knocked at the front door and asked if she could have a job. We used her intermittently at first, but with the passing of time she became more and more a member of the family, ending up our housekeeper, looking after both the original house where we met her and then the second house we bought later. She became an incredibly good friend. I think of her the way I think of Mary Benson, as a sister. She died five or six years ago, of a stroke. An inspiration when it came to writing the play. Of course, unlike in the play, there was no sexual or personal relationship between us, she was married and had a family of her own. But in her strength, she was my Marta. It's a portrait of her without the complications of a white philanderer in her life.

Dudu is my Port Elizabeth Katrina, an African woman who looked after the family there for 25 years, at The Ashram [Athol and Sheila Fugard's Port Elizabeth home], which we've sold. She is still alive, and we bought her a house of her own in the township. She and I talk to each other once a week on the telephone. And Mary – Mary Benson, oh my God, Mary was extraordinary, as a friend of the family, of myself personally, and of my work. London without Mary Benson is a place I feel very uncomfortable and awkward in. It's an enormous satisfaction to me that after I had written a working draft of *Sorrows and Rejoicings*, I had a trip planned and I thought I'm going to give Mary a little surprise, I've got a feeling she'll like this one, I'll take it with me; and then something said to me, don't do that, post it. I got back a wonderful response from Mary, and a few days later [in June 2000] she was dead.

So – just those three women in their different ways looked after me. They are the three sisters.

DW You've often said that women are very important for you personally, but also for your work. And that the portraits of women in your plays matter a lot to you. Can you explain how?

AF Well, the portraits all are rooted in – in *The Captain's Tiger* I spoke about the one abortive attempt I made to put my mother down as a character, put my mother's extraordinary story down on paper – my novel, which I threw into a lagoon in Fiji, and I thought that was the end of it. But what I actually realised with the passing of time was that all of those women I've written about are my mother. All of them in their strength, in those life-affirming qualities that they've got, in their defiance – like Lena's defiance, the fact that her spirit comes out at the end – all of those qualities are actually the telling of my mother's story. Though I failed to do it directly the first time. My mother was my muse.

DW Certainly she's your muse in *The Captain's Tiger*. Although you do this strange thing there, make her come to life as a young, seductive muse, not at all distant from the young writer-to-be.

AF Ja, ja. In some ways I regret giving *The Captain's Tiger* to that little theatre in Richmond [The Orange Tree, where the play had its UK premiere], because I allowed them to separate the Tiger and the Narrator. I should have held the play back for its moment. Because as time passes it will be appreciated for a lot of what it says about the craft of writing. How your page talks back to you. That is what I am dramatising there. When a writer sits down to write, or an artist stands in front of a canvas – you start a dialogue with yourself, a process of yes and no. The writer puts a line on a page and he says, yes, or he says no, and reshapes the sentence or just cuts it out altogether. An internal dialogue that goes on all the time in shaping the work of art. And in *The Captain's Tiger* I found the perfect way to dramatise that: by making my character come alive and take on a dialogue with the writer – happy with some of it, then very angry. Because you can violate the integrity of a character, and that character will immediately tell you that; and you can choose not to hear at your own cost, or else you've got to reckon with it.

DW And are these recent plays in dialogue with each other, too?

AF Oh, very much so.

DW They're commenting on each other in a way that reminds me of that Yeats poem – the Yeats reference in *Sorrows and Rejoicings* has made me think of Yeats – 'After Long Silence', in which Yeats refers to a time that has come to 'descant and yet again descant/Upon the supreme theme of Art and Song'. Isn't this your theme now, too? Art, and the Song as a rhythm in these plays. Contrapuntal, isn't it?

AF Absolutely. It's very true, in terms of the four voices in this play. Somebody said to me in New York: I don't know whether *Sorrows* is your middle or your late, but it's a string quartet. You listen to Denise [Marta], it's a cello; Jennifer [Allison] is a violin; you listen to Amrain [Rebecca] and you've got a viola; and old Marius [Dawid] is a bass. That contrapuntal quality. Funnily enough, talking to the actors during a late session yesterday, before the performance, I said to them, you've got to understand – there were one or two little carelessnesses with the text that I wanted to correct – and I said, you've got to understand, these are leitmotifs. Some of the things you chaps are just taking lightly are actually very deliberate leitmotifs, in the way that Bach uses leitmotif in his music . . .

DW Can you give me an example?

AF Look at how many times a *promise* turns up in the play. Right at the start Marta says Dawid made a promise to come back, then she promised him that when he came back nothing would have changed. 'He kept his promise, I kept mine'. Dawid then goes on to talk about a promise, to Rebecca . . . and later, Rebecca says to her mother, 'Well, I kept my promise' . . . there was another example, maybe it'll come to me.

DW One phrase which had a very powerful resonance, not only in this work but in relation to your others as well, and your whole idea of drama, which Marius Weyers slightly threw away at last night's performance, occurs when he talks about returning to the Karoo, to find 'space, time, and silence'. I would have paused after that.

AF That's right.

DW But I can see it's difficult for the actor. He has to come in at a certain emotional pitch, created after the two women have been talking for some time, and this is very demanding.

AF Ja. It took me a long time, you know, to find the form which allowed me to tell the story, and feel that I'd told the story I wanted to tell. I've got a draft of this play written in Port Elizabeth, written in a very orthodox fashion in the sense that it doesn't play with time or with memories at all. Dawid arrives home at the start of the play, and disappears from the play just before interval when he goes to his room to die. At that point, Allison returns from London, and the second Act concerns Allison and Rebecca.

DW It is so much better to do it through flashbacks, like a dream...

AF In order to fracture the story. So at one moment you see an ageing Dawid who just manages to get back home, and then in the next scene there's this vibrant, passionate young man who's on the point of going into exile; and then you see the drunk, wasted life; then the dying man – and then suddenly there he is again in all his glory, on the table [in the centre of the stage].

DW Although it is a horrifying speech he makes there, about the man who castrates himself. Do you think exile is a kind of castration?

AF No. Actually he is castrated by the system in the country. It's ironic that he cannot have a family after he leaves. And you know – look at Jeremy Cronin: Communist, and imprisonment didn't stop him writing, and he's still doing it now. The point is, some of the stories of exile show the flowering of a life, not the extinction of it. Look at Joseph Conrad, for God's sake, one of the great stylists of the English language, Nabokov, Eliot coming to England, Auden going to America....

DW But in the case of Dawid?

AF He is inspired by three figures in my life.[1] Poet Sydney Clouts: look what happened to him. Nat Nakasa. Perseus Adams, who travelled up Africa with me [in 1953]: never wrote again. And there was a Coloured poet, dedicated a poem to me, committed suicide in Oxford – Arthur Nortje. For the longest time I was puzzled, disturbed, fascinated by this phenomenon, of voices that had had so much promise in South Africa, silenced. I was intrigued by the possibility of a play, it kept occurring to me, and then the moment came to write it.

DW You don't feel you're in exile now?

AF No. Never.

DW You did say to me once you couldn't write outside Port Elizabeth, the Eastern Cape ...?

AF One of the freedoms that has come into my life since 1994 is that – I mean I could never write about anything but South Africa. You know, there is always that fork in the road. You've got to choose which way to go. You always wonder what would have happened if you'd chosen the other path. I had the opportunity to go into exile: they offered me an exit permit [in 1967], when they tried to get me out of the country, which would have been one direction. In a way this play is an exploration of what would have happened to me if I'd chosen the other fork. And it is the same device I used in *Hello and Goodbye*: Johnny has a chance to leave home, and stops on the bridge, thinks about his father, and can either go on to railway school and free himself from that bondage and find a life of his own, or go back – and he goes back. So in two plays I explore that other road, the one I didn't take. I hadn't thought about that....

DW It's a recognition: to meet the pain that is South Africa, that is what kept you going, to create your work. This is also a very painful play. I felt as if a layer of skin were being taken off, people exposing their pain in a way I haven't felt about your recent work, going back to the earlier plays.

AF That's absolutely right. *Valley Song* and *The Captain's Tiger* don't have that factor. But look at *Playland*: those are also flayed bodies – like in that exhibition in London now ['Body Worlds', Atlantis Gallery]. This is my exhibition of flayed South Africans.

DW I'd like to ask you about something we've discussed before, the visual aspect of your work, the originating image. There's often a single or even a cluster of generating, central images. What about for this play? The cover of the American published playtext shows Rebecca in the doorway, standing, as she stands throughout much of the play, barely moving.

AF I am fascinated by children, by life upon the threshold, and that is what Rebecca is: that doorway is a threshold, and she realises she must enter into it. That might well be – it's very metaphorical – the genesis. The whole theme of exile is one I've had inside for decades but just recently as I move within the reality of South Africa now, I've had this sense of the country's complex, problematic future, where so much can go wrong, so much can go right. I have a sense of the responsibility that new generation of South Africans face. If Rebecca's going to go around burning up the beauty of the past, as she burns up her father's poems in the play, it's going to be a very impoverished future, a very impoverished future.

There's a marvellous quote over the entrance to Georgetown University in Washington, about how important the past is: the only building material you have for the future is the past. You can't build your future out of anything else. And if you only choose the negative part of it, you're going to have a very ugly construction, finally.

DW Clearly memory is important to you, on a personal as well as on a broader level. It's become a key element in your work.

AF Memory is such a central and complex factor in creativity that I think every artist, in whatever medium, will have a different relationship to it. I experience it as a mixed blessing – as much a hindrance at times as a blessing. Firstly let me state the obvious, which is my total reliance on it because of the long gestation period that all of my plays undergo before they reach the page … *Sorrows and Rejoicings* is a perfect example … the memory of those early years of the apartheid struggle, when friends went into voluntary or enforced exile, etc. But conversely and at another level, I always experience the memory of past work as a very real hindrance when I sit down to write. At the level of craft, the craft of playwrighting, I think I can say in all honesty that nothing in the past has ever helped me write the next one and for the simple reason that the challenge, the demands of 'the next one' are always unique and require the forging of a new and unique set of tools to deal with it.

DW There's an image that comes to my mind, from Walter Benjamin's writings, where he says the images of the present are like images on a photographic plate that only the future will develop. So we cannot know how it will look.

AF That's very beautiful. It'll only be beyond us, when it emerges. Very pertinent. Like that last moment of Allison's, when she says to Rebecca that 'you and your "new South Africa"' are going to need all the love they can get, no matter where it comes from.

DW It's unexpected: just as we're experiencing a sense of loss, of the past dominating the present, there's this turn, to love. The play seems to be all about sorrows, but the rejoicings are also there.

AF If you're going to talk about South Africa, what two words can you use? Sorrows and Rejoicings! Christ, as South Africans isn't that what we experience?

DW So Eugene Marais is wrong in the end, that quote of yours from his 'Song of South Africa', the country that gives nothing but demands everything?

AF It's a beautiful poem: stark, and oh! But it's the right one to end with.

DW And I notice there's a screening of *The Guest* [about an incident in Eugene Marais' life, with Fugard as Marais] here at The Tricycle as well, coinciding with the play: it is a reminder that Marais came to London, too, and that you need luck to flourish.

AF Absolutely.

DW So where are you going now? What's your agenda?

AF I've got to move the New York production of *Sorrows* to the West Coast, to LA. Unfortunately I've lost my New York Marta and Rebecca, so I've had to audition and replace them. A big number in directing on my hands. But this is the *last* one. I let the work go after this ... although I'm sure that when I've written something I'll try to help, talk to the director.

DW Won't you find it difficult to give up that kind of control over your work?

AF Yes. I'll find it very difficult. And maybe unlike my drinking, this'll be a resolution I can't keep [laughs]. But we'll wait and see. There's no breaking the resolution about not talking about my work any more. That is what my instinct, my daemon has told me. What did he say to Socrates? Make more music. And to me: shut up. No more talking.

DW But writing?

AF To my dying day.

DW *The Abbess*? The play about Hildegard of Bingen that you've said you've been working on for some time now?

AF It's there. I think I use it as a kind of smokescreen, so that my conscious mind doesn't know what's bubbling up. That's exactly what happened. I was working on *The Abbess* and one morning I found myself saying, I'll just make a note about that idea about exiles again – I was astonished. I said to Sheila [Fugard], you know this one got written surprisingly quickly, what was it, three months? And she said: 'What do you mean? You wrote it in three weeks'. There's a note, after the first entry about exiles, which then turned into five pages of notes about exile, and at the end of three weeks there's another note which says, 'I now have got enough on paper to be able to phone Emily Mann at the McCarter and tell her that it's not going to be *The Abbess* in my slot, but a play called *Sorrows and Rejoicings*'.

DW The US production earned some quite negative comment, didn't it? Would you like to say something about the different reactions to the play there, and here, and in South Africa?

AF A good few years ago I stopped reading critical comment and reviews of my work, both journalistic and academic. I have never found them of any use to me as a writer. My version of the old joke is: '*The Blood Knot* is Dead! – Ken Tynan … Ken Tynan is Dead! – Athol Fugard'. I might add that *The Blood Knot* continues to enjoy a very healthy life and has I believe been described as a contemporary classic. But to get to your question: I think *Sorrows and Rejoicings* was not simple enough for the American critics. I know from past experience that they always try to see SA in very simplistic terms, to reduce it to 'white oppressor–black victim'. England is just that much more aware of the complexity and subtleties of the South African situation, and I think *Sorrows and Rejoicings* possibly requires an awareness of those complex subtleties more than any of my other plays. Directing an American cast in this play was for that very reason more complex than working with South African actors – it was 'their story', and they embraced it accordingly. And at the Baxter, the South African audiences claimed the play in exactly the same way as the actors – it was 'their story'.

DW The title came from Ovid, didn't it?

AF That was an accident. I'd already written this play, and I was playing with titles like 'Warm Brown Bread' [a phrase Dawid uses to show how everyday speech can be poetic]. Then browsing in a bookshop one day, a little paperback, *Sorrows of Exile* – ah! I'm writing about that. I couldn't believe it. I'd already written the section about Dawid walking around London, practising his Afrikaans, and there was Ovid, doing the same thing in exile, practising his Latin. And then this other poem of his, about what I'm going to do with my voice in exile – indict Caesar.

DW There are still indictments to be made, are there not? I saw you on Channel 4 News a few days ago, and a bit of fire came out about Zimbabwe and also about the HIV/AIDS crisis.

AF Ja, I don't think the government's too fond of me.

DW But it's not something you want to put in your work, this kind of statement?

AF I don't write about ideas. I don't take up polemic. Storyteller, regional storyteller.

DW Do you have an interest in any up-and-coming playwrights in South Africa today?

AF There's a lot bubbling up. Not one of them has produced something which has made me say – Ah, one to watch! I've seen a lot of things, and it's very healthy. A stew is really on the cook. But I haven't identified any one particular voice that for me seems to have the authority and ringing urgency that the new South Africa needs. Because a point I keep making is that the new South Africa is going to need the vigilance of writers every bit as much as the old – even more so, because it's a more complex situation, much more ... We've moved into a world of grey areas ...

DW It used to be 'vriend of vyand' [friend or enemy], to quote the play.

AF Yes! I never thought of that, but it is what the old South Africa was about. Now it's friend or enemy, or business associate, or diplomat, or whatever other categories you've got to add. It's a whole different ball game. That was the stark polarity of the old South Africa – 'vriend of vyand'. God, wasn't it simple? Only three words needed in your political vocabulary. Now you've got to have 'maybe', 'if', 'possibly', 'let me think about it'.

DW Some people miss this powerful polarity. Fatima Dike [the Cape playwright] said to me a few years ago that many didn't know what to write about now that the old order had gone.

AF I find that very silly.

DW But she herself has been running a Theatre Education Group in Cape Town ...

AF If you're not writing, that's what to do: give your skills to younger people.

DW Do you have, would you like to have, any connection with institutions where this might happen?

AF Institutions as such have never been important to me. Personalities matter to me. I don't know whether you know it, but when Mannie Manim was 15 years old, he pulled up the curtain on the first-ever production of that play of mine, *No-Good Friday* [1958]. He was earning pocket-money by doing a little theatre work. I had got permission to use the Brooke stage [in Johannesburg] one Sunday night to show this play of mine, with a star-studded cast – Bloke Modisane, Lewis Nkosi, and Can Themba playing a sax in the wings. The greats of Sophiatown. Mannie was there, and then later became my producer, my designer, a pillar of strength. If there is one thing that has categorised my life in the theatre then it is luck [with actors and creative associates]. I have a nickname among the Xhosa down in the Eastern Cape which means luck.

Zakes Mokae at the beginning, Yvonne Bryceland ... you know, I needed an absolutely extraordinary instrument in those first, those memorable female roles I created, Milly, Lena, Miss Helen. John Kani and Winston Ntshona. Latterly, Susan Hilferty, my first designer when I did *A Lesson from Aloes* at Yale Rep, she was in her final MFA year as a designer, she was assigned to that production, and we have worked together ever since.

DW And co-directed?

AF Absolutely. She is my most trusted eye in the theatre. And there was Barney Simon.[2] I have been so lucky in the people who've crossed my path at critical moments.

DW Any actors now who have that importance for you now? Jennifer Steyn was excellent last night.

AF Yes – and Marius [Weyers].

DW She was also in the American production of *The Captain's Tiger*, as the mother.

AF She was *so* funny in it. It's a comedic role. Marius I'm thinking of in terms of something I'm writing next. I don't know where my mind is going next, I'm always surprised. But he would be magnificent in it.

DW There is a man in your life you haven't dealt with, isn't there? The father.

AF That's right ... You know, one of the reasons for wanting to be silent after my 70th is because if I'm going to go on for whatever time that's left I've got to get it out fast. Not that I've spent any time in my life looking back, but there's a pressure to do it now. What is terribly important is that I just look ahead. You know Rilke in his *Letters to the Young Poet* talks about the need to recapture a kind of innocence when you confront blank paper again, and start a new journey. He is so right. If you let the past crowd you, that innocence will be impossible. You will imitate yourself, instead of being yourself. That's what happens to so many poets. That's what Harold Pinter does now, he imitates himself.

DW It's a paradox, isn't it? You need the past because you have to use it, but you have to keep looking beyond, to the future, too.

AF Ja.

NOTES

1 Sydney Clouts (1926–82), whose books are *One Life* (1966) and *Collected Poems* (1984) emigrated to London in the early 1960s. Nat Nakasa (1937–65), *Drum* writer and founder of the literary magazine *The Classic*, died after a fall from a high-rise building in New York. *The World of Nat Nakasa* (ed. Essop Patel) was published ten years after his death. Arthur Nortje (1942–70) died under mysterious circumstances at Oxford University (where he held a scholarship). His poems appeared in the posthumous collection *Dead Roots* (1973) and *Lonely Against the Light* (1973).

2 Barney Simon's own workshop productions for the Market Theatre included *Black Dog/In'emnyama* (1984), *Outers* (1985), *Born in the RSA* (1985) and *Score Me the Ages* (1989).

'Put me on the Stage'
Interview with Nomhle Nkonyeni
Winchester 20 July 2001

DAVID KERR

Nomhle Nkonyeni has had a long acting career, almost uninterrupted since 1963. Although the interview she gives is mainly chronological, it needs to be emphasised that not all her achievements have been covered by it. She has missed out some of her most famous acting roles, including the old woman in Zakes Mda's *Dark Voices Rising* and Freda Jama in Fatima Dike's *The First South African* (Kruger 185–6 and 162–3). In addition she has directed and written plays.

In this interview Nkonyeni somewhat belittles her television career, yet it has made her an extremely well-known personality, not only in South Africa, but throughout the region. Despite her fame, she remains very down-to-earth and in touch with ordinary people, as I witnessed, watching her in the un-glamorous context of training AIDS orphans in devised drama techniques in the dusty yard of a charity centre (Chiredzi, Zimbabwe, May 2001). Her eagerness to progress is shown by her recent undertaking of a Masters Degree in Theatre for Development (at King Alfred's College, University of Southampton), a new field which she feels will become increasingly relevant in twenty-first century South Africa.

A little background in South African theatre history might be useful in order to locate her interview within its appropriate social and political parameters. Although black involvement in mainstream drama activities can be found as early as the 1930s in the activities of the Bantu Dramatic Society, by the early 1960s various pieces of apartheid legislation had made it virtually impossible for blacks and whites to collaborate in drama, and effectively restricted African involvement in performance to the politically sanctioned areas of 'tribal' song and dance.

For a young African man or woman interested in training for and acting in the theatre there were really only two choices, either the liberal art theatre associated with progressive white directors like Athol Fugard and Barney Simon, or the township musicals of director entrepreneurs such as Gibson Kente. Nkonyeni opted for the first option with the Serpent Players. For the next generation, in the 1970s, there was another important option, the resistance theatre of the late 1970s and 1980s, initiated by the Black Consciousness movement of the early 1970s. Nkonyeni was a member of the Pan-Africanist Congress in the 1960s and was closely associated with the Black Consciousness movement (which she refers to as BC), even though she did not join any of the formal resistance theatre companies such as Soyikwa or Bahumutsi. Instead she chose to provoke formerly white-dominated theatre companies or broadcasting institutions into changing their policies. Much of the interest to be found in Nkonyeni's interview comes from seeing her recall the pressures she underwent as she struggled to sustain her radicalism within a liberal, white-dominated theatre landscape.

Some of the references Nkonyeni makes to this theatre history are worth explaining in advance to reduce the need for footnotes. The reference to Zionists is to the Zionist Christian Church (ZCC), a very popular separatist movement, founded in the 1920s, which mixes Christian and indigenous African elements, with the latter including performance features such as costume, song and dance. The white organisations that Nkonyeni joined and helped transform were part of a highly bureaucratic and authoritarian state system. Theatre fell under the aegis of various regional arts councils; she refers to two of these, the Performing Arts Council of Transvaal (PACT) and Cape Arts Board (CAPAB). During the mid-1980s, this racist monopoly began to break down. Nkonyeni's important decision to join The Space Theatre at the invitation of artistic director Brian Astbury became possible because of the 1986 lifting of racist provisions in the Entertainment Act. A similar but much slower process took place in broadcasting. The monopolistic South African Broadcasting Corporation (SABC) had a racist policy of different radio stations (and, later, different segments of TV channels) for different ethnic groups, a system which Nomhle complains about; its reform was one of the first cultural changes made by the democratically elected government of 1994.

Nomhle Nkonyeni is a very theatrical speaker, using a full repertoire of verbal and visual expression even in normal conversation; the performance quality of her interview has challenged my ability to translate these elements into a description of her gestures and vocal interjections. Her interview (conducted in English) has received minimal editing, in order to retain the flavour of her communication; she carefully collaborated with me in that editing process. The interview is peppered with local words or phrases from isiZulu, isiXhosa or Afrikaans. Most of these I gloss in the text, but a few merit a little explanation here; where I do gloss I use square brackets, leaving round brackets for Nkonyeni's own parentheses. When Nkonyeni is referring to a male comrade or friend, she often prefaces the first name with the word 'buti' an Africanised version of the Afrikaans word 'boet', meaning brother. 'Sisi' is the female equivalent. The word 'dorpie' is a playful variant of the Afrikaans word 'dorp', meaning small town. The word 'shebeen', derived from Irish Gaelic, but very common in South Africa, means an illicit drinking place often run from a private home.

Nkonyeni thrives in an interview context where she receives few interventions from the interviewer, but is allowed to build her own narrative drive. This is all reflected in what follows. The reader also needs to note that at several points throughout the interview she uses a technique of recalled direct speech (often without introductory phrases). This provides a vivid, impressionistic reconstruction of earlier conversations, but is, of course, not meant to be a totally accurate verbatim account. In addition, I thought it necessary to provide a few explanatory footnotes, though keeping them to a minimum to enable the reader to enjoy the full flow of Nkonyeni's narrative.

DK When did you join the Serpent Players, Nomhle?

NN I joined the Serpent Players in 1963, and the first production was *The Caucasian Chalk Circle*, where I played Grusha. I never thought I would be an actress. I just did it I suppose because people said, 'Nomhle, you have potential.' But when you see people ... [*comic gesture of gossiping*] you get discouraged. Then the aim of the Serpent Players was to bring people to the theatre, which thereafter we managed to do. But when we did *Chalk Circle* we performed to ... [*laughing*] you know ... twenty people.

DK Where was that?

NN In Port Elizabeth. My beginnings were in Port Elizabeth, until 1972 ... no, the beginning of 1977 when I came out of prison... My second play was *Antigone*. I then played that young hot-headed girl, Antigone. Like we were getting people by word of mouth: 'There's this group ... Athol Fugard' and so and so and so and so [*gesture of gossiping*].

DK Athol directed both?

NN Ja. You see, when Athol Fugard came back to Port Elizabeth, we had an association, which was called New Brighton Arts Association, NBAA, and what the older guys, who were mostly teachers, wanted to do was to take the children off the streets, sort of give them something to do. I know, Sundays we had activities, because everybody was available. Line dance, ballroom dancing, drama... There wasn't much of visual arts, but that was what was happening, and music. And when Athol Fugard came back to Port Elizabeth those guys got to know. He had been working with the Phoenix Players in Johannesburg. They went and approached him. Athol knew they wanted to learn more about theatre so he became involved in the Serpent Players. That's when we started doing the first play, which I wasn't part of. The second play, that's when I was recruited and brought into the group for *The Chalk Circle*. And then it was *Antigone*.

In between, Athol would give us some theory and master classes, pronunciation. He would say, 'If you guys want to be actors you may have to ... because most people who go to the theatre are white people who are not tuned to hear "sarenda". So if you say "sarenda", people will say: "What? What?" So we say "surrender".' So these were the kinds of classes, not in a formal way. We would go to his house, every day. If you wanted to be together for so many hours you have to apply for a licence. So we used to go to Athol's on Mondays, Wednesdays, Sundays. At times we'd just have fun. I was not a drinker then – I was very young. Those who drank, drank, and that's where Athol got most of his material about New Brighton, and they wrote about New Brighton, because people were like, 'Ao! This nice white man!' He was sucking things from us then.

DK Who were the people there, apart from yourself?

NN Norman Ntshinga, bless his soul! That is the man, who brought the idea of *The Island* to the Serpent Players. Simon Hanabe, bless his soul! He also died. He was in Robben Island. Reverend Keyki Njikelana, he was a teacher then, before he became a minister of religion. Monde Mbikwana, he was also a teacher. It's like all the money we used to make, we had a kitty, and the aim then (that was Athol) the aim was to send each member to RADA. We managed to send *buti* Monde. Then there was *buti* Shark Mququlwa, he's also dead. Monde and Keyki are still alive. Then there was *Buti* George Mnci, *buti* Michael Ngxokolo, who was in charge of music. He was a composer, a renowned composer, classical music. He is dead also. There was Daphney Majojina, also a teacher. Mr Sogoni, who was a lawyer. *Buti* Frank Thomjeni, also a teacher. Those are the people who recruited me. They were my teachers. There was Sarah Nyati, who also died. There was May, wife to *buti* Norman Ntshinga. May Magada was the singer, using her maiden name. She's still alive. There was Liziwe Duru. I think she did one production, *The Caucasian Chalk Circle*. There was Nombulelo Mjuza, she was also part of one production. They often didn't last long. And there was later, after I joined the Serpent Players, my ex-husband, Mangi. There was John Kani, Winston Ntshona. Oh, and the old guys – these were: Fats Bokholane, still alive and very active, George Luse, Zacharias S'kweyiya, that was the guy who brought us the idea of *Friday's Bread on Monday*. That's about all.

DK When was the first devised production you were involved in?

NN I think the first devised production was *The Last Bus*, the second was *Friday's Bread on Monday*, and then *The Coat*.

DK How was *The Coat* devised?

NN Let me start with how the coat was brought to our attention, the very coat, because there *was* a coat. In 1963 *buti* Norman was arrested. *Buti* Norman, *buti* Welcome, *buti* Simon, they were arrested. There was a big swoop in 1963, the second swoop in '65. So *buti* Norman was among the first group of Pan-Africanist members. So he was part of that. When his case..., you know political cases were not conducted in Port Elizabeth. They were conducted outside PE in neighbouring cities or towns. In his case, it was in Cradock. Most of them were done in Humansdorp, small dorpies. I suppose they didn't want any crowds there. We couldn't get there unless, in Sisi May's case, Norman's wife, Athol used to transport her to Cradock.

So on this particular day when we went to listen to his case, there were three men, one recognized May; the three of them were from New Brighton. One recognized May, and he had this jacket, because his family was not there, to listen to his case.

'May,' he said, 'I need you to take this to number 21 Mnqandi Street in New Brighton. I know you are Norman's wife. Please take this jacket and give it to my wife. Tell them I've been sentenced to five years.'

So May said, 'Okay, fine, fine.'

May comes back, tells Athol, 'This is the case, this man has given me the jacket, so I'll have to take it to his house when we get back home.'

The following day, when we were at Athol's place, they tell us the story that there was a man who was sentenced yesterday and May was given a coat, a jacket, to take to his family.

'Let us look at this coat, guys,' Athol said, 'What do you think we can do with this coat?'

We started debating about the coat. That's how the coat became *The Coat*. We started debating, talking. Athol said:

'Everybody go home, think about this thing. If you were in this woman's shoes... Nomhle, if it was you, in this woman's shoes, what would you have done? May, being given the coat for that woman, what are you going to say?'

The others are neighbours – '*s'bonda*' what is it? Headmen. Because in the township at that time they used to have, they still have, what do they call it? Councillors, that looked after the township. So there would be headmen who would go round checking if you'd paid your rent and da di da. And so we all put ourselves in that situation. So every night we discussed it. This is how we would write down whatever we would feel, as the person allocated.

'You are that woman, Nomhle. We leave you in that house.'

We started doing a sort of Joe Blag [a play devising game for creating characters]. That's how *The Coat* was born. It comes from the cells of Cradock, through New Brighton... So we gave it some life.

Then *The Last Bus*... We used to rush for this bus. There was a curfew. Nobody was allowed to be in town after 10 o'clock. If you were caught in town after 10 o'clock you'd get a criminal case. So we'd go to Athol Fugard's house, which is right in town on the other side of town. But we had to rush back. There was this bus, which leaves at 10 o'clock exactly, it gets out of the city centre. So if you miss that bus you're in big shit. So Athol would go to the terminus and if we missed the bus, he'd chase the bus, because if you're caught on the streets... so we rode. One beautiful thing was the people in the bus, because everybody used to complain. Some of them used to visit their wives in town. They were working in kitchens in the white homesteads. If they had lovey lovey dovey [*comic gesture of embrace*] with their wives and forget about the time, they're in big trouble. If they sleep at the house in the yard, the white man can call the police and they're still in trouble. So everybody was 'Man, man, man, if only this law could be changed!' So that's how *The Last Bus* became.

Friday's Bread on Monday – another piece that we did. Zack, who lives in New Brighton, works in Korsten, so Zack felt there was no point for him to pay bus fare, so he can walk from home to Korsten. (Don't ask me kilometers or miles. To me when I was younger, it could have been a walking distance.) So Zack used to walk. There was a neighbouring shanty township, called Emaplangeni, it's now called Fordsville. Very posh houses now. But then, houses built in planks, so low, low-income housing – very poor. People from there used to send their children. Just across the veld, there was a bakery in a white area, a bakery called Britos. They used to sell stale bread for five cents. So Zack used to notice these kids scantily dressed, only in shorts in the middle of winter running behind him when it was very dark. And one day he asked them, 'Hey, guys, where are you going to?'

'*Ai, tata,* [father] we're going to Brito'.

'Why Brito?'

'We're going to buy bread'

'Why can't you buy it in the café next to you?'

'Ah, because Brito sells bread for five cents.'

So that's why we decided to call it *Friday's Bread on Monday*. Yes. I think it was an exaggeration on our part to call it *Friday's Bread on Monday*, if it slept on Sunday. Nobody buys on Sunday. It was quite cheap. For five cents, they'd get about four loaves. Or if there was a surplus, they'd get four loaves on Monday. So we called it *Friday's Bread on Monday*. We looked into that situation, and we came up with a production about it.

DK So it was the same process that produced *The Island* and *Sizwe Bansi*?

NN It was the same process, but now in isolation. [*pause*]

DK So how did that happen, the isolation? [*pause*]

NN We'd been persecuted, man, by the police, the Special Branch.

DK Because of the drama?

NN Ja. Oh, the Serpent Players were like [*seeking the right word*] a cell, a political... Ja they were under that impression. Those police guys must've been stupid. And one other thing was they were aware that we were conscientising people politically. To them we were mobilising whatever was happening in the township – it was because of the Serpent Players. If the Serpent Players would just shut up, nothing would like... all the uproar that was happening in the township, it would just shut up. Nothing would happen, they'd just say, 'Yes, *baas* [boss], yes, *baas*!' But here is a group of people who're working with a communist! [*laughing*] Which is Athol!

So we had a big problem. Every time we do something the Special Branch would know. [*TAPE switched off while Nomhle explains her suspicions about a police informant in the group*] We did a play by Camus, *The Just*. We adapted, and localised it, and we were actually bringing in the exiles, long before you know... that was 1972. And the police felt... The script was taken. The man I mentioned before [*when the tape was switched off*] said his script was taken. The Special Branch came to his house. The script was taken and they said we should stop doing this play. But we did not. We felt there was nothing wrong with the play. And if they'd taken the script, which was the original script, it's talking about Russia, it's not talking about South Africa. *Ours* was South Africa. Anyway, every time they even knew the venues. They'd come to my house.

'Yes, what are you doing?'

So when we'd see in advance, that they were coming, because we'd rehearse with the curtains open, when we'd see cars and people walking in, we'd start singing and they'd say:

'Why don't you do what you were doing?'

'This is part of what we're doing.' We'd sing like Zionists, and say, 'This is part of what we're doing.'

And I remember in Grahamstown, we put up the show, and they came; they were watching the show. They stopped the show, the Special Branch. So everybody felt that was the time to go, you know... to go underground. Just let everything cool down, after some members of the group were jailed for political reasons.

Now, going back to *buti* Norman and the creation of *The Island* and *Sizwe Bansi is Dead*, *buti* Shark, who was playing Haemon in *Antigone* (on the day they arrested my brother). And when *buti* Shark got there, after he was on trial for a year, he was sentenced and sent to Robben Island. When he got to Robben Island he started telling *buti* Norman, *buti* Welcome and *buti* Simon what the Serpent Players were currently doing. They usually had a get-together, I think on Sundays on Robben Island. So *buti* Shark was insisting to *buti* Norman and *buti* Simon that they should do this play. But he couldn't remember Antigone's lines. He couldn't remember anybody's lines; he could remember Haemon's lines – *his*.

So the others said, 'Man, Shark, look we don't have the script.'

'Man, of what I remember let's start rewriting *Antigone* in jail for these guys.'

And then they performed; it was their own thing. It was not a gathering that was permitted in jail. *buti* Norman told us later that when they were applauding it was like... [*gesture of rubbing hands together instead of clapping*]. But they managed to get something out of what *buti* Shark was telling them. That's how *The Island* was... The men coming back from prison telling us about what the guys in prison were doing. Until Athol, who's got this at the back of his head, when we were told to go underground after being persecuted doing Camus in 1972. The bulk of the men came back. Athol, along with Winston and John, who were members long after the Serpent Players were founded, started doing the play.

And it's again *buti* Norman who was friendly to Styles, the photographer in *Sizwe Bansi*. And *buti* Norman was a good storyteller. He would make a joke about the real Styles, his friend. [*conspiratorially*] And they would take note of it. And when they said 'Let's go underground, let's relax', they knew that now they were moving away from us, and they were creating these two productions. That is how *Sizwe* and *The Island* were done – without us knowing. We got to know that these plays were happening when they were here, in the West End. John and Winston had gone to the West End. And we all went our different ways.

DK And Norman wasn't acknowledged?

NN Norman wasn't acknowledged at all for a long time. He died without being acknowledged in his lifetime. He died two years ago. I remember Winston coming to me when we were now at loggerheads with Athol, and me saying, 'You know, cousin, I'll never forgive you for one thing – for not acknowledging *buti* Norman. He died without due acknowledgement.' I said that to John as well. I don't know. [*sigh*] But that's how these things happened.

DK How did you get arrested?

NN In 1976 some guys... Well, when I was not involved in theatre I used to run a shebeen. My shebeen was just to discuss issues that were paramount in our community. And there were these youngsters, people who were expelled from Fort Hare – oh that's another phase – who would come to my home and say, 'Sisi Nomhle, why don't we start the Serpent Players again?' . When I invited John and Winston, they were big names now. And I said 'Hey, guys, there are people, youngsters, who are really...' [*gesture of enthusiasm*] And when the kids came to so-called rehearsals, I gave them such a lecture. Whatever Nomhle says is right.

'This is not what we want,' they said. 'We came to Nomhle, she didn't give us that. Winston and John, are you going to help us?'

'Ah, but we will come. Just work with Nomhle for the time being.'

That's it. So I had these kind of associates. We'd have like debates – anything, everything. And when the riots erupted – I was then associated with the BC. – when the riots erupted in Johannesburg, the youngsters said:

'Guys, Eastern Cape was always known to be the administration block.[1] What are we doing about it?'

So everything was planned in that house. And amongst these youngsters, one must have gone to the Special Branch and said, 'This is what is going on'.

I was taken in. They wanted to know who holds meetings in my house.

'No, no,' I said, 'I don't hold meetings in my house. I sell liquor. People who go there, go there only to drink.'

'Who are the people?'

'There's Temba.'

'Temba who?'

'I can't remember, because I don't know his surname.'

'Who else?'

'Sipho.'

'How many Siphos do you know?'

(Sipho, Zola, these are the common first names.)
'Surnames?'
'I don't know their surnames.'
'Where do they live?'
'I don't know. They live somewhere. They just come to my house to drink.'

I was beaten up. That's where it ends. I don't want to go into the sea with a sack over my head. I've had nightmares. So I was kept in prison for nine months.

When I came out of jail, my mother said, 'Come to Cape Town. Just leave Port Elizabeth for a while.'

So I left. I just wanted to see some live performances. The first performance of *The Just* had just happened at The Space. That's when they'd just opened The Space, and I decided to go to there. 'Somebody please accompany me.' So I went to the Space. I walked in. Brian Astbury said, 'My God, the woman I've been looking for.' Since there was a play, *Medea,* being directed by Barney Simon... I did *Medea*, playing Gora, directed by Barney Simon. And there was another play in the pipeline for me. It was going to be directed by Dimitri Valorakis. And a play written by Fatima Dike, *The First South African*. So I've never looked back.

And thereafter, I played at The Space. Before I moved from Cape Town, I worked for a film company, doing magazine programmes. That's when I started doing my little bit of writing, like short scripts, but not too demanding of me, magazine programmes. I'd go out, research and write a piece. They'd shoot it, and I'd present it.

Before The Space closed I phoned CAPAB, and said, 'My name is Nomhle Nkonyeni, I'm an actress, I'm looking for a job.' That was before they opened theatres for black people. You could only work for the Space Theatre. They said, 'Nomhle, we've heard so much about you. Can you come over?' They said, 'Can you prepare three pieces for an audition?' I'd never been to an audition, so I asked my friends in the theatre, 'Guys, what do you do for an audition?' So Jacqui Singer was among the people who helped me.

'It's simple, Nomhle. Some of the things you have done.'

I did that. I went back to them. And they employed me. That's when I did *Poppie Nongena*, opening the theatre for black people, acting for the first time on that stage, a multi-racial audience, and a mixed cast.

DK But you'd performed for integrated audiences before, with the Serpent Players.

NN Integrated, but invited. Because the law did not allow integrated paying audiences. So it was invited and donations. Nobody should pay. [*laughing*] And no integration after the performances. So discussions after the show were like *zilch*, though we'd go to someone's house and discuss, but not in the same complex.

DK What about *Poppie Nongena*?

NN To me it was hard, because *Poppie Nongena* was in Afrikaans, and I didn't know Afrikaans. That was my first production in Afrikaans. Do you know how I got that job? I went for an audition, and thereafter there was [*lip sound*], quiet. Nothing from management. My second husband was in Lesotho in exile. So I went and joined him. I stayed there. I got a call, so my mother called me.

'Hey, there's some people from Cape Town phoned you from CAPAB. They said please, can you phone them.'

I phoned the following day at CAPAB.

'Nomhle, where are you?'

'I'm in Lesotho.'

'Nomhle, we need you back. We want you in Cape Town.'

'For what?'

'We've got a role for you. We are going to do *Poppie Nongena*.'

I was excited. I'd read *Poppie Nongena*. It was serialized in *Fair Lady* in English. I said 'Ooh, if anyone decides to adapt this book into a play, I'd love to play this part'.

So I said to this guy, 'Is it in English?'

'No, it's in Afrikaans.'

'Ah, count me out, guys.'

'Praat 'n bietjie Afrikaans met my, Nomhle'.[2]

'Nee, Peter,' I said, 'Ek kan nie suiwer Afrikaans praat nie'[3] I could only speak like local...

'You've got the part,' the director said.

'No!' I said. I panicked.

'You've got the part,' he said, 'Where do we send you the ticket? How do we get hold of you? Do you want to give us your number?'

I wanted to consult.

'Okay,' I said, ' I'll phone you. Give me like a day. I'll call you tomorrow.'

So I consulted. I was with BC people.

'Guys, this is the situation – to come back to South Africa for da da da.' [*gesture of summation*].

'Go for it, Nomhle.'

But I was referred to the South African-based members of the BC. 'Find out, if it's okay,' the Lesotho comrades said, 'and what is the situation. Are the theatres open to black people?'

'Oh no, that is okay,' the BC people said. 'That new law is about to pass. By the time of performance the theatres will be open.'

So I phoned CAPAB. 'It's okay.'

Everything was arranged. I flew from Bloemfontein to Cape Town, and I started rehearsals. When I looked at the script, I said, 'My God, what have I got myself into? The play's about a non-Xhosa speaking Xhosa woman. We call them Oorlams. They can't speak Xhosa properly; they've got used to Afrikaans. You get these people in the Northern Cape, into the Karoo, and then a lot of them in the Eastern Cape. When I received the script I could read it, but I could not make sense. I could not understand what I was reading. So I had some Afrikaans actor friends. They said, 'Nomhle, we're prepared to help you.' I overcame that. I made it, and I got myself an award. When I got to understand the language I stopped acting. You could not act that, you can only live it. If you understand what a mother can go through, you don't act it. That is how I tackled *Poppie Nongena*. You know, with *Poppie Nongena*, I didn't have to do any research – it was every black woman's experience. You look this way, there's a Poppie Nongena, you look that way there's a Poppie Nongena. So it wasn't really difficult.

And so I moved to Johannesburg. PACT was a bit stiff about employing black actors. So I worked for SABC as a dubbing producer for a year. But I felt, 'Man, there's something missing in my life.' If you haven't been on stage for five years you lose part of yourself. Jacqui Singer, Aletta Bezuidenhout, Clare Stopford were working for PACT and they were commissioning to do a work-shopped piece they said with Nomhle Nkonyeni. They brought me there then, they decided to employ me. We did this wonderful piece called *Chameleon Jive* (*uLovane Jive*). We did that, and PACT did not want to part with me. And then, I had an agent in Johannesburg. When I was doing *uLovane Jive* she got me a job at the Market Theatre to do *Diepe Grond* [Deep Ground] by Reza de Wet. It was a walk-on. But whilst I was working doing this project, I thought I'd be able to do that, but PACT decided to contract me for a year, and I was offered a beautiful role, playing Winnie Mandela, in *The Time of the Hyena*.

DK Was it possible to use her words in the play?

NN It wasn't about Winnie, right. It was about her lawyer and his wife, who befriended her, and you know these Afrikaners, this lawyer was an Afrikaner and she had a get-together with all the prominent liberal Afrikaners. She invited Winnie without her friends knowing. It was just a little piece; it was underwritten. Then these Afrikaners – [*imitation of their gasps of horror*]. 'Ah, communist party member!' Winnie was like very relaxed. The lawyer's wife, who told me the story came to see me, and she said, 'Exactly, that's exactly her.' I tried to get into Winnie. I have a debt to her up to now. I have tried to get into her … to get her opinion… I was going to represent her out of ignorance. So I wanted to be accurate, and you could not get anything on television about Winnie at that time in 1986, so I wanted to have it first-hand. But no, there was always a barrier. I couldn't talk to her. She was a banned person, and was not allowed to give interviews. Then the lady, the lawyer's wife was quite impressed with the way I portrayed her accurately.

DK The lawyer and lawyer's wife came to the show?

NN Ja, they came to see the show all the way from the Free State.

DK Where was it performed?

NN At the Windybrow... and at the State Theatre. It was when they were opening up. The play was written by an Afrikaner woman, Mitzi Booysen. Ja, it was 'the change of times'. To me the change of time was not when they released Mandela, it was when they opened theatre to non-whites.

DK What about your roles in film and soap operas?

NN Films? Soapies? Well, for one, in South Africa there was a 'rule and divide'. There was a Nguni channel for Xhosa and Zulu-speaking viewers. At first, I didn't want to do a thing, because of that, because there wasn't one body. The best was TV1, which was for English-speaking Africans. In the rank and file, 2 and 3, which was not well-received – why the separate channels?

The first reception of television was 1975 in South Africa was it? I didn't want to be part of that, because politically it would have been very wrong. I became involved in television in 1982, when I was doing this magazine programme, and I wasn't working directly with SABC. SABC was like taboo. If you wrote for SABC you were a sell-out. I wasn't working directly with SABC, but the programmes we were doing were for SABC because it was the only outlet on television, and SABC didn't have studios in Cape Town. I worked for this private company. And luckily for me, the producers said, 'Nomhle, if only you can use subtlety, say what you want' (it was all said in Xhosa), 'Say what you want, but be careful.' So I was given that leeway. As a result we got an award for best production in the Cape, because we were tackling issues that were of primary importance, important to people, the community. We'd tackle such issues, when we go out we'd say, 'But how do I approach this theme so that SABC accepts it?'

Our producer said 'As long as you are subtle. If you want to say 'fuck you' say 'fuck you' in a very subtle manner. You don't have to say 'fuck you' but 'Oh man, this was a disservice, da da, da, da, da" [*gesture of boring circumlocution*].

So I worked for the company like that, which gave me leeway. I enjoyed that. And when I became involved in the dramas, the first that I did was a children's programme, *uMakhulu uyasibalisela* [Granny Is Telling Us Stories] about this matriarch, this mama, who was in control. I didn't want anything... any character that's going to belittle black people. It was this black woman who was [*gesture of strength*]. She was a queen in her own right. So I accepted such roles. I would look at roles and turn them down if I feel, 'No, no, no, no – it's putting down black people.'

Though that was not my first love. Theatre was always my first love. Why I did that, it was for money. They were paying more money. As long as the script is good for me and for the black people. I would do it. And I would do like *The Wrath of the Gods*, which is a Xhosa legend.

Ah, now, soapies, *ag*, that's another thing! The first soapie I was involved in was *Egoli* [At the Place of Gold, viz. Johannesburg] and they brought in this family, intact, you know a respected family, again nothing that was going to put down the black people. Okay it's a family that's trying to improve its lot. That's the kind of role in that soapie that I played. And the next soapie was

Generations. Oh, for *Generations* I was very careful in my own funny way, but it was the money. It's always been the money. I would do the soapies, and I don't care about the overall storyline, but the roles I played had to be meaningful.

DK Did you find you had to have different working techniques and acting styles for the TV work?

NN Television is dead. There's nobody there. You have to do it for the camera and think, 'Ah, yes, there's an audience over there.' But the audience is not giving you anything back. On the stage when you give something there's an immediate response. It may be a movement, it may not be vocal. It may be a body shift. And so you say, 'Yes, I've got you.' But with a camera, it's dead. You have to think, 'Behind that lens is my audience, therefore, communicate, connect!' Unlike the stage.

Ag, the stage is beautiful! *Ag*, David, put me on the stage, oh my god! [*gesture of excited fulfilment*].

NOTES

1 For resistance against apartheid.
2 'Speak a little Afrikaans with me, Nomhle.'
3 'I can't speak a pure Afrikaans.'

BIBLIOGRAPHY

Kruger, Loren (1999), *The Drama of South Africa: Plays, Pageants and Publics since 1910*, London & New York: Routledge.

Noticeboard

Compiled by JAMES GIBBS

The Noticeboard section provides opportunities for the sharing of information about theatre in Africa and by Africans. As will be seen from the pages that follow, a variety of sources, including Internet sites, correspondence and newspaper cuttings have been used in attempts to draw attention to issues and achievements.

REPORT FROM THE 2002 GRAHAMSTOWN ARTS FESTIVAL

As in the previous year, the Grahamstown Festival 2002 opened under ominous clouds that gathered following Standard Bank's announcement that it was withdrawing as the Festival's main sponsor. 'Reliable rumours' had it that the 2002 Grahamstown Festival would be the last one, and that in future the Festival might be held somewhere else.

This possibility was dispelled, however, by the chair of the Festival Committee, Mannie Manim, who was able to report that the Eastern Cape government had committed itself to joining Standard Bank, and would be co-sponsoring the Festival for 2002 and 2003. In Manim's view this should give the Festival a new lease of life, and it should survive – in Grahamstown – for another 28 years!

Doubts about sponsorship did not account for all the storm clouds. The Grahamstown Festival has been widely regarded as a barometer of the creative power of South African arts and theatre, and it has been suggested that there has been a falling off in artistic activity and intensity. Some commentators have pointed to a reduction in the number of productions on the Main Programme and to productions following a predictable formula. Writing in *Cue* on the opening day of the 2002 Festival and under the title 'Is there a cure for this hangover?', Alan Swerdlow asked if the South African arts community had brought itself into a dangerous situation by failing to dissociate itself from the past. He wrote: 'Are the lingering effects of "protest theatre" killing genuine creativity?' And continued: 'Without reciting a history lesson, let me remind you of the golden age of agit-prop plays that flourished in the mid-1980s. That work – brilliant, angry and inventive – was the challenging of a collective spirit in response to very specific circumstances.'

Swerdlow ended his article by inviting responses. Two days later he got one from Gwen Ansell under the heading

'Confront the hangover'. She asked if the didacticism of protest theatre was totally negative, and suggested that Swerdlow's restrictive approach '[came] dangerously close to a sort of "cultural imperialism"'. In her view, protest theatre would be around as long as there are evils worth protesting against. She asked, rhetorically, 'In a democracy with many strands, shouldn't we be defending the space for all dramatic styles – including those "lessons" – to flourish?'

Another issue that was raised in various discussions was whether the Festival was becoming more of a Jazz Festival than a Theatre or General Arts Festival. My impression was that there remained a healthy mix of forms of artistic expression, with a reasonably well-balanced blend of indigenous and imported shows. I also felt that when theatrical successes of the past were revived they had been 'touched up' to avoid appearing dated. This was certainly the case with Paul Slabolepszy's *Mooi Street Moves*, which was very well received by capacity audiences.

Other 'older hits' included *Boesman and Lena*, which was 'brushed up', and *King Lear,* that appeared in African clothing. Noel Coward's *Private Lives* fared less well, although the play was highly acclaimed as a theatrical perfor-mance. It was described by Lance Claasen in *Cue* as 'superbly irrelevant'. He added: 'It is sad that a play written in the 1920s and set in Europe, by a playwright that is long dead, is accorded this privilege.'

William Kentridge's dramatisation of Italo Svevo's novel *Confessions of Zeno*, adapted by Jane Taylor and produced in collaboration with the Handspring Puppet Company, has been long awaited. It is an avant-garde, multi-media production, somewhat confusingly described in the Festival programme as an 'opera' – there is music composed by

Kevin Volans. The production made great demands on the large audiences it attracted, and elicited a wide range of responses: highly praised by some, received with incomprehension by others. The person sitting next to me described it as: 'Disruptive and depressing!' I found it intellectually and technically fascinating.

Physical theatre modes and dance featured fairly frequently in the programme. There appears, as Andrew Gilder pointed out in a *Cue* review of *Mainland*, to be a gradual shift in South African choreography from a classical, ballet-oriented dance style to a more theatrical expression.

The ills of new South Africa were also visited in this year's programme. One could not escape from the Aids pandemic, from poverty, violence, political and sexual ineptitude, and the gender issue was brought to the fore in a number of productions. For example, male identity was explored in *Male Order Performance*, and masculine chauvinism was dealt some healthy blows in the fringe performance *Inimba Mafazi*. Some of the men in the audience looked distinctly uncomfortable.

Among the new South African plays, Zakes Mda's *The Bells of Amersfoort* was given a mixed reception by both critics and audiences. On the other hand, John Kani's debut piece as a playwright, *Nothing but the Truth,* was a distinct success. In Janice Honeyman's well-balanced production and with a strong cast that included Kani, Pamela Nomvete and Dambisa Kente, the play explored the effect of the recent past on present reality in South Africa. This great theatre was rewarded by standing ovations. Together with Yael Faber's *He Left Quietly, Nothing but the Truth* was among the outstanding productions at the festival.

The Grahamstown Festival is projected as a 'general arts festival', and it presents a rich tapestry of music – jazz as well as classical, dance, film, and the visual arts. Above all, however, it remains the country's major shop-window for theatre. It would be a great shame, and an incalculable loss to South Africa's cultural life, if it were to disappear.

Rolf Solberg
Stavanger University College

GRAHAMSTOWN FESTIVAL IN TRANSITION, A REPORT ON 2001

The 25th Standard Bank National Arts Festival, the Grahamstown Festival (1999), was celebrated with particular gusto and a stronger-than-ever international dimension, but by the end of June 2001 uncertainty hung over the Settlers' Monument following the decision by the Festival's major sponsor, Standard Bank, to reduce the level of its support.

Over the years, the Bank's money has gone into the Grahamstown Foundation that establishes the infrastructure for the Festival. For example, during Festival week it seems as if all the scaffolding in the country has been moved to the Eastern Cape to transform assembly and dining halls into theatres by the introduction of raked seating. In addition, the Foundation's enlightened offer of 50 per cent of the funding for selected shows, on a rand-for-rand basis, has made it possible for many struggling companies to participate in the Festival.

If international participation peaked in 1999, by 2001 productions from abroad were few and far between. These were distinguished, however, and included Zinnie Harris's important

Further than the Furthest Thing about the experiences of the inhabitants of Tristan da Cunha. Presented by Tron Theatre Company (Glasgow) and the Royal National Theatre (UK), this production provided many echoes of local concerns, though clarity was sometimes lost because the minuscule cast enforced some unconvincing stretching of roles.

It was in the relatively informal street market behind Grahamstown Cathedral that a pervasive and genuine sense of 'international participation' was embodied. There festival-goers patronised the stalls set up by Kenyans, Somalis, Nigerians, Zaïreans, and Senegalese who have progressively taken over this 'informal section' and given expression to a vigorous, pan-African trading culture.

At the 2001 Festival, Europe was present not only through Harris's play but also as a liberating force in the texts of Jean Genet's *The Blacks* (presented by the Market Theatre and the Stockholm Staadsteater) and Beckett's *Waiting for Godot*. The former, subtitled 'a clown show', was presented in a riveting production at the Rhodes Theatre, and the latter, in a sense another 'clown show', was brought to vigorous life at Graeme College where Lionel Newton and Seputla Sebogodi in the major roles gave the play freshness and originality. Both productions attracted very large, in some cases capacity, audiences that, in age and racial composition, promised a bright future for the festival.

By contrast a pretty 'mature', almost all-white audience felt the hand of Chekhov settle over the reverential and suffocatingly self-conscious *On the Lake*. Reza de Wet's play engaged with traditions of Naturalism and Realism in a way that seemed to expect audiences to care about such isms. In *Dearly Beloved*, another South African playwright, Fiona

Coyne, took the risk of building a play around a poet, albeit a mediocre one. She seemed to satisfy a supportive, again almost entirely white audience. Presumably the two plays provided highbrow and middlebrow audiences with what the Festival has offered them over the years. Neither production seemed likely to ruffle any feathers or create much excitement.

The ebullient but calculating Nicholas Ellenbogen has built up a following at the Festival for his *Raiders of ....* series. The eleventh *Raiders* jumped, as far as the title was concerned, on the Harry Potter bandwagon, and was, essentially, lively storytelling theatre. 'A whacky action adventure', it was pitched unerringly at a faithful following.

Few of those who came for *Raiders* stayed on for Ellebogen's more challenging *President Khaya Afrikha*. Performed by a cast that wore its 'SADC character' on its sleeve, the production extended the kind of narrative theatre Ellebogen has been working with for years in a way that appeals to international funding agencies. The 'whackiness' was diluted by a variety of 'languages of the theatre' in a piece that was astutely, or opportunistically, directed at ecological issues. Supported by a quiverful of NGOs active in Southern Africa, *Afrikha* had enjoyed international exposure before the 2001 Festival and had a European tour set up.

Living in Strange Lands, Anton Robert Krueger's play about Dimitri Tsafendas, the parliamentary messenger who assassinated the then Prime Minister, Hendrik Verwoerd, was among the triumphs of the Festival. One can only hope that the production's qualities, particularly the moving central performance by Renos Nicos Spanoudes as Tsafendas, was recognised. The unpromising venue in which it was presented, 'B2 Arena', has provided a

launching pad before.

The intensity of Krueger's play made a startling contrast with the much-hyped *Big Dada*, written, directed and designed by Brett Bailey. Premiered in Umtata, whence it had been lured by sponsorship arrangements, the show arrived at Grahamstown with an invitation to London's Barbican in its pocket. Unfortunately it ran out of steam in the second half and one left thinking that the talented Bailey had taken on too many roles. Perhaps the hectic accounts on the web about his visit to Uganda, one of which was headed 'White boy looking for Big Dada 1/06/01', should have provided a warning.

South African history was inevitably in evidence, providing the background to *Ushaka KaZulu* and *Makana*. The former, written and directed by Bongani Linda, was presented by a large cast from the Victory Sonqoba Theatre Company. It was extravagantly hyped as 'the plea by generations of Dingane to the spirit of Shaka to forgive us and bring to an end bloodshed that has become our daily bread today'. However, the performance hardly went further than the synopsis in the programme.

Presented some way from the town centre, literally on the other side of the tracks, *Makana* was altogether more adventurous and challenging. A hard-working cast of four played effectively with what they called 'the creative toys of the theatre' to examine the reputation of the nineteenth-century Xhosa leader Makana, whose decisions profoundly affected the history of the Cape and whose presence haunts Grahamstown. I emerged impressed, though confused by the discrepancy between the allocation of the script credit to Andrew Buckland, and the description of the piece as examining 'recorded stories of the period mixed with our own imaginations, and directed towards making theatre'.

In a previous issue of this publication, the Noticeboard offered an insight into the *Sarafina 2* fiasco, drawing attention to the controversy surrounding the exuberant, misbegotten HIV/AIDS awareness-raising musical. One would have thought that in a post-*Sarafina 2* South Africa, no- one could work in the theatre without an awareness of the impact of the pandemic. However *The Stadium*, devised and directed by Smal Ndaba and Phyllis Klotz with the East Rand's Sibikwa Players, showed prostitutes and clients without indicating that we live in a situation in which unprotected sex may be a murderous or suicidal act. The piece began to lose credibility as soon as the successful shebeen Queen left her purse lying on the counter. It entered the realm of pure fiction when she accepted an uncashable cheque. Kwaito music composed by Junior Sokhela and a bold set by Sarah Roberts could not rescue the production or give it a sense of engagement with the issues it touched on.

Often the gutsiest shows were in the smaller venues, and in this connection *Amajita* was a tough act to be compared with. The 'glue sniffing' postures into which the gifted members of the Melisizwe Community Theatre collapsed between episodes provided a sadly eloquent background to the exploration of the life of street kids.

Further away from the main stream were new groups, such as Laduma Arts Productions who put on *Kuse-Njalo, Our Arts Our Healing*. Howard Dladia and his cast were clearly struggling to reconcile the realities of the 'new South Africa' with the expectations, real or imagined, of the Festival organisers and audiences. Although living in a country where white rugby players hunt down boy trespassers, they seemed to feel compelled to fumble towards an inclusive ending. Their performance left the audience of two convinced that the theatre in South Africa would only grow by honestly confronting the nation's contradictions.

Grahamstown, as the view from Settlers' Monument reveals, is not just an historic town or an educational centre. Locals, including some from the 'extensions' that stretch away over the low hills, are employed by Festival organisers to oversee venues and to watch parked cars, and this allows some 'trickle down' of the Festival income. In 2001 there were opportunities for tourism with a local flavour that will undoubtedly grow. For example, at the St Aidan's Guest House Project, 'one of the biggest youth (NGOs) in the country' offered a meal and cabaret (*Umtshotsho*) that brought together 'the scintillating colours of a customary Eastern Cape performance, complemented by a traditional three-course meal'. Their publicity material summoned festival-goers 'to encounter and explore expressions of the AmaXhosa'.

The strength of AmaXhosa musical culture was certainly apparent, both at the supper and at the International Library of African Music where the Ngqoko Women's Ensemble gave most remarkable performances as part of 'Mmino Fest'. For those familiar with Es'kia Mphahlele's observations about the limited appeal of Negritude in South Africa, it was a revelation to see the reappraisal of 'traditional culture' going forward. The new ingredient was the commercial dimension.

The Festival has vigour, variety, and a buzz of critical comment in the daily issue of *Cue*. It attracts audiences and provides genuine opportunities for theatre people to take risks. But, on the evidence of 2001, its vision is still limited, and it fails to engage with its environment.

The map of the venues showed just three outside the city – about 2.5 km along Raglan Road and the programme offered at those venues revealed both a failure of nerve and a lack of imagination. Only a performance by the Pretoria Chorale indicated recognition of the desirability of taking quality performers to the Extensions. For the rest the policy was circuses, circuses, circuses: the programme consisted of screening Kung Fu and Hong Kong action movies!

'Street entertainers' Ellis Person and Bheki Mkhwane, who attracted substantial crowds to their 'interactive' performances of *iLobola* on the lawn behind the University's Drostdy Arch, had no performances scheduled in more challenging parts of the town. Clearly the 'new South Africa' is only slowly emerging from the old. Perhaps Standard Bank, who said they were moving their sponsorship because more of their customers are interested in jazz than theatre, were in touch with reality.

FIFTH D'AGASTO INTERNATIONAL FESTIVAL

The Chingola Arts Society (CAS) from Zambia was one of the 43 theatre groups from nine different countries that participated in the Fifth D'Agasto International Festival held in Maputo, 21–31 August 2002. In the September 2002 issue of the invaluable *CAS News*, Peter N'gambi, CAS Productions Manager, reported that the participants were well looked after and that the Zimbabwean 'ambassador' gave a reception and dinner for the group.

N'gambi indicated that the well-organised festival covers music and the plastic arts as well as performances, and that, in 2002, participating countries included Belgium, Brazil, Cape Verde, Spain, Lesotho, Portugal, Zambia, Zimbabwe and, of course, Mozambique. Workshops and discussions were included in the programme and were, understandably, mostly in Portuguese.

Reporting on the Festival, N'gambi noted that 'One of the new experiences as far as members of CAS were concerned was performing in an open-air theatre.' Because of the climate, he noted:

the people in Mozambique have a preference for open-air theatre in an enclosure. For instance out of the eight venues used for the festival only Teatro Avenda is indoors.

As for Zambian theatre's own contribution: 'The invitation Festival was not a competition and had no rules. However CAS performed very well and was rated sixth in the top ten and came out third in the African groups category.' N'gambi noted that 'Our friends have a lot more theatre lights than we have here.' And he asked 'Is it because of their proximity to South Africa?'

N'gambi was clearly impressed by the level of official support and felt Zambia had lessons to learn. He observed that 'Theatre commands a lot of respect from the people and the government, with a lot of professional artists. The audiences are large.' And he added, a little wistfully: 'I hope things will one day change for the better in Zambia.'

The financial arrangements underpinning the festival were not made clear in the newsletter. However, N'gambi reported that: 'At the end of the Festival, all the participating groups contributed 30 per cent of their total box office takings to a local HIV/AIDS organisation.... The Mozambican Minister of Tourism and Culture received the money and thanked all the participants for their kind gesture.'

NEW APPOINTMENT: PLAYWRIGHT, DIRECTOR, TEACHER

An example of the way in which Southern African theatre is influencing drama work in other parts of Africa is provided by the career of Mufunanji Magalasi. Born in Malawi, Magalasi, like many Malawians before and since, left for South Africa after completing secondary school. An opportunity to move into theatre work came through the Afrika Cultural Centre, and he completed diploma courses there in the first half of the 1990s. He subsequently moved on to drama teaching and to further studies, first as an occasional student and then on an MA programme at the University of Witwatersrand. There he worked with Professors Bheki Peterson and Malcolm Purkey, wrote a long essay on Black Theatre of the 1970s, and presented a thesis that focused on 'Politics, Performance, and Narrative in the Plays of Dukuza ka Macu'. This academic writing went hand in hand with acting, directing and creative writing. For example, he was directed by Maishe Maponya in *The Journey to Self*, and by Benjy Francis in Ngugi wa Thiong'o's *This Time Tomorrow*. His director credits include productions of *This Time Tomorrow* at the Afrika Cultural Centre and the Wits University Box Theatre, of *Maid in the New South Africa*, and of Ola Rotimi's *The Gods Are Not to Blame* (Johannesburg Civic Theatre, 1999).

Magalasi has also directed his own plays. *Stop Press* was put on at Wits University Theatre Complex (1997) and *Wrong Day*, a farce, at the Bachaki Theatre, Johannesburg (2000). Since taking up a lectureship at Chancellor College, part of the University of Malawi, Zomba, he has adapted Steve Chimombo's text *Chamdothe, Child of Clay*, as a musical, and has also put on Soyinka's *Trials of Brother Jero* (both 2001).

His homecoming was linked with the search for a Malawi production that could represent the country internationally. For the 2000 Southern African Theatre Initiative (SATI), *Last Temptation* by Alabama Theatre of Blantyre was selected. In an article on 'Malawian Theatre at the Crossroads' that appeared in *The Journal of the Humanities* (Zomba, 2001), Magalasi acknowledged the 'innovative storyline and controversially adventurous topic' of that production while observing that the performances 'appeared rushed and unpolished'.

In the same article he also discussed Du Chisiza's contribution to the theatre, and began to provide a context for the consideration of developments in the Malawian theatre in the new millennium. SATI's decision to hold a playwriting workshop in the country in 2001 indicated one of the ways in which support for the development of theatrical skills was being provided, and in which Southern Africa's theatre people were working together..

Magalasi asks: 'What legacy did Drama for Development leave for Malawi stage drama?' This question invites an assessment of the contributions of David Kerr and Christopher Kamlongera, who preceded Magalasi in the Department of Fine and Performing Arts at Chancellor College. Kerr's work is well known through his writing, some of it in this publication, and one hopes that there will have been opportunities for him to take it up again since returning to Zomba in 2002. Kamlongera's achievements are less widely publicised but of great importance.

SADC, CCD, PRCA, THE FAO AND SDRE: ALPHABET SOUP

At the time of writing, Kamlongera is Director of the Southern African Development Community (SADC) Centre of Communication for Development (CCD). Based in Harare, and funded extensively by the Food and Agriculture Organisation (FAO) and the Italian Government, the Centre's approach found expression in a handbook entitled *Participatory Rural Communication Appraisal: Starting with the People* (1998). The approach, abbreviated to PRCA, draws inspiration from initiatives associated with the name of Augusto Boal and with the FAO's Extension, Education and Communication Service (SDRE). In the handbook, authors Chike Anyaegbunam, Paolo Mefalopulos and Titus Moetsabi draw attention to some of the relevant intellectual and organisational background by acknowledging the technical guidance of SDRE's Phillippe van der Stichele, and the support of the Italian government.

The handbook is one of several that draw together principles with suggestions for practical activities. One might mention in this context the *Stepping Stones Project Handbook* put together by Alice Welbourn, and *Participatory Approaches to Reproductive Health and Nutrition* compiled by Gill Gordon and Pat Pridmore of the Institute of Education, University of London (1998). The CCD handbook is particularly thorough. It draws on the postgraduate work Anyaegbunam carried out at the University of Iowa on development perspectives and what he called 'Bolekaja Intellectualism', on Mefalopulos's experiences in Bolivia and in upland conservation projects, and, finally, on Moetsabi's experience of veld products management and of participatory rural appraisal in Botswana.

PRCA has been described as 'a flexible, multidisciplinary and participatory way to conduct communication research either to improve ongoing projects or to assist in the design of new projects with the people'. One of its main tenets is the importance of involving all those concerned in the research process to ensure that communication is effective. The authors claim that 'since it was initiated and developed in 1994–5, PRCA has been applied with success in various development projects dealing with agriculture, animal husbandry, soil conservation, poverty alleviation, food security, adult education, health, family planning, water and sanitation, etc....'

Seeking to define its distinctiveness, especially *vis-à-vis* the Participatory Learning and Action (PLA) programmes that emerged in the 1970s, the authors of the handbook identify their unique focus 'on rural communication systems and (methods) of (improving) information sharing among all stake holders in a development effort'. An example is provided by the use of knowledge about responses to long-standing sexually transmitted diseases, such as VD, when waging HIV/AIDS awareness campaigns. A second illustration is of a honey project that failed because the target audience associated the masks provided for beekeepers with costumes worn by Nyau masqueraders. (See Kamlongera, SADC CCD *Case Study 3: Learning how to use Folk Media in Development in Malawi*, 2000.)

ORFA

Acronym soup is not limited to Southern Africa. West Africa is very familiar with it. From a report compiled by the 'Festac News Agency' (Nigeria), it would seem that during the Third Book and Art

Festival, organised by the Committee for Relevant Art (CORA), a memorial event for Ola Rotimi was held. At a press conference plans to establish the Ola Rotimi Foundation for Arts (ORFA) were announced, and project coordinator Muyiwa Osinke spoke of the determination with which he and others were facing the financial implications of the project. This will be an organisation to watch and learn from.

NATIONAL THEATRE, LAGOS

Joint editor of this publication, Femi Osofisan, has been given the task of managing the National Theatre, Iganmu, Lagos. Apart from 'facing the financial implications', Osofisan is in charge of a building designed for another country (Bulgaria) and another climate. He has had to cope with problems caused by long-standing structural faults, particularly leaking roofs, and with mechanical breakdowns, notably of the air-conditioning system. The security system is inadequate, and expensive, hard-to-replace lighting equipment has been stolen.

Theatre in Lagos has been through some hard times. In 1994, when he was preparing for a Lagos production of *The Beatification of Areaboy,* Soyinka was told that Sani Abacha's net was closing around him and he left the country. He was able to attend the eventual 1995 Leeds premiere of the play, an event that coincided with one of Nigeria's darkest hours: the execution of the Ogoni Nine.

In 2001 some of the cast of *Areaboy* came together in Lagos in a new Soyinka play, *King Baabu.* Much had changed by this time. Soyinka directed with Swiss support, particularly in technical roles, and with a cast that included five London-based performers as well as

actors who have made their careers in Nigeria. It opened in Cinema Hall 2 of the National Theatre.

Writing in the *Saturday Punch,* Olumide Iyande produced the following provocative résumé:
King Baabu is a comic take on Nigeria's recent history. It tells the story of a mythical country where sheer savagery was made an official policy. Its protagonist is King Baabu, who, assisted by his scheming wife, Maryia, is transmuted from an army general, Basha Bash, to become King Baabu.
The extent to which the play begins and ends as 'a comic take on Nigeria' was a central theme in several reviews. Baabu clearly took his place in the long line of identifiable tyrants with whom Soyinka has populated his stage. Indeed, the play is descended from *Kongi's Harvest, Opera Wonyosi* and *A Play of Giants,* all of which illustrate that within Soyinka there is a constant battle between the instinct to personalise and the recognition of the need to generalise. Moving from the particular to the general is particularly difficult in a situation in which political debate has been stifled, and in which everything put on stage invites code breakers to get to work.

In his piece for *Ace Magazine* ('When King Baabu came to town', 17 August 2001), Yemi Oladeinde described the play as dealing with 'the obsession with power', with how the populace should react when tyrants rise to power. He drew particular attention to the influence of wives on tyrants and emphasised parallels between Baabu's death at the hands of women and Abacha's demise (a leavetaking which seems to have given a whole new meaning to the expression 'companions for the chief'. JG).

Oladeinde provided details of the plans for the show: after the four performances scheduled in the National Theatre, it was to be taken to Ibadan and

Benin City, before moving on to Zurich and Dusseldorf at the beginning of an extended international tour.

Oladeinde reported that the venture had been by mounted by Nawao Productions and received support from the Swiss Development and Cooperation Agency, Prince Claus Fund, Pro Helvetia (the Arts Council of Switzerland), Stanley Thomas Johnson Foundation, Theatre-spektatel Zurich, Zurich Canton, Nestlé Nigeria and Panalpina. Clearly there had been a massive and imaginative fund-raising effort 'behind the scenes'. It was recorded that Governor Bola Ahmed Tinubu generously purchased 250 tickets but did not himself attend.

The progression of King Baabu included its performances in Cape Town and Roma, Lesotho. However, apparently because its Swiss funders felt the Nigerian government might take offence, the play was not presented in Johannesburg to coincide with the World Summit on Sustainable Development in September 2002. As might have been anticipated, Soyinka was angry about this. In a sense, however, he had moved on, having presented a version of *Oedipus at Colonus, Oyedipo at Kholoni,* in Greece during July.

WSTS, NANTAP AND PACT, MORE ACRONYMS

The Wole Soyinka Training School (WSTS) is the National Association of Nigerian Theatre Arts Practitioners (NANTAP) a 'concrete, creative artistic effort and platform for arts scholars, researchers, and practitioners to discuss and further the development of Theatre in Africa'. These words introduce an initiative funded by the Ford Foundation that took off in March 2001.

Best wishes to it and to the School's

publication, *Perspectives in Crosscurrents in African Training* (PACT) which was launched with an issue on *The Essentials of Rotimi's Theatre.* The editorial contact is Dr Austin Asagba, Department of Theatre Arts, University of Benin, PMB 1154, Benin City, Nigeria. austinasagba@yahoo.com

The involvement of a major American donor in this and other projects (See *Yaa Anansewa* below) is to be warmly welcomed. The history of funding the theatre in sub-Saharan Africa has yet to be written, but when it is the roles of such organisations (and 'fronts') as the Goethe Institute and the Rockefeller, Ford and Farfield Foundations will have prominent places and come in for close scrutiny.

The chronology will have to include 1983, which saw the foundation, in hope, trust and expectation, of the Union of African Performing Artists (UAPA) following a conference in Harare, and 1986 which saw accusations of misuse of UAPA funds and the withdrawal of support. These charges marked the demise of what was potentially a wonderful expression of pan-Africanism in the creative arts.

May 1995 will also have its place, since that month saw the convening of a Conference on Culture and Development at Rockefeller's Bellagio Conference Centre in Italy. Despite the experience of UAPA, those present from donor agencies signed up because they felt there was 'a future for donors to African culture'.

By June 2002, however, the crisis in funding cultural initiatives in Africa was acute and was discussed at a meeting in Oxford of some of those concerned with African publishing. It became clear that many who had shared the vision of 1995 had moved on and that their places had been taken by people who might have said: 'Whenever I hear the word "culture", I put my cheque book away.' It is good that there were some funders who gave against the tide rather than being swept along by it, and excellent to see Ford's involvement with theatre in West Africa.

TRANSLATIONS

Despite the remarkable accomplishments of multilingual Africans, the linguistic fissures that divide the African continent are rarely traversed when it comes to the formal theatre. F. K. Fiawoo's translation into English of the work he first published in Ewe remains an example that has rarely been followed. And the number of 'movements' in the 'other direction', from English or French into an indigenous African language, remains depressingly small.

Appeals to African writers to translate works written in English and French into indigenous African languages are issued regularly, and there has been some response. For example, Akin Isola's *Ikú Olókùn-Esin* (*Death and the King's Horseman*) proved itself on the stage in Olusegun Ojewuyi's 1994 Lagos production, and, confident that it could find a reading public, Fountain Publications, Ibadan, issued the text in the same year.

Translations into English and French are always likely to offer quicker rewards than work that goes in the other direction. The encouragement to translate into a language with a large readership and one which will make a text accessible to a large audience will always be present and tangible. This was illustrated by the competition organised in 2001 by the Gate Theatre.

The Gate Theatre in the Notting Hill area of London is tiny, but there is some justification for its claim to be 'London's home of International Theatre'. By hosting a striking production of Ama Ata Aidoo's *Anowa,* it played a part in making African theatre in English available to a metropolitan audience.

Over the years, the Gate has been active in organising awards for translations (initially with the help of the brewers Allied Domecq), and in commissioning and putting on translations of foreign classics and contemporary plays. Since 1990 a remarkable number of the commissioned scripts, 35 out of 50, have been published. In October 2001, the theatre launched the 'Gate Translation Award' with a prize of £2,000 for the winner to be selected by a distinguished panel of judges and with guaranteed staging at the Gate. The relevant press release also promised the following: 'Shortlisted plays will ... be given a staged reading which will ensure that these submissions reach a wider audience providing an important springboard to other stages in the United Kingdom'.

Reflecting the process by which many plays 'arrive' in English, the invitation was to 'translators and playwrights working from literal translations'. It is to be hoped that this competition will become an annual event and that 'The Literary Director, The Gate Theatre, 11 Pembridge Road, Notting Hill, London W11 3 HQ', will remain a relevant contact for African translators and dramatists for a long time to come.

At the same time, the example of Isola should also be recognised, and the address of Fountain Publications (32 Adenuga Street, Kongi, Bodija, Secretariat, P.O. Box 29263, Ibadan, Nigeria) should be noted. Perhaps sponsors will be found (possibly among the local equivalents of Allied Domecq) to help show the way for those involved in translating in different directions.

SOUTH AFRICANS TALKING BACK 1

Taking advantage of the ease of communication available in the last few years, Zakes Mda was 'in virtual residence' at the Africa Centre, London, during November–December 2001. Members of the public were able to send in questions, and the correspondence was posted on the Internet. For example, asked about the use made of his work in Ghana and about the attention given to *The Girls in their Sunday Dresses* in Toronto (November 2001), Zakes Mda e-mailed the following very full and helpful response:

I am glad to hear that they give some attention to my plays in Ghana. I met a Ghanaian student at our performance in Birmingham who told me that When People Play People, *my handbook on the ulitilisation of theatre as a medium for development communication, is the 'bible' (that's the word she used) of theatre-for-development scholars and practitioners in Ghana. I was not aware of all this. I am unlikely to get any royalties from all this 'popularity'. I suspect they just photocopy the books. It doesn't matter though.*

As for Toronto, Canada: yes, the AfriCan Theatre Ensemble got the rights from DALRO (Dramatic, Artistic and Literary Rights Organisation – a South African body that administers performance, reprographic and related rights). Actually AfriCan sent someone to South Africa to negotiate the rights. I am not sure what royalties they have agreed upon because I am too busy to really follow these things. I let DALRO handle everything without coming back to me. I will only know at the end of DALRO's financial year when they send me the statement and the cheque. AfriCan flew me to Canada for the gala night of the play. The facilities of collecting my royalties rest with DALRO who also work with similar agencies in various countries. However in future I plan to transfer these facilities to my London agents, Blake Friedmann Film, TV and Literary Agency, because I think they are in a better position to negotiate better deals for me.*

SOUTH AFRICANS TALKING BACK 2

The London International Festival of Theatre (LIFT) 2001 brought *Women in Waiting* from South Africa to the United Kingdom and the author/actress was interviewed by Jenny Murray for BBC Radio 4. Murray asked Thembi Mtshali about her experiences and her reactions to experiences, guiding the interview to provide a background for the creation of *Women in Waiting*. Thembi's side of the conversation went something like this:

I grew up with my grandparents because my parents were working in Durban. My mother was a domestic worker; she was taking care of the white people's children and she could not have me with her. I used to see my parents once a year at Christmas time. I was very lonely in the village, and I used to talk to birds. Because birds could fly, I figured they could go everywhere and I could give them messages to take to my parents. I would say 'Tell my mother to buy me shoes, OK? And don't forget the size this time, because last time she brought me shoes but they didn't fit me.'

We lived in a very close community and I thought that was it until I moved to live with my parents at about 12 or 13. The first time I saw a white person, he was driving the bus from the village to Durban. When I saw a white person, I thought he was an albino, because we had a guy in our village who was an albino, and I thought the driver was another one.

When I got to Durban, I realised that life was completely different.... Coming from a non-political background you try to figure out whether things were supposed to be just like that. But later you grow up and you say 'Something is definitely wrong here.' I had a child, but I had to leave her to go and take care of the white children myself.... You get angry but you can't get ulcers. You ask: 'Why are things like this? Is it like this in the whole world?' Only when I started travelling outside South Africa did I find that there was something completely wrong.

[When I got work as a performer] our performances were only for white people. Black people didn't have theatres. My parents never saw me perform until I had been overseas. My father used to ask: 'What is it that you really do?' And I had to explain that I sang and talked. But when I was growing up I was very shy and my father said: 'You hardly talk here in the house. How can people pay to listen to you talk?'

Political plays happened long after. I remember in 1976 when there was the uprising in Soweto, when children were fighting against being taught in Afrikaans. At that time Ipi Tombi was going to open on Broadway.... When we got to New York and South Africa was in the news, everybody wanted to know what was happening in South Africa. They said: 'We don't want to see this song and dance....' That's when I realised that I can sing and dance but that I really have to tell the truth about what is going on in South Africa. So I started writing songs that really reflected my own experiences.

[Working on Women in Waiting] with Yael Faber was a very great and weird experience. Elle is very young – she is younger than my daughter, and when we started writing this piece we were both living in America. Yael had been inspired by seeing women waiting outside the Truth and Reconciliation Hearings, waiting to hear what had happened to their loved one, their husbands, their children. So she called me and said she would love to do a piece

about women waiting because waiting has been like a history of South African women. And I said to her: 'I am a part of that South African history of waiting. I've been waiting for something since I was a child when I used to wait for my parents.' So we started writing using my own experiences. There are things that happened when I was writing. I found that remembering things that had happened was like .... 'Oh God'... Sometimes I remember with Yael, she would ask me a question and I would burst out crying and she would burst out crying too because of things that came back that were very painful. For the first time I realised how much I had missed by not raising my own child. Now each and every performance is like reliving my life, each and every line is like I am saying it for the first time.

When my grand-daughter saw the production, she didn't believe a word of it. She said 'Granny was that the truth that you told in the show?' I said 'Yes.' She said 'I thought maybe you just wanted to make people cry.'

SOUTH AFRICANS ON THE MOVE

While Mda's work held the stage in Toronto and *Women in Waiting* was presented at the New Ambassadors (London) during June 2001, students from the University of Witwatersrand were also on the move. During October 2001 they took productions of *Umm ... Somebody Say Something* and *Venus Hottentot* to London and Bristol.

The University of Bristol and Goldsmiths, University of London, with sponsors such as the Ernest Oppenheimer Memorial Trust, made the visit possible, and the double bill was remarkable for the honesty with which it tackled issues confronting those living in the 'rainbow nation'. The testimonies in *Umm ... Somebody*, a devised piece, were often poignant, and deeply moving. Building on the pattern of work established by *Born in the RSA*, and by the strong female dimension of *You Strike the Woman, You Strike the Rock*, the five women in the cast carved out a space in which the present could be examined with wit, insight and passion. Areas for future examination were hinted at, and the attitude to them was expressed in a programme note about those involved that concluded:

Drama school is just the beginning. We are all destined to be revolutionary!

Venus Hottentot was, as one might expect, inspired by the story of Sara Baartman. It drew on the contributions of the performers and on a play text by Suzan-Lori Parks. The power and awareness of *Venus Hottentot* suggested reasons why South Africa continues to be the richest source of African theatre for most of the rest of the world. For example, the programme for the 2001 Perth International Arts Festival included the Baxter Theatre Company's *SUIP!* , and Ellis and Bheki in an open-air show for all the family, *Boy Called Rubbish. Big Dada* arrived in 2002. Meanwhile *The Island* continued to make an impact wherever it was produced. Venues included the Old Vic (London) and the Theatre Royal in Bath (2002), and a younger generation of South African performers took London audiences by storm with a production based on the Chester Cycle, *The Mysteries*.

YAA ASANTEWA

Exporting UK productions based on African material and using African idioms of music and dance has become a feature of the work associated with the West Yorkshire Playhouse. The following account of *Yaa Asantewa*, a production that started in 'the Athens of the North', appeared in the *Accra Mail* on 18 December 2001:

The story of Yaa Asantewa (circa 1835– 1921) Queenmother of Ejisu who led the Asante war against the British colonialists, is brought to life through music, song and dance, in a spectacular, awe-inspiring performance that leaves you almost overwhelmed with excitement, in the stage epic Yaa Asantewa – Warrior Queen written by Ghanaian-born international writer, Margaret Busby, alias Nana Akua Ackon I. Sponsors included the Ford Foundation and the Arts Council of England among others, a solid technical team, including: Geraldine Connor – artistic direction; Nana Danso Abiam – musical direction; George Dzikunu – choreography; and Robert Bryan – lighting design. Great colourful lights, sound and theatrical movements add a special magic to the stage performance expertly executed by the London-based Adidzo, the Pan-African Dance Ensemble. The costumes used, designed in amazing masquerade techniques, pay a tribute to African heritage, and the imageries depicted in the presentation speak volumes of the greatness of African women, and their role in the flow of life. The show played at the National Theatre in Accra, and was presented in a special showing at the Kumasi Cultural Centre in Kumasi last Saturday. It was quite an event. This is a must-see production, even if only for its spectacle and splendour. The messages in it, universal and contemporary, are equally poignant in spite of the 'showbiz' aspects of it.

Missing from this report is the resourcefulness displayed by the director and stage crew in coping with the challenges of staging the production in the National Theatre, Accra, and in the National Cultural Centre, Kumasi.

Problems at the former included

rigging lights: the British equipment taken over for the production was not compatible with the system installed by the Chinese who constructed the theatre. At Kumasi, arrangements had to be made to reproduce Akomfo Anokye's historic *coup de théâtre* – the acceptance of a Golden Stool that descended from the heavens – in an open-air theatre with minimal above-stage facilities.

There were also problems with publicity. Despite the efforts of George Dzikunu and others, some of the advertising material remained in the hands of the customs authorities even after the performances had finished.

James Gibbs

CONFERENCE REPORTS

Drama Papers at the ALA Conference, 2001

At the African Literature Association Conference held at Richmond (Virginia) during April 2001 a number of drama panels were convened. Patrick Ikoye chaired a session on Political Drama, at which he presented a paper on 'Drama and the Language of Social Commit-ment'. The others panelists were Juliana Okoh of Smith College ('Redefining Cultural Traditions in Nigerian Feminist Drama'), P. Jane Splawn of Beaver College ('Reading Ritual in . Contemporary Black Women's Drama'), and David Cho Wanki of the University of Yaounde 1 (on Bate Besong's work).

The panel on Translation in Drama, chaired by Katiwa Mule, brought together Akintunde Akinyemi of Obafemi Awolowo University, who spoke about Olanipekun Esan's trans-lations of Plautus and Sophocles, and John Tiku Takem (Bayreuth) whose

paper was subtitled 'Translating Change in Femi Osofisan's Drama'. Mule, from Smith College, looked at Amandina Lihamba's *Mkutano wa Pili wa Ndege* (*The Second Conference of the Birds*).

James Gibbs

'THEATRE IN AFRICA: FROM PROTEST TO LIBERATION AND BACK?' AN EVENING WITH LESEGO RAMPOLOKENG, FEMI OSOFISAN AND JANE PLASTOW MUNICH, 6 APRIL 2001

The City of Munich has arranged a series of cultural events as addendum to 'The Short Century: Independence and Liberation Movements in Africa, 1945–1994', a multi-faceted exhibition curated by Okwui Enwezor which encompasses fine arts, film, photography, architecture, music, literature and theatre.

Friday, 6 April 2001, was devoted to theatre and the performing arts, conceptualised and introduced by Martin Rohmer, the author of *Theatre and Performance in Zimbabwe* (1999). The evening opened with a performance by the South African poet Lesego Rampolokeng, followed by a public debate on African theatre between Jane Plastow and Femi Osofisan.

Rampolokeng's performances have filled venues in Germany for almost a decade, and those familiar with his work were delighted to see him back with his poignant, often acid, verse, yet with a number of previously unexplored issues. Most striking was an altered performance presence that clearly aimed at transcending his former, by now somewhat outworn image of the 'angry young man'. Tongue-in-cheek references to his wearing glasses or early poems he wrote 'as a child' were light-hearted allusions to a serious issue.

Now in his mid-thirties, Rampolokeng wants to be perceived as a 'respectable and respected *Dichter* [poet]' and as a continuous force to be reckoned with. Though his uniquely musical poetry which, as Rohmer rightly pointed out, is at its performative best without the accompaniment of music, still blends elements of global youth culture with long-established African performance idioms – mixing, for example, rap, dub poetry and seSotho recitals (*dikotho*) – Rampolokeng markedly distanced himself from the label 'rap performer' used in the festival brochure. 'I don't really want to be classified. It was said a long time ago, so I feel obliged to go with it, but I don't really feel comfortable to be expected to join in a monkey dance'.

Rampolokeng's poems and comments have lost none of their edge, still addressing subjects considered off-limits in his country and elsewhere: the hagio-graphic reverence for the former South African president ('What are politicians for if you can't even make jokes about them?'); Thabo Mbeki's attempt at 'dictating renaissance to us'; the purportedly 'new [South African] consciousness' as well as the increasing xenophobia in his country, especially towards Nigerians, which led him to perform a poem about Fela Anikulapo-Kuti.

Other issues addressed included the role of academia ('Even this person posing with a pipe [Thabo Mbeki] has turned critic and has been saying nasty things about what I and other people do'), the uses and abuses of oral poetry, and his discomfort with his own role in the 'rent-a-poet enterprise'.

Rampolokeng teased his audience without making them feel uncomfortable (as happened in his previous performances). This might have been due to the distance of the predominantly European audience in the heart of Bavaria from the topics he considered. To the Africans present, however, the topics were very pertinent. It is therefore regrettable that Rampolokeng was not given his own question and answer session; his presence was apparently forgotten when the floor was opened after the discussion about theatre. Performance poetry is part of theatre in Africa, and we should not have to wait until Rampolokeng's work is on stage or in print before recognising him as a man of the theatre.

Jane Plastow and Femi Osofisan engaged in a dialogue intended to map out broader issues of African theatre practice for a non-specialist audience. Among the general topics they addressed were the functional aims of African theatre as opposed to European notions of 'arts for arts' sake'. The point was made that apart from providing relaxation and entertainment, African theatre was also concerned with the 'health of society' in that it addressed 'moral, political and social issues' (Osofisan). The aesthetic forms employed were different to European forms as they blended European influences (dialogue-based drama) with African performance elements such as music, dance, masquerades and mime. Rigid Western categories such as 'drama', 'opera' and 'musical' could not be applied to the African context. In discussing the question of audiences, Osofisan emphasised that they were much more part of the performance than could ever be conceived in the northern hemis-phere. Spectators commented on and reacted continuously to shows, at times mercilessly interfering with the performance if they did not approve of the conduct of the characters 'on stage'.

To avoid suggesting that the continent [and by implication all African theatre practices] presented 'one, homogeneous whole', Plastow steered the discussion towards Osofisan's specific working context. Who, she asked, was Osofisan writing for if theatre had a purpose, and quite often a political intent? Drawing on the overarching theme of the Munich exhibition – resistance and liberation – Osofisan elaborated on the background of Nigerian history to conclude that his target audience was primarily the educated class, in particular the student population. Highlighting Nigeria's deplorable post-independence state of affairs in his work, he suggested, would encourage this group 'to take on the fight' for a better society. This was the message of most 'second generation' Nigerian writers, as opposed to that of the 'first generation' (Achebe, Soyinka and Tutuola) who, in his view, were primarily concerned with the anti-colonial struggle. This was a rather reductionist argument, especially concerning the authors' engagement with political topics, but perhaps it was necessary to map out broader issues for uninitiated members of the audience.

The final points raised were the ever-present question of language, now rekindled by the Asmara Language Declaration, and the influence of (predominantly American) popular culture. While Plastow provided the historical background to the language debate – African languages vs. European ones – Osofisan pragmatically announced that in a multilingual country like Nigeria, declaring one of the local languages as *lingua franca* would be equivalent to declaring civil war. In order to address the nation, not only one's own ethnic group, the writer had to use the language spoken across local language divides, namely English. English, he maintained, was by no means an exclusively European language: it had long been turned into an African language.

Still, Plastow asked, why continue with theatre in the light of the impact of foreign popular material, the harassment faced by theatre practitioners, especially women, and the minimal financial rewards? This, Osofisan concluded, was a question he was unable to answer, apart from his deep-seated knowledge that humankind longed for theatre and art. 'Why are you all here?' he asked. 'You could be enjoying yourself elsewhere! I believe that the artistic impulse is something deep down in the human psyche and cannot be destroyed.'

All in all, the debate proved informative for the general public, even if occasionally it was in danger of slipping into platitudes (Western theatre forms being equated with stuffy naturalist drama, for example, as opposed to the exuberant African theatre scene with its multiple performance elements and enthusiastic audience participation). Yet it was evident from the feedback that the discussion had hit a raw creative nerve and that there was a patent need to learn more about theatre practices in Africa. One theatre pedagogy student requested information about exchange programmes. For the insider audience too, there was food for thought.

Onookome Okome, who was a visiting professor at the Iwalewa House in Bayreuth, pointed out that every time a statement about foreign popular culture in Africa was made, it seemed that the continent was a passive recipient of the Western (and Asian) media output. He pointed out that African audiences did not absorb everything indiscriminately, but were highly selective. 'They take only those things they can infuse, and when they infuse it, it ceases to be American or European.' This creates a problematic not unlike the pragmatic appropriation of non–African languages, if you look closely. And if you think of Fatima Dike's *So What's New?* and the way she integrates the notorious soap *The Bold and the Beautiful* in her play, or how Yoruba theatre companies have appropriated hospital series (Barber 1987; 2000), it seems we need to readdress the links between popular culture and African theatre. As Osofisan pointed out, we cannot simply condemn globalisation as 'dangerous'.

NOTE

1 The House of World Cultures, Berlin, The Museum of Contemporary Art, Chicago, and the PS1 Contemporary Art Center in New York also hosted the Short Century exhibition.

REFERENCES

'Asmara Declaration on African Languages and Literatures' (2001) in *African Theatre: Playwrights and Politics*, Oxford/Bloomington/Johannesburg: James Currey/Indiana University Press/Witwatersrand University Press, pp. 207–8.

Barber, Karin (1987), 'Popular Arts in Africa', *African Studies Review*, 30, 3: 1–78.

— (2000) *The Generation of Plays: Yoruba Popular Life in Theatre*. Bloomington: Indiana University Press.

Dike, Fatima (1999), 'So What's New?' in Kathy Perkins (ed.), *Black South African Women: An Anthology of Plays*, Cape Town: University of Cape Town Press, pp. 26–46.

Christine Matzke
University of Leeds

Introduction to
Cont Mhlanga's *Workshop Negative*

JANE PLASTOW

Workshop Negative by Cont Mhlanga was first performed in Bulawayo, Zimbabwe, in 1987, as one of a continuing string of plays emanating from Mhlanga's phenomenally popular Amakhosi Theatre Company. The success of Amakhosi needs to be seen in the context of Zimbabwean theatre in the years after the country finally achieved independence in 1980. After decades of the severest censorship of all black art under the apartheid regime run by Ian Smith, theatre and literature blossomed in the 1980s, with some two hundred companies affiliating to Zimbabwe's two umbrella community-based theatre organisations.

Cont Mhlanga himself was originally a factory foreman who ran a karate club in his township area of Makakoba, Bulawayo. In 1980 he was annoyed when his regular club slot was taken over by a National Theatre Organisation workshop. He went along to see what was going on, and promptly got hooked on theatre. Subsequently his young company pioneered a hugely physical style of theatre, incorporating the karate work, but also using high-energy dance and music. Mhlanga has been endlessly inventive in developing his work. When he found that the rapid turnover of actresses in the company was because husbands and boyfriends were concerned that their womenfolk were becoming involved in what was seen as a potentially licentious activity, Mhlanga organised a party to which he invited the men to explain how women were respected and protected within the company. He was then able to build up a core of women who have worked with Amakhosi over the years. He then discovered that while Amakhosi had a strong youth following, the older people were staying away. He engaged in a consultation process that resulted in an old man being commissioned to teach the performers the traditional dances which had been lost to urban youth culture.

Amakhosi's plays always premiere in their township base at Makakoba, but they tour throughout the country and beyond, to neighbouring countries as well as Britain and Scandinavia. The company have become the leading Ndebele group in Zimbabwe, with their plays written in what Mhlanga calls 'Ndenglish', a fusion of languages which makes the work accessible to all Zimbabweans. Mhlanga sees his mission as being a voice for the *povo* – the ordinary people, and it is this which drives both performance style and content.

Politically much Zimbabwean drama moved from supporting the independence government to criticism of its rapidly emerging corrupt practices within a very few years. The play which preceded *Workshop Negative, Nansi le Ndoda* (Here is the Man), won the National Theatre Organisation Festival in 1986 and dealt with some difficult issues of youth unemployment, nepotism and the sexual abuse of women. But it was *Workshop Negative* that brought Mhlanga into open conflict with the government.

Workshop Negative looks at the situation of two workers, the black Zuluboy and the white Ray Graham, both of whom are employed in the workshop of an apparently socialist MP. Initially the men view each other as the enemy, since they fought on opposite sides in the liberation struggle. But we rapidly come to see that it is the hypocritical exploitative MP, mouthing socialism while practising the most oppressive capitalism, who is the real enemy in independent Zimbabwe.

The government announced it was banning *Workshop Negative* from touring to the West, and Mhlanga has subsequently been consistently pressurised not to put on such controversial material. However the company has continued to produce work criticising both social and political oppression in Zimbabwe, and has extended its work by becoming a centre for the promotion of African arts in Bulawayo.

Workshop Negative

CONT MHLANGA

CHARACTERS
Mkhize *workshop owner*
Zulu *toolmaker*
Ray *toolmaker, white*

The action takes place in a tool-making workshop which could be in any part of the country five years after independence. In this workshop we find Ray Graham, a thirty-year-old white Zimbabwean, at work. The song *Tshotsholoza* is heard in the back-ground.

Ray This song reminds me of those long-gone days of madness and murder, days of – blood and tears. When I was still in the Rhodesian Defence Force
All Operation Zambezi!!
(*Ray dives for cover throwing explosives as sounds of return fire and bomb blasts are heard from offstage*)
Ray Kill the damn terrorists! But there were no terrorists. It was a revolution. a black child uprising.
All Amandla!!!
Ray To me it was kill and kill again. But to them, theirs was a path of no return. And that song ... Tshotsholoza!!
(*Ray starts to sing* Tshotsholoza. *Others in the background join in, with Ray dancing like mad. Soon he changes the song to* I Remember. *The words of the song are as follows:*)
I remember,
Day after day,
I remember,
Days of long ago.
Yes it's true,
I remember all I used to hear in those days.
Rhodesia will never die.
No majority rule in
A thousand years

112

Rhodesia is super.
(*Laughs*) *Hei madoda*[1]
Times are changing
Things are changing
But people don't change.
(*Ray starts singing the song* Times Are Changing *as he gets down to work on the grinding machine*)

Ray (*Laughs*) Really times are changing, today me, Ray A. Graham, is employed in this tool-making workshop by an African. A *muntumnyama*[2] (*Laughs*) I can't believe it. Who can? A descendant of the white settlers, employed by an African! Even Rhodes and Jameson would turn in their graves if they heard that a Graham is employed by a native. A native. (*Laughs and walks towards the exit pauses and turns towards the audience*) A native!!
(*Exit Ray. Enter Mkhize, followed by Zulu*)

Mkhize You have seen it all Zulu, from down there, right up to here is my Tool Manufacturing Firm.

Zulu Yours ...

Mkhize Yes, mine alone.

Zulu Great Mkhize. And the place is very representable.

Mkhize Not only representable young man, but also worth thousands of dollars.

Zulu Did you build this when you returned from the bush, Comrade?

Mkhize No-o man. I bought this property from a Mr Rowland.

Zulu A Mr Rowland. What got into his head, to give away a business like this?

Mkhize He left for South Africa, for reasons best known to himself and his wife.

Zulu Some of these whites are really diehards. So the Rowland emigrated to the South simply because he didn't want to accept what our revolution brought in 1980.

Mkhize It is not my problem or concern why Rowland emigrated Zuluboy. My problem and concern right now is getting the right guy to replace David Grey who died in a car accident last week. And that is why I'm engaging you with effect from now.

Zulu He died?

Mkhize Do you read the papers?

Zulu Yes ...

Mkhize He was on last Sunday's front page. The car that left the road ten kilometres from Harare, hit a tree and caught fire.

 Zulu Heavens!

Mkhize I lost a real master of metal in that guy. So you take his place. Ray Graham ... Now where is he? (*calls*) Ray! Ray Graham!

Ray (*Calls back from off-stage*) I'm in the toilet!

---

1 Hey guys.
2 Black man.

Mkhize Hurry up you! My production is at a standstill here. (*To Zulu*) He is another whizz-kid with metal, this Ray. If I lose him I'd better quit manufacturing tools and try some other business. But *hei*! Don't ever tell him that. He could start blackmailing tactics or whatever. You know how some of these pigs are.

Zulu Pigs. (*Laughs loud. Enter Ray zipping up his overalls*)

Ray I'm here Mr Mkhize.

Mkhize Say Comrade!

Ray I'm sorry Sir.

Mkhize (*Emphatically*) I'm sorry Comrade!

Ray Sir!

(*Mkhize sucks his teeth angrily. Meanwhile, Zulu is staring at Ray*)

Zulu I have seen this man before.

Ray Yes, I have seen you before.

Mkhize Ha-a! Great! So you two have met. How nice ... Now why don't you shake hands and start pushing my production?

(*He is met by silence as the two stare at one another*)

Mkhize Aaa ... why? Trying to remember where you two met (*Dead silence from the two*) Where did you two meet?

Both Operation Zambezi!!

Mkhize Come on now! What does that mean?

Zulu See what, Comrade Mkhize, when I was still a freedom fighter ...

Ray A terrorist!

Zulu A terrorist! You − I will ... (*Jumps on Ray. Zulu scores with a hard kick. And quickly Ray returns a hard blow. Mkhize moves in and stops them*)

Mkhize Ray! How dare you talk like that?

Ray Mr Mkhize ...

Mkhize Say Comrade!

Ray I'll try and remember that next time. But what I'm trying to do is put history correct from my side. At that time, to his people, he was a freedom fighter. But to my people he was a terrorist.

Zulu A group of the rebel regime's troops tracked us into the Zambezi Valley. And they captured me ...

Ray A terrorist! (*Zulu moves in to attack him once again but Mkhize blocks his way*)

Zulu And he was in command.

Ray I was doing my national service.

Zulu He tortured me until my comrades came to my rescue.

Ray And the bloody *magandanga*[3] killed eight of our boys. I was the only survivor and he made me run 200 ks on foot, the ruthless murderer!!

Mkhize So that's where you two met! Here I have a problem.

Ray I'm not the problem Mr Mkhize, or if you like Comrade. I have worked for you for five years, and I have never given you a headache. Him is the problem.

(*He rushes for Zulu and smashes him head-first onto the working bench. Zulu leaps*)

---

3 Terrorists.

up and catches Ray with a head-butt. Ray goes down on his knees)
Zulu I will go crazy on you!
Ray Better go crazy you grandson of a *bhaka!* [4]
(*They jump on each other. Mkhize seperates them*)
Mkhize If this is my workshop this nonsense must stop. And if this is your workshop, go ahead – fight! I say fight! And I'll fire both of you right now! (*There is a silence.*)
Ray I'm sorry Mkhize.
Zulu *Ngiyaxolisa baba Mkhize* but *inja le kumele izikhuze.* [5]
Ray What did he say? I don't understand that language.
Zulu You must learn the language. Comrade Mkhize is the Managing Director, not an interpreter.
Mkhize This negative attitude must stop. What would become of this country if everybody started opening up old wounds?
Both But Mkhize … ! How – how …
Mkhize You both shut up! I don't want to hear any of it! The leaders of this nation speak of reconciliation every now and again. And it must start right here, in this workshop! (*There is silence*)
Ray OK. It's over Mkhize.
Zulu It's finished comrade.
Mkhize Actions speak louder than words.
(*The two move in to shake hands. But Ray pulls away his hand before they touch*)
Ray Nice to meet you. Hope you'll enjoy yourself here.
Zulu Nice to meet you, I'm happy to get a job at last. I've not been employed since I was demobilised from the army.
Mkhize Now Ray, show him around and start pushing my production.
Ray Yes Comrade.
Mkhize How far have you gone with my 5,000 2/8 screwdrivers?
Ray I've just started on them.
Mkhize Heavens, that order is urgent! Metals Limited gets them in two weeks' time or they cancel the order. Now show him around and push my production.
Ray Yes Comrade. (*Mkhize walks out*)
Ray Now what shall I show you first?
Zulu Just show me what I must do first.
Ray Wait … you boys from the bush, I'll show you the toilet. It's where you piss … come!
Zulu Who said I want to go to the toilet you silly bugger?
Ray Don't call me silly, you idiot!
Zulu Idiot you say. Me idiot?
Ray You Africans will always be idiots.
(*This is enough to start a fight. A small chase round the benches and they are in the open. They close in and roll down on the floor. Zulu gets a good grip on Ray's arms*

---

4 Bugger.
5 Forgive me father Mkhize, but that dog needs controlling.

and throws him off. Both are on their feet. Zulu scores in the belly and Ray goes down. Ray comes up with a big stick. Mkbize coughs and walks into the workshop. The two quickly pretend to be hard at work)

Mkhize How are things going Ray?

Ray (*Breathlessly*) Oh fine Comrade. And Zulu is really wonderful. (*Turns round sharply and hits Zulu in the belly with the wood*) I'm sorry!

Mkhize Zuluboy, how is the work going so far?

Zulu Great Comrade, and Ray is really wonderful. (*Turns round sharply and hits Ray with his elbow in the belly*) I'm sorry!

Mkhize Lovely – push my production guys. Here Ray, another job card, 7,000 hammers c.v. 16. You are working up to 10 p.m.

Ray Yes Comrade. (*Mkhize walks out*)

Ray (*Throwing the job card on the table and getting down to work. Zulu is working on a rod on another bench*) A-a-ahh man. Everyday working till 10 p.m. Saturdays, Sundays, no days off. Does he think people are animals? Mistaking me for a donkey. And the salary he pays us is peanuts. Ah-h-h-man!!

Zulu That's what your fathers did to our fathers. See now why we went to the bush?

Ray Shut up you. I'm not talking to you.

Zulu Nor I.

Ray This is too much work, and this slavedriver does not want to employ more people. (*A few seconds pass as they both concentrate on what they are doing*)

Zulu I'm finished with this rod. (*Ray walks over to Zuluboy. And speaks a sentence in Afrikaans*)

Zulu (*Looking puzzled*) I don't understand that. (*Ray repeats himself in the same language*) I don't understand that language. What do you mean?

Ray You must learn the language. I'm an engineer and not an interpreter.

Zulu I'll tell Mkhize! (*Rushing off the stage. Ray blocks him*)

Ray No! Please Zulu, don't tell Fox. Please!

Zulu Out of my way!

Ray Here Zulu, have this five bucks.

Zulu I'll tell Fox.

Ray Don't tell Fox. I was just joking.

Zulu (*Takes the five dollar note smiling to himself*) Next time don't joke like a fool, sonny.

Ray You sharpen it over there. (*For a minute or two they get down to work. Zulu pulls out the five dollar note, laughs and puts it back into his pocket. Later he keeps looking at Ray as if he wants to ask something but cannot bring himself to do it. It becomes obvious that he needs to go to the toilet as he tries to reduce the pressure by trying to work with his legs crossed*)

Zulu Eh Ray, where is the toilet?

Ray You can find it yourself. You made a fool of me when I was going to show you. (*They work on, but Zulu can stand it no longer*)

Zulu Ray! (*No answer*) Ray!!

Ray Stop bothering me. You can do it right there on the floor.
Zulu Please Ray! Show me the toilet!!
Ray You give me back my five bucks.
(*Zulu passes the five dollar note to Ray*)
Ray Now, go ask your grandmother.
Zulu I'll tell Mkhize! (*Runs off but Ray grabs him. They struggle going round and round*)
Ray Please don't, don't tell Fox. (*But Zulu breaks loose and runs off-stage, shouting*)
Zulu Toilet! Toilet! I want the toilet! (*Ray runs after him, shouting*)
Ray It's to your right, Zulu. To the right!
(*As Act One ends, the political song* Ilizwe, *which leads on to Act Two, is heard in the background*)

ACT TWO

All the characters, Mkhize. Ray and Zulu, move out of character. Ray is singing the Ilizwe.
Ilizwe ngelethu
Imali ngeyethu
Amandla ngawethu
Konke ngokwethu.[6]
(*The actors dance a mixture of isitshikitsha, isikokotshi, imbube and irabi*)
Ray So we sing at rallies.
Mkhize So we dance at rallies.
Zulu Mkhize is coming to address a rally.
All About socialism (*as they sink down on their knees*).
Mkhize Here he comes.
(*Actors demonstrate Mkhize arriving in style. Actor 1 and 3 drive in style to the far corner of the stage. Actor 2 follows them and parks in the centre. All in mime drive with car sounds coming from their mouths. After parking ...*)
All Luxury drive!
Mkhize But I walked five kilometres to this rally.
Zulu I walked six.
Ray I walked eight.
(*The actors walk towards stage centre and suddenly stamp hard with their right feet pointing to the audience and asking the question ...*)
All But who is Mkhize?
Mkhize Ex-freedom fighter, high command.
(*Ray and Zulu move to attention shouting 'Hawu' and then all actors demonstrate toyitoyi[7] with Mkhize calling the command words*)
Mkhize Freedom fighter!
All *Hawu! Hawu!*

---

6 The land is ours, the money is ours, the power is ours, everything belongs to us.
7 War dance.

Mkhize   *Yinyamazana!* [8]
All   *Hawu! Hawu!*
Mkhize   *Ihlale gangeni!* [9]
All   *Hawu! Hawu!*
Mkhize   Idle – Capitalist!
All   *Hawu! Hawu!*
Mkhize   Change gear!
   (*All actors come to a sudden stop stamping hard on the ground with their right feet*)
Mkhize   Those were Mkhize's Youth days, and now a Political Commissar for Socialism!
Zulu   A member of the Politburo.
Ray   A member of the House of Assembly.
Mkhize   A member of the National Defence Council. And the chairs!!
   (*Zulu jumps over to pick up a chair and places it in the centre of the stage. He is the first to sit on it as they all rotate to sit; each one shouting the name of the organisation in which Mkhize is Chairman*)
Zulu   Provincial …
All   Chairman!
Ray   Drought Relief Aid …
All   Chairman!
Mkhize   Southern African States Development Council …
All   Chairman!
Zulu   National Cooperatives Society …
All   Chairman!
Ray   Blue Bombers Football Club …
All   Chairman!
Mkhize   And the shares … (*Ray moves off stage centre to the back with the chair, making the three actors form a triangle on stage. Another bit of mime here. Actors carry shovels and are heaping money as they shout the names of the organisations of which Mkhize is shareholder*)
Mkhize   Chrome Industries …
All   Shareholder! (*Thrust the shovels down and load …*)
Zulu   *Khula ntaba ye mali.* [10]
Ray   Grow money mountain. H & H Auctioneers.
All   Shareholder! (*Thrust the shovels down and load …*)
Zulu   *Khula ntaba ye mali.*
Ray   Grow money mountain. Grow money mountain.
Zulu   National Finance Group.
All   Shareholder! (*Thrust the shovels down and load …*)
Zulu   *Khula ntaba ye mali.*
Ray   Grow money mountain. Aviv Motorways.

---

8 Animal.
9 Living in the forest.
10 Grow money mountain.

All Shareholder. (*Thrust the shovels down and load …*)

Mkhize Owner of Truemans fashions. (*All thrust the shovels down and load …*)

Zulu *Khula ntaba ye mali.*

Ray Grow money mountain.

Zulu Managing Director of Progress Tool Manufacturers. (*All thrust the shovels down and load ….*)

Zulu *Khula ntaba ye mali.*

Ray Grow money mountain.

Mkhize Fast jobs and drug smuggling profits. (*All thrust the shovels down and load …*)

Zulu *Khula ntaba ye mali.*

Ray Grow money mountain. (*All the actors fall down flat on their backs lifting up their right hands and feet, and as they rise back to their feet …*)

Ray This is the money mountain.

All *Intaba ye mali!*

Ray For just one person …

All Umkhize!

Zulu Owns three farms and a mansion.

Ray One wife and one child.

Mkhize Two Jaguars and two Mercedes.

Ray Employs 12 domestic servants.

Zulu He is swelling with luxury and wealth. (*All actors demonstrate the swelling bellies as they get closer*)

Mkhize Wrong framing comrade.

Ray Yah …!

Zulu Hah …!

Mkhize He is swelling on the sweat of the toiling workers.

Ray Who work from six to six.

Zulu And cannot even organise a decent breakfast for their families. *Uyahuquluza!* [11]

Ray Yah …! He is capitalising.

Mkhize Shut up you! Mkhize is addressing a rally!

All He – hee – he! (*Ray and Zulu run into the audience. Mkhize remains on stage to address the rally*)

Mkhize All of us here must be for socialism.

Zulu & Ray Yee down with capitalism! Down with imperialism!

Mkhize All of us must work and contribute to our nation with socialist principles and ideology in mind. (*Zulu and Ray shout and clap*)

Mkhize All of us here must see to it that there is no room for capitalism and the capitalists in our society. In this country we are striving for a classless society.

Ray & Zulu Yes, yes, (*clapping*) tell them comrade, *Batshele!!* [12]

Mkhize I don't want to see in Zimbabwe what I saw in Rhodesia. The other

---

11 Crook.
12 Tell them!

side of town, you get three people sharing a fifteen-roomed house. Yet on the other side of town you get fifteen people sharing a three-roomed house. The other side of town dustbins stink with leftovers, yet on the other side of town people go to bed with empty stomachs. On the other side of town a stream of flashy cars flows into the city centre. Yet on the other side of town a stream of bicycles flows into the city centre. That alone drove the sons and daughters of the soil to the bush. And where is the white man's regime today?

(*Zulu and Ray clap and shout and whistle*)

Zulu Where is it comrade?

Mkhize Low class, middle class, high class, or whatever nonsense. We are bringing socialism for you to sweep that out.

Ray & Zulu Equality! Equality!

Mkhize I am here for a socialistic life for all. Therefore we must share the country's wealth just like workers sharing a mug of beer after a day's hard work.

(*Zulu and Ray run up on the stage. Zulu picks up a mug of beer and the three actors move closer together as each sings a line in the song* Bayayazi)

Zulu *Uyayazi*[13] socialism ...

Mkhize *Bayayesaba obhushwa bonke*[14] ... All the bourgeois fear it.

All *Ngoba befuna ukusetshenzelwa ngabanye.*[15] (*They all laugh*)

Ray Pass the mug.

(*Zulu passes the mug to Ray who drinks*)

Zulu Hey man, are you from the rally?

Mkhize Ya, and Mkhize was the speaker.

Ray When did he say the wages increase is?

Mkhize He never talked about that. He talked about working conditions and advised people to share equally the wealth of the country like people sharing a mug of beer.

Ray Share the country's wealth ...

Mkhize ... like people sharing a mug of beer. (*They all laugh*)

Zulu Hei, pass the mug.

(*Ray passes the mug back to Zulu who drinks*)

Mkhize But the mug hasn't moved this way gentlemen.

Ray Why? You did not press for your round.

Zulu *Kawuhlabanga.*[16]

Mkhize But *madoda*, I'm broke. I have twenty cents in my pocket.

Ray You bring it here.

(*Mkhize digs for the twenty-cent coin from his pocket and gives it to Ray*)

Ray That buys you two gulps.

Mkhize Ha-a madoda ...

---

13 You know ....
14 All the bourgeois fear it.
15 They want others to work for them.
16 Press (i.e., pay).

Ray & Zulu Yah—h!

(*Mkhize takes the mug and prepares to pour down as much beer as his throat can allow to pass through. Ray gets ready to count the gulps as the beer goes past the throat, and Zulu gets ready to count the beer as it lands in the stomach. Mkhize sucks down the beer*)

Ray One!

Zulu One!

Ray Two!

Zulu Two!

Ray & Zulu (*Grabbing the mug from Mkhize*) Ah! ah! hee! (*Zulu takes the mug*)

Mkhize Come on gentlemen, socialism *madoda*.

Ray Does socialism mean you don't press for your round?

Mkhize *Madoda!* Let's do as Mkhize says.

Ray & Zulu What! You!

Ray Let's do as Mkhize does.

Mkhize and Zulu What! You!

Mkhize Gentlemen, Mkhize is a man of substance. I see no wrong in doing as he does.

Ray & Zulu Rubbish!

Zulu Gentlemen, we are also people, we can reason. I see no wrong in doing what is good for us.

Ray & Mkhize Rubbish!

Ray Gentlemen, let Mkhize teach by example. If he does not, I see no wrong in doing as he does.

Mkhize & Zulu Rubbish!

Mkhize Gentlemen, you are both drunk. Some beer *madoda*, my throat is dry.

Ray You are getting nothing.

Zulu Nothing at all.

Mkhize Ayia – I'll empty that mug.

Ray & Zulu *Ah maya!* [17]

Mkhize I'll kick it over! (*Springs at the mug. Zulu moves it out of his way. The two make a fool of Mkhize as he tries to reach for the mug and empty it. They pass the mug to one another, drink as they bump him away with buttocks and legs. On the last move they send him crashing to the floor and they exit. He follows them, in pain*)

ACT THREE

(*It is February. A few minutes before the workshop opens. Mkhize is sitting on the only desk in the workshop reading the morning paper. Zulu enters carrying his overalls. He starts to dress for work*)

Mkhize Morning Zulu.

Zulu Morning Comrade.

Mkhize Please, when it's here, and just the two of us, call me Sir.

---

17 No! (Slang).

Zulu (*Almost to himself*) Sa-a-a-h! (*Seconds go by then Mkhize speaks again*)

Mkhize You are so early to work today Zulu. Why?

Zulu I need to talk to you.

Mkhize Talk to me about …

Zulu Working conditions in this here workshop, they … are … bad!

Mkhize (*Throwing his newspaper aside and getting on his feet to face Zulu squarely*) What? You say what is what?

Zulu Working conditions in this workshop are …

Mkhize … bad you say?

Zulu We work long hours. And many government regulations are not observed to this …

Mkhize You shut up! Who do you think you are under the sun to come and tell me about conditions in my workshop?

Zulu Mkhize!

Mkhize Mkhize *ukuthini*? [18] We work long hours we … we … we … Who is this We, Zuluboy?

Zulu I mean Ray and I.

Mkhize So is it Ray who sent you here to come and tell me this rubbish?

Zulu How can you say it's rubbish Mkhize when …

Mkhize *Hei* man! I said did Ray send you here?

Zulu No.

Mkhize That big obstinate head of yours is misleading you young man. I have worked with Ray for so many years and he has never come to me puffing up like this. You have been here for only two months, and you come vomiting about working conditions and government regulations. What do you know about government business, you?

Zulu It's not a matter of knowing government business, but a matter of how things are run.

Mkhize A *nyonyoro* [19] of how things are run. Zuluboy, if you feel conditions in this workshop are no good for you, you can just sign a resignation form and get the hell out of my workshop. You can go and work for your government or your grandmother.

Zulu Let me remind you of something, Mkhize. We fought a bloody war to remove such attitudes towards workers. We deserve to be listened to, both in the workshop and in the running of the country.

Mkhize I'm sorry for you, sonny. You played your part by staying in the bush *bhundu* with bombs and guns. Now why not let others, clever ones like me, do their part, that of running the country?

Zulu Mkhize! Do you really understand yourself? Do you know that if I push this matter you could end up in serious trouble?

Mkhize To hell, son of poor stock. Do you have enough money to push a man of my weight into trouble?

Zulu What! Son of poor stock?

---

18 Mkhize what?

19 Nonsense word.

Mkhize *Ungumtanomyanga!* [20] Zuluboy.

Zulu That's an insult, Mkhize.

Mkhize *Hayi,*[21] that's the truth Zuluboy. It's a fact. And if you want facts, facts I will give you, Zuluboy. Fact number one; the most expensive thing your grandfather ever owned is a three-speed bicycle. Fact number two; the most expensive thing your father ever owned is a scotchcart. Fact number three; the most expensive thing you ever owned is a Tempest stereo under a lodger's roof. (*To the audience*) Do I call that rich stock?

Zulu (*Shouting angrily*) Mkhize! Mkhize! Do you want me to jump on you?

Mkhize Jump if you feel like it. Come on jump, and I'll show you that money speaks.

Zulu I better take this matter to the Ministry of Labour and the Union.

Mkhize (*Laughs*) Mfana, who controls the Labour and the Union? If it's not me, it's my connection. Now go out and report. (*Pushes him*) Go out and tell whoever you want and you will know what it means to have money.

Zulu Is that what you say when you are in public?

Mkhize You shut up Zuluboy. It's almost time-up. Start pushing my production. (*Zuluboy shoves his hands into his overall pockets*) Ah-a-yiya Zuluboy, If you feel you are not gonna work for this workshop because there is no Workers' Committee, there is no this and that condition, please without much talk, follow me to my office, fill in the forms, get your money and get out into the street. There are thousands of people searching for jobs. (*Turns to walk out*)

Zulu Mkhize!

Mkhize (*Turns to Zuluboy*) I said follow me.

Zulu Mkhize! People have eyes, people have ears, they hear what you say and see what you do. One day (*Swears*) *Mncgwi!* You will meet your fate.

Mkhize Zuluboy, if you don't want to come for the form I'll bring it right here for you, sonny! (*He walks out. Zulu starts work on a machine close by, talking to himself*)

Zulu Mkhize! This fox. Just the kind of person I can't get along with. With his stinking mouth, he is for socialism, yet in this workshop he is just the opposite Mkhize! *Skelema!* [22] Dangerous day-time socialist and night-time capitalist. I wonder why some people just can't do as they say.(*Enter Ray carrying his overall and starts to dress for work*)

Ray Morning Zulu. (*No answer*) Zulu! Morning. (*No answer*) Heyi, What's the matter? Are you sick?

Zulu I'm OK.

Ray Coffee?

Zulu No thanks.

Ray What's up Zulu?

Zulu Nothing.

---

20 Son of a poor peasant.
21 No.
22 Rogue.

Ray (*Mockingly*) No–th–ing–!

Zulu Don't be funny with me Ray.

Ray Who is being funny? You come to work in the morning and you act as if you received a telegram from the devil.

Zulu (*Grabbing Ray and pulling him closer*) Don't be funny Ray, I'll smash you!

Ray Look man, are you angry? It's a joke.

Zulu (*Pushing him away*) I'll crush your head.

Ray Must I not joke with you Zulu?

Zulu Not when I'm in this mood.

Ray What's up Zulu?

Zulu You are paid to make tools and not to ask me questions. (*Turns to work at his machine*)

Ray Yebo …[23] (*For a few moments the two concentrate on their work. Zulu breaks the silence*)

Zulu Ray, how do you manage to get along with this Mkhize?

Ray Are you paid to ask me questions?

Zulu I don't understand how you could go along with this mad man for six years.

Ray Mad! Mkhize mad?

Zulu Yes.

Ray Zulu, you talk like that and you are asking for trouble. Do you know Mkhize?

Zulu I knew Mkhize before the white race would share the same toilet with the black race.

Ray So you knew Mkhize before you came here?

Zulu What! Him. Mkhize and I walked half a thousand kilometres to the border, joined the armed struggle together, trained together in the bush. We parted when I was drafted to go and learn tool engineering in Libya and he went to learn to be a socialist political commissar in Cuba.

Ray (*Laughs*) Mkhize a socialist! (*Laughs again*) Mkhize a socialist? (*Laughs loud and exits. Zulu is so angry that he starts talking to himself*)

Zulu If Mkhize comes here, I'll ask him one question. Mkhize are you a socialist? *Ngiyabuza*,[24] Ah-ah, Do you practise socialism Mkhize? Ah! you are starting your thing again. You want to fight? Right! Fine! Let's go. I'll show you. (*He starts shadow boxing*) You get that, and that! Game down! Now get up Mkhize. I'll give it thick to you.

(*Enter Ray carrying two cups in a tray only to find Zulu shadow boxing. He starts imitating him as he drinks from his cup. Enter Mkhize*)

Mkhize (*Shouting.*) Heyi you … (*They all freeze*) What the hell are you two doing here during working hours?

Ray It's Zulu, Mkhize, ask him. I'm also wondering.

Mkhize (*To Ray*)What!!

Ray I thought maybe he is gone mad. You can never know with these ex-

---

23 Yes.
24 I ask.

combatants.

Mkhize Are you not in-charge of him Ray? Are you not?

Ray I am, but it's Zimbabwe now, and everyone thinks they can do as they please anytime.

Mkhize Is that the reason why you let him turn my workshop into a boxing gym?

Ray It's Zuluboy, Mkhize. (*Turning towards Zulu*) But you Africans are a problem. (*To Zulu*) Hey man, tell him why you are shadow boxing during working hours.

Zulu Africans a problem ... ! (*Misses him with a blow*) I'll smash your head.

Ray (*Jumping away*) See him Mkhize, he is gone lunatic.

Mkhize Zuluboy, is this a boxing gym or workshop? Sonny, you don't have to bring your jungle behaviour onto my premises. Okay!! What's wrong with your head?

Zulu You are the wrong with my head.

Ray *He-e-e madoda.*

Mkhize Zulu, I don't understand your behaviour today.

Zulu You don't have to understand it.

Mkhize Zulu you don't talk to me like you are talking to your kid.

Zulu Does it matter?

Mkhize Zulu, I don't think we will go on for another minute before I blow off that big head of yours.

Zulu And when you blow my head off, I'll be clapping my hands to that. (*Jumping about and striking his head*) Blow ... blow ... blow ... me ... hela ... hela ... hela ... Boom! Oh I'm so sorry, you traitor of our Revolution.

Mkhize What Zulu! You come to me begging for a job and now you want to be my equal. Do you know that I can fire you right now?

Zulu Fire me Mkhize! I'm not afraid of that. But before I go, I will expose this workshop to the eyes of the nation. I'll put it right for those who will come after me.

Mkhize (*Pulls out a form from his pocket and gives it to Zulu*) You bloody fool, take this form, fill it in and get out. I want to see what you will put right and how you will put it right. (*Zulu takes the form from Mkhize. Studies it for a few seconds. Then tears it and throws it into Mkhize's face. Ray walks out seeing that this will end up in a fight*)

Zulu Even if it means using my ten pounds hammer (*Shows him the big fist*), I will do it without fear or mercy.

Mkhize Out! No more talk from you, out! (*Pushing him*)

Zulu Don't push me. I know my way out.

Mkhize Right then, out!

Zulu You are just the kind of people that Marx and Lenin referred to as ...

Mkhize Shut up! And just get out. (*Pushing him*) Your Marxist-Leninist theories are driving you mad. Go and be crazy about it in Russia and not in my workshop!!

Zulu Mkhize, how many times a week do you shout to the masses to read that literature? You hyena of the nation.

Mkhize Hyena! Me, hyena of the nation, Zulu? (*Mkhize swiftly picks up a weapon and finds that he has picked a tray. He smashes Zulu in the face, then on the back and in the face again but this time Zulu grabs it and throws it away. Mkhize picks up a broomstick and moves in to attack Zulu. Ray runs in from off stage and grabs the broomstick from Mkhize and separates the two*)

Mkhize Out of my way Ray ... I want to ...

Ray No *madoda!* No, stop this! Hei-ei!

Zulu Let him come Ray. I'll show him.

Ray Look *madoda*, this is very inhuman. Be men of reason. Talk this out round a table. Settle your differences without violence.

Mkhize This guy is stupid.

Zulu Just come on Mkhize. I'll show you where the sun rises.

Ray Stop provoking a fight and talk things over responsibly. You come from the same area. You grew up together. He is black and you are black. You speak the same language and you fight one another like animals. How do you think I could respect your kind in this workshop!!

Zulu If black can exploit black, I see no reason why black cannot fight black. (*He starts to dance around ready for a fight*)

Mkhize Zulu, if you talk crazy stuff like that I can make you disappear without trace!

Zulu There you go. The Smith regime made your father and my father disappear without trace. For good. And you say it shamelessly that I will go the same way. What is the difference between you and the Rowland who ran this workshop before? (*Pause*) The only thing that has changed in this workshop is the name!

Ray Please, how long will this go on? We have done no work since morning. Your firm is losing thousands of dollars.

Mkhize Because of this fool. (*Pointing at Zulu*)

Zulu What! (*Moving in to attack. Ray who is between them stops him*)

Mkhize Let him come Ray. Just let him come. I'll fix him.

Ray Mkhize, you said you had a meeting with the Ministry today ...

Mkhize Oh yes ... (*Looks at his watch*) Ten minutes to get there. Thanks for reminding me Ray. Push my 14,000 trowels, you are working till ten p.m. today. If he is stubborn Ray, just forget about him. He is out! I'll get someone for you, this time a white guy. You cannot work out profit-making strategies with these black fellows. Socialist literature is spoiling them. (*He walks out in a hurry. Zulu cannot believe his ears. He is so angry, he cannot breathe easily*)

Ray Ten p.m. ... ten p.m. everyday. To hell with this slave labour. (*Turns to Zulu*) Come on Zulu, stop puffing like a buffalo. Let's have some action!

Zulu Please, I know what to do.

Ray Right then, do it. (*The two get down to work on a big, very noisy machine casting metal handles*)

Ray (*Shouting rhythmically*) *Shova we ndoda!* [25]

---

25 Push you man.

Zulu *Ha-la-la-la Hezo!*

Ray *Shova-shova-shova …!*

Zulu Come Friday, *Umsebenzi mawunda wunda Imali ungayibona!* [26]

Ray Push …*msebenzi!*

Zulu *Ha-la-la-la kuzwa!* (*Suddenly Zulu stops the wheel*) This is first–class modern slavery.

Ray *Shova lomsebenzi* you. You fought for this. Work for the prosperity of your country.

Zulu And who gets the lion's share?

Ray Mkhize of course, he owns the joint.

Zulu A capitalist, yet he moves around preaching socialism.

Ray Mkhize's socialism is theory, not practical. You must understand that.

Zulu Then he must come out of his sheep's skin and be a hyena openly, so that people will treat him like the hyena that he is.

Ray Zulu, the way you talk has no diplomacy. Those statements are very offensive to some people.

Zulu There comes a time when we must put diplomacy aside and call a spade a spade, for the good of our nation. (*They go back to hard work and this time they move faster with the shouts. Ray stops*)

Ray *Hei!* Coffee time.

(*Ray walks off stage with the two cups to bring tea. Zulu remains doing his boxing act, bobbing and weaving. Enter Ray. Zulu reaches out to receive the cup from Ray but instead Ray puts it on the table and proceeds to sit on a working bench to drink his coffee*)

Zulu Right Ray, you are working till ten p.m. today. Me, no! After five I go womanising and drinking.

Ray Ayia – a-a, is that a boycott or a strike? Mkhize will sack you.

Zulu So then he can employ a white guy this time. (*Laughs*)

Ray (*As if talking to himself, Zulu and the audience*) Employ a white guy, what does he mean a white guy? Why a white guy?

Zulu Because you white guys cannot say anything in this country. You lost the war. If you speak, you will be reminded eleven times of that, and you will quickly be reminded of what your ancestors did to our ancestors. If you don't zip *lo* mouth *kawena* [27] you will be quickly reminded that you are free to follow the rest down South.

Ray Why must it be my generation that gets the boot? Yes, we fought a war and lost. Were we there when our ancestors came here and shot the natives? We were born in a land at war, given a gun and told to defend it. We did not choose to see things as we see them. We were taught how to see. We were taught to live in Africa and see Africa and Africans as we do. We were taught to see the world as black and white.

Zulu What else did they teach you?

Ray Rubbish! I'm not talking to you. I'm talking to nobody. I'm talking to

---

26 No job no money.

27 That mouth of yours.

myself.

Zulu So they taught you to talk to yourself. (*He laughs*)

Ray Who am I, in this workshop?

Zulu You are a human being, just like me.

Ray Can I not have freedom of thought? Freedom of action? Can I not preserve my culture? Can I not go back to my roots?

Zulu If all that means doing here what your ancestors did in Rhodesia then you better start changing, because this society will always boot you.

Ray Change! change! What's wrong with me? Where do I belong? In Europe because my skin is white, or here because I was born here and I grew up here? And my deeds, must they be of a man who stays here or who stays in Europe?

Zulu If you live here because of this country's wealth, then you will always be afraid. But if you live here because you were born here and grew here, then it's your home. Get involved in national problems and celebrations of this place. Be at home with everyone and everything. Starting right here in this workshop with fighting these working conditions. (*They get down to work. This time even faster with more of the shouting coming from Zulu than Ray. Suddenly Zulu stops and throws the hammer down*)

Zulu I'm going.

Ray Fox will sack you.

Zulu Then he will employ a white guy this time. I'll never forgive him for his policies towards workers. I'm gone!! (*He hurries out*)

Ray Maybe he is right. Maybe he is mad. This workshop is in total disorder. Bankruptcy is the next thing. (*He sings the first two lines of the song* Tshotsholoza) *Tshotsholaza, kulezontaba Sijikele zeZimbabwe.*[28]

(*As he slowly walks off stage. Mkhize rushes into the workshop in a very furious mood. He is kicking, throwing, and smashing everything next to him in the workshop as he moves about furiously. He stops on the far side of the workshop. Enter Zulu, who wonders what has been happening in the workshop. He picks metal blocks off the floor and makes a sound, Mkhize turns on him*)

Mkhize You! (*Pointing at Zulu*) I don't want nobody in my workshop today. You get out.

Zulu But the workshop opens in two minutes Mkhize.

Mkhize I said go out please!

Zulu So the workshop remains closed today?

Mkhize These days this workshop opened or closed, it just makes no difference. Now you get out before I drive you out ten times faster than you came in. (*Turns his back on Zulu, both his hands in his jacket pockets*)

Zulu Why so emotional Comrade?

(*Mkhize turns swiftly with a gun in hand aiming at Zulu's head. Zulu screams, dives for cover. Rolls on the floor, drops off stage and disappears into the audience*)

Mkhize Bloody *nyamazana*. One of these days I'll kill an idiot!

(*Turns to face off stage. Behind him enters Ray. He picks up a metal block from the*

---

28 Tshotsholoza, in those mountains from place to place in Zimbabwe.

floor to place it elsewhere and he makes a sound. Mkhize turns to face him)

Mkhize And you ...

Ray He-e-e!

Mkhize Is that the reason why you remained behind when Rowland went to South Africa?

Ray Reason, what reason?

Mkhize What reason? As if you know nothing. Why did you remain behind when Rowland moved down South?

Ray What are you talking about? I don't understand, Mkhize.

Mkhize You don't understand, Ray? I see. That is why you come in two minutes late. Do you think this is Rowland's workshop?

Ray If it's that I'm sorry. There was a roadblock on the Morningside Road.

Mkhize Roadblock Ray? Today I don't want nobody in my workshop.

Ray Wha—at?

Mkhize By the way Ray, when did you last have contact with Rowland?

Ray Contact ...

Mkhize Don't blush, answer!

Ray Six years ago. Why?

Mkhize Ray you are English. I expect you to understand this language best. I did not say when did you last see Rowland? I said when did you last have contact with him?

Ray That time.

Mkhize Which time, you pig?

Ray Six years ago! *(Shouting)* And stop calling me pig! What in hell am I supposed to have done wrong?

Mkhize Ray, don't try to be smart. *(Pulls a letter out of his pocket)* This letter dated five days ago is from Rowland to you.

Ray I don't know about it.

Mkhize You don't know about it when I took it from your dustcoat yesterday!

Ray Let's see it. I don't remember getting a note from Rowland.

Mkhize Rubbish! *(Throws the letter at Ray's feet)* Is that the reason why you remained behind when Rowland went down South?

Ray *(Picking up the letter)* I remained here because this is my home.

Mkhize Your home ... As if you know where you belong. Now Ray, tell me what is written in that letter?

Ray I don't know. *(Tears up the letter)*

Mkhize You don't do that! *(Tries to grab the letter from Ray)*

Ray I'm gonna flush it down the toilet!! *(Runs off stage)*

Mkhize No-o-o-o! *(Takes a few steps after Ray and then stops)* Pig ... Pig ... This pig has destroyed all my valuable evidence. I'll catch him. I'll fix him. *(Enter Ray)*

Mkhize You pig ...

Ray Stop calling me pig.

Mkhize You pig, you secretly make tools in my workshop and export them to Rowland.

Ray I don't know that.

Mkhize Ray you are a thief.

Ray I'm no thief.

Mkhize Shut up! The letter says it all.

Ray What letter?

Mkhize Ray, stop fooling around.

Ray I'm not fooling around. I'm asking.

Mkhize One ... You use my raw material. Two ... You use my machinery. Three ... You use my time. Four ... You use my business name, to supply tools to all SADCC countries. One ... Without my knowledge Two ... Taking all the profits. Three ... Me paying you to run your own business in my own business. With the Rowland being your distributor in South Africa. Don't you see you are heading for a loss of your job.

Ray Loss ... loss ... loss ... Do you think losing a lob means anything after losing so much in this country? War we lost, power we lost, our wealth we lost, top jobs we lost and we are still losing. For how long must we go on losing?

Mkhize There you go, grandson of a coloniser. So you sabotage our economy because the new order doesn't give you colonial advantages?

Ray No, *boog*[29] features. We do it because we have the skill, the technology and the means.

Mkhize Ray you dare talk like that to me. (*Throws a hard blow at Ray's face. Smartly Ray blocks it*) You bloody get out! I'll get a team to investigate your case thoroughly. I'll give it to you thick. They call me Fox. Now get out, while there is still time. (*Turns his back on Ray*)

Ray You better make sure I don't tell them about the mandrax you have got in this workshop. (*Mkhize swings round with a gun aimed at Ray. Ray drops for cover rolls off stage and disappears into the audience*)

Mkhize I better close down this workshop. (*Quickly walks out*)

(*Zulu and Ray recite the poem 'Workshop Negative' from the audience. Mkhize responds from behind curtains. The stage is left empty throughout the reciting of the poem by the actors*)

Mkhize Workshop!

Ray Negative!

Zulu This workshop

Mkhize A paradise of production.

Zulu This workshop

Ray Pride and hope of the nation.

Zulu This workshop

All Productive no more!!!! (*There is a roll of African drums*)

Zulu Men ...

Ray In the...

Mkhize Workshop!

All Men in the Workshop, Men in the Workshop, Men in the Workshop.

---

29 Not Ndebele.

Zulu Negative
All Hawu ... hawu ... !
Ray Attitudes
Zulu Negative
All Hawu ... hawu ... !
Mkhize Principles
All Hawu ... hawu ...
Zulu Negative
All Hawu ... hawu ... !
Zulu Ideas
All Hawu ... hawu ... !
Zulu Negative
All Hawu ... hawu ... !
Ray Directions
All Hawu ... hawu ... !
Zulu Negative
All Hawu ... hawu ... I
Mkhize Energy
All Hawu ... hawu ... !
Zulu Watch out!
All Hayi ... hayi ... hayi ... hayi ... !
Mkhize Men in the workshop ...
Ray Want no oneness.
Mkhize Men in the workshop ...
Ray Want no reconciliation.
Mkhize Men in the workshop ...
Ray Want no peaceful talks.
Mkhize Men in the workshop . . .
Ray Want war! Fighting! Confrontation!!
Mkhize Men eating men. (*drums*)
Zulu Is that good for the workshop?
Ray & Mkhize No!
Zulu Is that productive for the workshop?
Ray & Mkhize No!
Zulu Is that progressive for the workshop?
Ray & Mkhize NO! NO!

(*Actors sing 'Masibambaneni' as they dance onto the stage. The lines of the song are:*
   Masibambanenei
   Sibemoya munye
   Sakhe indawo yethu
   Sifanane lamajuba.[30]
When the song stops Zulu and Ray are on stage, just coming in for work in the morning)

Ray So you finally told Fox about my secret production, you fool.

---

30 Let us unite/And have one spirit/To build our place/And be like doves.

Zulu You leave me alone, you idiot.

Ray For five years I have pushed my stuff with Grey and nothing ever went wrong. Now with you here, everything explodes.

Zulu *Wena* Ray, you always went to Mkhize and urged him to sack me, because I have bush behaviour, I'm rude, and have a socialist mind. But I never came to you complaining. And here you are vomiting rubbish. I'll break your jaws, *nja!*[31]

Ray *Lawe nja!*[32]

(*They are just about to attack each other when Mkhize walks into the workshop*)

Mkhize So you two fools are at it again. And now in my workshop. Now two of you, out!

Ray You are also a fool.

Mkhize What?

Zulu The two of you are fools.

Mkhize Ah, you two, I'll smash you!

Ray You two, I'll smash you!

Zulu You two, I'll smash you!

Mkhize Heavens! What do I hear? You and you are in for a rough ride.

Ray Joking! You and you are in for a hard time.

Zulu Daydreaming. You and you are in for a tough time.

All Fighting!!!

(*A very fast and fearsome fight erupts among the three men in the workshop. They pick up whatever they can reach in the workshop to use as weapons. As Ray and Zulu grab each other Mkhize picks up a short chain from a nearby workbench and slams it on the bench. Ray and Zulu separate*)

Mkhize I'm sick and tired of you two in this workshop. (*To Zulu*) Especially you. (*Swings the chain to smash him but Zulu dodges on to the floor. He swings chain down to smash him but Zulu rolls out of the way. Mkhize then manages to separate himself from the melee. He is on his knees*)

Mkhize Why must I be fighting in my own workshop. A workshop that I run with my own money and brains.

(*Ray and Zulu attack each other. Both actors are finally down on their knees. They are exhausted*)

Zulu Here I am, fighting again. But why? I spent my youthful days in the bush fighting. And in what today is a free place I'm fighting. Was I born to be fighting where others are driving around, building money mountains day and night?

Ray What am I doing fighting? Why am I causing trouble here?

Zulu Fighting my own brother! But why?

Mkhize A man of *my* class, a man of my standards, a man of *my* calibre, I cannot be seen fighting like an animal here. Are there no better ways of ending this problem once and for good?

Zulu Hell! But why have I been saying all these things?

---

31 Dog.
32 Dog yourself!

Ray Talking ... talking ... talking, saying things that I should have kept to myself. Why did I open my heart and let out what was inside. Shame on me. (*Turns his back on the audience*)

Zulu Shame on me. (*Also turns his back on the audience*)

Mkhize Did I have to say all this? I just talked of things that should best have been left unsaid. (*Turns his back to the audience. Short silence. Mkhize gets up on his feet*)

Mkhize I'm closing down this workshop. It's the best way of stopping this madness. You two can start thinking of how you will make a living.

Ray (*Sitting up and facing the audience*) Do you really mean closing down?

Mkhize I'm closing down and selling this whole joint.

Zulu (*Getting up to his feet amazed, puzzled*) Mkhize you are simply closing down this profitable joint because you don't want to improve working conditions.

Mkhize What I have said I have said. This place goes on sale, now you two blokes can go and talk about working conditions elsewhere.

Ray (*Getting up*) This place on sale? Mkhize are you serious?

Mkhize I'm going to contact my lawyers and agents to get rid of everything here!

Ray If it is like that, good! I'm buying this workshop as it is.

Mkhize You buying it?

Ray Serious. I'm going to contact my lawyers and arrange for loans. I can't miss such a bargain. (*Turns to rush out and stops*) By the way, for how much are you giving it away?

Mkhize You will see that in the papers in a few days time.

Ray Please Mkhize, don't tell anybody about it. In me you have a sure buyer. (*To Zulu*) I can imagine this workshop with a new sign out there infront, 'RAY GRAHAM TOOL MANUFACTURERS' (*Laughs and rushes out*)

Mkhize This place I sell.

Zulu Are you sure you want to sell it to Ray?

Mkhize I don't care who buys it.

Zulu Sure Ray will buy it.

Mkhize Does it matter?

Zulu Mkhize, it does matter. Don't you realise that this workshop is slipping back into white hands. It was a Rowland and now it will be a Graham.

Mkhize You contributed to this, why worry?

Zulu Mkhize, this is no time for pointing fingers. Think quick and act. This workshop must not slip back into white hands. Your ancestors, your generation, will both curse you.

Mkhize I can't stand this nonsense going on in this workshop. No more!!

Zulu But Mkhize, failing to run this workshop smoothly and productively does not mean you must give it away like this. The wealth taken from white hands that controlled it, and then giving it away like this. Then what did the sons and daughters of this land stay in the bush for?

Mkhize I'm sick and tired of the disorder in this workshop.

Zulu You know well the problem facing this workshop, Mkhize. All you

have to do is make a new decision that will bring about a new order. You just can't give away this workshop simply because you don't want to change, yourself and these working conditions. No ... o ... o ah ... man!!
(*Enter Ray now dressed in a smart suit and carrying a briefcase*)

Ray So far so good. My lawyers will meet you any time you are ready. (*To Zulu*) I'm positive I'm buying this workshop *mfana*.

Mkhize I'm sorry Ray. You can't buy it.

Ray But why?

Mkhize Maybe because you are white.

Ray (*Losing temper*) What is that now? Racism? Can I not buy a business in my own country without being referred to by the colour of my skin? Can I not be equal to you or Zulu in the country of my birth? Where do you want me to go? Does losing the war mean we have to be slaves for you black Africans, and only then can we qualify to be called true homeboys by you? As long as we are white, to hell with us you say. Ah–a-a-aah man! (*Kicks the working bench next to him*)

Zulu Stop boiling and exploding Ray. Maybe Mkhize has a better reason why he is not selling the workshop to you.

Mkhize Better reason, yes a better reason I have, Ray Graham, I better be frank and open with you. This workshop was in white hands, since then it moved into my hands, black ones, not only at the expense of thousands of dollars but also at the expense of thousands of innocent lives.

Zulu (*Moving next to Mkhize*) Tell him Comrade!

Mkhize So it will be total madness if I let it slip back into white hands so easy. My ancestors and my generation will curse me.

Zulu Tell him Comrade. Yah let me go to the toilet. (*Exit Zulu*)

Mkhize If a Mambo there, or a Khumalo here, or a Monomotapa came to buy this workshop I would give it away without thought. But if a Livingstone, a John Cecil, or a Carrington came to buy this workshop I would tell them what I'm telling you now, and they would turn away disappointed.

Ray So I am kept in this workshop only for my skills and abilities? You just need me for the survival of the workshop, and not because I belong here just like you and Zulu.

Mkhize (*Laughs mockingly*) Skills and ability which I accordingly pay you for ...

Ray You bloody fool! We work like slaves under the worst conditions and you talk like a lunatic. You bastard!!

Mkhize Now who is this 'we', Ray?

Ray Zulu and I, you bastard!!

Mkhize Ray, you don't have to call me names. After all you steal resources from my workshop ... I will ... will ...
(*Rushes on Ray to attack him. Ray meets him with a double punch on the belly. But Mkhize still manages to send Ray back with a good knee kick on the ribs. Kicks fly all over amd Mkhize is caught with a hard punch on the stomach. He goes down. Ray lifts him and pulls him on to the table and strangles him. Mkhize shouts for*

Zulu to come and help him as he gasps for breath)

Mkhize Zulu! Zuluboy! Come Zulu! Zulu-lu-lu!

(*Enter Zulu. Runs in to separate them. Mkhize still wants to attack Ray. Zulu struggles to keep them apart*)

Zulu No *madoda*, you just can't do this! Can't you talk this over reasonably without violence? Are you mad?

Ray Do you hear him Zulu? He employs us under the worst conditions, pays us the worst salary. And here he is boasting about it. I'll eat him alive!! (*Rushes for Mkhize. Zulu pulls him off*)

Zulu Come on *madoda*. Are people in this workshop mad?

Ray I'm not mad.

Mkhize I'm not mad.

Ray Shut up! You are mad. (*They rush for one another and Zulu stops them*)

Zulu Sure, people in this workshop are mad.

Mkhize Stop saying that before I shut you up with this. (*Shows him a fist*)

Zulu No matter what you say or do to me Mkhize, let's face facts. This is total madness. One; when I came into this workshop, I fought Ray, and you Mkhize separated us, stressing that violence was no way of solving matters. A clear sign that you are not for violence.

Mkhize Of course I'm not for violence.

Zulu There you are. Secondly, (*To Ray*) when I attacked Mkhize you separated us, also stressing that violence was no way of solving matters, a clear sign that you are not for violence.

Ray Of course I'm not for violence.

Zulu There you are. Thirdly, you Mkhize and Ray are attacking each other here like animals. I am separating you, also stressing that violence is no way of solving matters. A clear sign that ...

Ray You are not for violence.

Zulu There you are. So what are we doing here, provoking division, hatred and violence with the careless speeches that we vomit? Is that not madness?

Ray Maybe you are right Zulu.

Mkhize Maybe.

Zulu Mkhize, do you want this kind of violence going on in this workshop?

Mkhize No!

Zulu No! Ray, do you want this kind of violence going on in this workshop?

Ray No.

Zulu No! I don't want it either. So the question is, what do we do about it now? (*Silence*) I'm asking you gentlemen, what do we do about it now?

Ray Put our differences aside and maybe come out with a solution.

Zulu Ah-h- man! That is not working. The question is, what do we do about it now?

Mkhize Gentlemen, we can work for unity and peace.

Zulu Ah-h man! That is not working. The question is, what do we do about it now?

Ray Let's be careful about what comes out of our mouths. We find a common cause that will bring us together in reconciliation, unity and peace.

Zulu Ah-h man! That is not working.

Ray The question is, what do we do about it now?

Mkhize We must finish this workshop madness.

Ray Ya-a, but how?

Mkhize For instance Ray, you have connections in town, you can raise money and buy shares in this workshop.

Ray Aa-h-a-a.

Zulu And how do I fit in?

Mkhize How will you fit in? The problem with you Zulu is you don't have money. All you have are socialist theories. And the odd thing is that they also need capital to be implemented. Anyway Zulu, we will improve conditions and observe Government regulations which is what you are fighting for.

Zulu Ah-h man! That is not working. The question is what do we do about it now?

Ray (*Losing his temper*) Now stop asking the same question over and over again, like a fool. Now you tell us, what do we do?

Zulu What do we do? OK gentlemen, we do this ... (*He pulls both of them to the centre of the stage and taking one hand from each, the three put their hands together making a strong hold*)

Zulu Now say this after me.

Ray This after me.

Zulu Be serious, Ray.

Ray OK sharp *zinto*.[33]

Zulu Together like our hands, forever we should be.

(*Mkhize and Ray repeat what Zulu has just said*)

Zulu United we stand, united we advance. (*Ray and Mkhize repeat this*)

Zulu United!

All We Stand

Zulu United!

All We advance!

Zulu Together forward *madoda*.

(*They all pull in different directions as they shout and chant 'Sho-o-va-! Push, Pull! madoda! but they don't move an inch until they break their hold and fall over*)

Ray We are still not advancing.

Mkhize Something is wrong.

Ray Yes, different ideas.

Mkhize Taking us in different directions.

Ray He is going that way; you are going that way, and I'm going that way.

Zulu So what do we do about it now?

Mkhize Let's get a new plan that will unite us. On the class, racial and political spectrums.

Mkhize And with all the ideas that the world has taught us, we put them together for the new plan. Only then can we head for one destiny.

---

33 Slang for things.

Zulu A new plan the West has never known.

Ray A new plan the East has never known.

Zulu A new plan the past has never known.

Mkhize A new plan, good for us all who are in this workshop most of our lives.

Zulu New plan!

Ray For one direction.

Zulu New plan!

Mkhize For one destiny!

Zulu Better done than said, *madoda*! Together forward.

(*They rush in and hold hands but again end up pulling in different directions with Zulu and Mkhize lifting Ray up, their arms passing right under his thighs and groin. Ray screams and they break the hold*)

Mkhize We are not advancing.

Zulu Let's give it another trial *madoda*.

(*They rush in shouting and chanting and this time they find themselves in a worse tangle as they pull from side to side in different directions*)

Mkhize This is a waste of time.

Ray Something is wrong somewhere.

(*They break the hold, falling over*)

Zulu So what do we do about it now?

Ray In order for the unity and plan to succeed we need to be new men, this world has taught us a lot of things differently.

Mkhize So we have different beliefs, concepts, conclusions and directions!

Ray Now let's put together all we have and all we know for the success of the plan.

Zulu You are right Ray, we need to forget our present selves and our present ambitions to be new men.

Ray And that is not easy *madoda* ...

Mkhize Of course it's not easy man! Ah – forgetting all I have accumulated. What! You! Do you mean that I have to forget my three farms and a mansion? And you Zulu, what have you to forget? Ah-h-h man! (*Turning his back to them*)

Zulu Mkhize! Do you want unity?

Mkhize Of course.

Ray Mkhize, do you want peace and progress?

Mkhize Of course.

Zulu Then do something about it now!!

(*Slowly Mkhize walks off stage, Ray and Zulu remain surprised as they mime questions to one another. Just then Mkhize walks back*)

Mkhize Forward with unity! Forward with peace and progress! Come on guys – action now. Don't stand there like aimless fools. Let's take pens and files and work on the new plan.

(*They turn to move towards the workshop administration desk. Ray stops them*)

Ray Stop! As I said for anything to be successful here we have got to be new men.

Zulu Yes Ray!

Ray I then propose that we be made new men in front of everyone here.

Mkhize & Zulu Agreed, Ray! Yes! yes! Agreed.

Zulu Do you have an idea of how it can be done Ray?

Ray Yes! yes. We draw a line in front of us. Right! We make an oath and then cross the line. On the other side we become new men.

Zulu Yes Ray. Do as you say. (*Ray draws the line in front of them*)

Ray OK, I start. (*He kneels down*) Lord strike me dead if I cross that line without a true and honest intent of being a new man.

(*Mkhize is the next. Kneels down and raises his right hand up as he speaks*)

Mkhize Lord strike me dead if I cross that line without the true and honest heart of a new man.

Zulu (*Kneels down*) Lord strike me dead if I cross that line without the true and honest heart of a new man.

Ray Right, let's all cross the line and then start working on the details of the new plan.

(*The three of them walk up to the line. Zulu and Ray cross but Mkhize does not*)

Zulu Come on Mkhize, cross,

Ray Cross the line.

Mkhize Just give me a second gentlemen. I'll be back to cross the line. (*He walks off stage*)

Zulu Mkhize! What is he up to?

Ray Why does he not want to cross the line? (*There is a loud scream from Mkhize who is now off stage and then a gun shot. Zulu dives for cover*)

Ray It's a gunshot.

Zulu Run and have a look. (*Ray runs out and quickly returns quite frightened*)

Ray It's Mkhize. He is dead. Shot dead.

Zulu Mkhize dead! No-oh-oh.

(*They run off stage and soon come back looking even more frightened now*)

Ray Who shot him?

Zulu I don't know. Were we not together here?

Ray Sure he did not shoot himself. There is no gun anywhere near the body. Now who shot him and why?

Zulu This is a set-up. I have a feeling you know something about it Ray.

Ray (*Grabs him by his shirt*) Don't talk like that. You arranged to get him shot.

Zulu Look Ray, Mkhize is dead, now what do we do?

Ray (*Letting him go*) What do we do? That is what we should be talking about, not whether I set up his killing. Anyway you have been against him since you came.

(*Then there is a cough off stage. Silence as the two respond, gripped by fear, to the sound of the cough*)

Zulu What's that?

Ray Who is there? (*Silence*). Let's go and have a look.

(*They walk a few steps up with Zulu in front. Quickly he changes position as he pushes Ray in front*)

Zulu It could be the man who shot Mkhize.

(*They move out very slowly, quietly and with fright. Then there is big laugh off stage as the two shout 'Mkhize! Mkhize!' The three enter on stage laughing shaking hands and stamping feet*)

Zulu Mkhize!

All The new man.

Mkhize The dying of one man is the birth of another.

Ray So now, let's cross the line and be ...

All New men!

Mkhize Now for the new plan.

(*They all cross the line and just then there is a loud sound of a drum and the actors collapse dead. Three different strong voices are heard each shouting at the same time*)

Voice 1 People of this land be for unity, but is it easy?

Voice 2 People of this land, be for reconciliation, but is it easy?

Voice 3 People of this land be for peace, but is it easy?

THE END

Book Reviews

Every attempt has been made to provide full bibliographic details with the help of the Africa Book Centre, 38 King Street, Covent Garden, London WC2E 8JT. UK prices have been provided where available. All editions are paperback except where otherwise stated. Books listed as distributed by African Books Collective are available from them at Unit 13, Kings Meadow, Ferry Hinksey Rd, Oxford OX2 0DP.

Karin Barber, *The Generation of Plays: Yoruba Popular Life in Theater*
Bloomington: Indiana University Press, 2000, 485 pp.
HB ISBN 0-253-33807-7, £37.95/US$49.95; PB ISBN 0-253-21617-6, US$29.95

Karin Barber has given us a series of works concerned with popular theatre in West Africa (see also Karin Barber (ed.) *Readings in African Popular Culture*, James Currey and Indiana University Press, 1997; and Karin Barber, John Collins and Alain Ricard, *West African Popular Theatre*, Indiana University Press, 1997), but this must be her greatest labour of love to date. *The Generation of Plays* is a meticulously detailed history of the Oyin Adejobi Theatre, as well as a guide to life with, and examination of play creation by, the company. The text follows the company from its beginnings as an amateur, biblical musical theatre group in 1953, through its professional existence dominated by secular dialogue drama from 1963 to 1988, and on to the most recent work in video production. However the most in-depth examination of play 'generation' to use Barber's own term – covers the period between 1981 and 1984, when the author spent considerable amounts of time on tour and performing with the company.

The result is a unique elucidation of the life of a popular theatre company, from the perspective of one who became an occasional member of the group, and who relishes using extensive direct quotes from company members. The reader is consequently challenged to move beyond the usual Eurocentric dismissal of much popular African theatre as 'mere' entertainment, and to look at the work produced on its own terms from within the Yoruba artisanal context which Barber takes such pains to establish.

The Generation of Plays begins with a most useful history, in chapters one and two, not only of the owner of the company, Oyin Adejobi himself, and his theatrical development, but also of how Yoruba popular theatre came into existence, flourished (or 'effloresced' as Barber rather unfortunately terms it in her early chapters), and was then eclipsed in the 1990s as the economy collapsed, street violence became endemic, and people turned from public performance to watching videos at home.

Chapter three looks at the actors in the company, using extensive interview material.

Here a picture is built up of a company of concentric rings of influence. Oyin Adejobi remains central. His voice and ability to compose musical drama enabled the founding of the company, along with his relatively superior educational status. However, as secular improvised drama gained the ascendancy, the company became increasingly dependent on the theatrical artistry of manager Alhaji Karimu Adepoju, with his ability to create a play out of the stories written by Adejobi, and his immense versatility as an actor. As has been evidenced in much research into African theatre, the status of acting as a profession is low, and like others such as the most famous of Nigerian popular theatre managers, Hubert Ogunde, Adejobi was forced, against his Christian inclinations, to marry a number of wives to provide actresses for his company. What is fascinating is the actors' own repeated belief that they are teachers and preachers of morality through their work.

Chapters four, five, six and seven describe the process of play making and touring. The enormous effort and financial precariousness of the enterprise are evident, but most interesting is the insider view on just how plays are 'generated'. Alhaji provides a vision of the play and coaches the actors according to their level of experience. However, these plays are by no means fixed. Barber takes us in detail through the evolution of *Besotted Bridegroom*, a play she often featured in. We see how actors constantly adapt the parts, responding to audience interest. Moreover, the company has no difficulty in slotting Barber or other occasional performers into roles as they become available, and all core actors are able to substitute for each other. Barber has tremendous admiration for the professionalism and skill of the company. I was particularly interested to recognise some strong similarities of acting style, across a whole continent, between the Adejobi company and popular theatre troupes whose work I have witnessed in Tanzania. Perhaps a next step for this kind of insider academic research into popular performance is to try to move on to more comparative studies.

Despite their ambivalence regarding the status of professional actors, the members of the audience confirm Adejobi's actors' belief that popular theatre is seen, crucially, as educational. These moral plays apparently offer distinct lessons for particular types of people, on which audience members say they will act, believing that they can learn from the 'experience' shown in the plays. We also see how characters are determined not by individual introspection, but by a very different worldview, which values particular roles, status, aspiration and a belief system that actively includes concepts of destiny, divine will and the malign influence of evil wishing.

Further chapters examine issues such as gender, politics, work, literacy, language and morality. Many of these topics have been touched on earlier, but through Barber's use of interviews, extensive excerpts from plays – in both Yoruba and an English translation – and the technique of approaching a subject from several different angles, an immensely strong picture emerges of the worldview of the Yoruba artisan class that both made up the company and provided its audiences. We experience the longing for education and self-improvement amongst these people situated in a strong, albeit often conservative, morality, a conjunction which Barber describes as a desire for 'enlightenment'. As I read these chapters I could not help thinking of the workers' improvement societies of the British industrial age, though Barber as an exacting cultural anthropologist would never allow one to make simple parallels. The drive to be one's own master and the religious mix of Islam, Christianity and pre-existing religious beliefs provide some very different aspects in the matrix.

Filtering through this book is Barber's love of the Yoruba language. She has particular admiration for the actors' command of 'deep' Yoruba, using the language in all its complex richness, and she frequently quotes audience members who also revere such skill. For Yoruba speakers I am sure this text, with its extensive quotations using 'Yoruba scholarly "best practice"' in the rendering of tone marks, will have an added value, sadly not available to me.

What is most refreshing, and indeed challenging to disciplines such as postcolonial literary studies, is Karin Barber's insistence on viewing this theatre from inside. Inside not only the company, but even more centrally inside Yoruba culture as a whole. This is a confident culture. It has indeed 'borrowed' from Western ideas, as well as from its own precolonial past, but Barber rejects the notion of therefore calling it a 'hybrid' culture. Rather, she insists it is 'modern', and consistently demonstrates its confidence, at least until the collapse of the economy in the 1980s, in its own value judgements. Barber's approach to cultural and performance study requires a deep commitment of time and open-mindedness. The dividends it pays are everywhere evident in this book, which constantly supplies fascinating insights into Yoruba culture as well as the Oyin Adejobi Theatre. Rather than negotiating mainstream cultural or literary theory in any obvious way, Karin Barber consistently tries to name the experience with the Oyin Adejobi Company in ways which seem truthful to her. Hence we have the 'generation' of plays, a particular sense of 'enlightenment', and a particular consciousness of what constitutes a 'modern' society.

The single significant question I have about Barber's 'insider' approach to this text relates to her apparent reluctance to make any negative judgements whatsoever in relation to Yoruba popular theatre and culture. Her love and admiration of many aspects of the company's work come shining off the page, but criticism is much more tentative. Reluctantly she confesses that she doesn't actually like *Besotted Bridegroom*, a play central to much of her analysis, and we come to see that slapstick horseplay is probably one of her least-favourite aspects of this kind of theatre. However, this is as far as personal criticism goes. I quite see that Barber is seeking to elucidate the worldview of the actors and audiences of popular theatre, but she skirts the issue of a plethora of plays – my experience of popular theatre in other African nations readily suggests further examples – that condemn women who don't know their proper, submissive place. This is symptomatic of an approach that celebrates the positive wonderfully, but seems uneasy about how to deal with less appealing aspects of this popular culture.

This is a big book, packed with detail and a sheaf of helpful photographs. *The Generation of Plays* is a superb and unique resource for learning about all aspects of Nigeria's once-vibrant, now sadly eclipsed Yoruba popular theatre. Karin Barber remains a leader in a slowly growing movement of researchers who wish to move beyond libraries and constricting postcolonial theorising to study African performance forms on their own terms and in *situ*. More power to their pens.

Jane Plastow
University of Leeds

Catherine M. Cole, *Ghana's Concert Party Theatre*
Bloomington: Indiana University Press, 2001, 208 pp.
HB ISBN 0-253-33845-X US$52.95; PB ISBN 0-253-21436-X US$21.95

West Africa in the colonial period was a hotbed of cultural innovation. People adapted existing genres and invented new ones in response to the emergence of new, wage-earning, urbanised publics. Popular fiction in English and in African languages proliferated, often in the form of thin pamphlets printed by local presses. New styles of popular music – palmwine music, highlife, *juju* – spread all over the region. Radically new styles of visual art – figurative, 'realist' and two-dimensional – were pioneered in commercial centres where such images supplied both advertising and ambience for hotels, bars and businesses. Theatre was one of the most spectacularly creative and expansive genres of this period. And among popular theatre genres, Ghanaian Concert Party was one of the earliest to be established, having its inception in late nineteenth-century music-hall-style entertainments in the culturally hybrid coastal towns. It was also one of the most dynamic and vibrant forms, going through rapid stylistic and thematic transformations as it spread, travelled the whole country, and became a professional, commercial and wildly popular phenomenon that is still going strong today.

Concert Party in the colonial and early post-independence period has been relatively well documented. Efua Sutherland's brief biography of Bob Johnson, one of the founders of the genre, was followed by a longer study by K. N. Bame and numerous books and articles by John Collins. The Togolese variant, which had its origins in Ghanaian Concert Party, has been brilliantly covered by Alain Ricard. Between them, these scholars have mapped out the history of the genre, described the theatre companies' organisation and mode of operation, documented the principal themes, characters and plots, supplied a number of synopses and several more-or-less complete transcribed play texts, and evoked audience reactions. But Catherine Cole's book shows how much more there is still to be said. In the first place, she adds a wealth of new material to the existing documentation. Her excellent research, based on newspaper archives as well as participant observation and personal interviews with elderly practitioners of the genre, has been able to correct the record and fill out the picture at numerous points. She penetrates further into the early history of the genre than anyone has previously, providing valuable information about the composition of early audiences and their attitudes to the concerts. More importantly, she brings to the material an imaginative and acutely questioning approach. She seeks to understand the Concert Party as a historical product of its time, but also to uncover its role as an active agent in the formulation and dissemination of new ideas and experiences, that is, as a participant in the construction of a peculiarly West African 'modernity'. She argues that Concert Party was a 'forum for the creation, dissemination and contestation of identities among Ghanaians in the colonial and early postcolonial eras', helping Ghanaians to 'reinvent modernity with a critical difference' (p. 6).

Her approach is interdisciplinary, bringing a performance studies perspective to bear on a historical narrative. This enables her to engage with questions of identity and modernity from a fresh angle. She argues that identity is not forged only at the level of ideas. Identities are performed, and discovered or consolidated in the performance: 'embodied knowledge and behaviours were central to the transmission and formation of new subjectivities in colonial Ghana' (pp. 36–7). Ghanaian Concert Party, then, should not be reduced to texts from which ideas about identity and modernity can be read off. Rather, the emergence of new identities can only be coaxed out from the history through an approach sensitive to the nature of Concert Party performance. Her questions begin from her own personal interests, assumptions and standpoint, which she is then able to modify in the light of her discoveries. As an American, she was initially puzzled by Concert Party actors' use of blackface, assuming that it had the same pejorative significance as in the American vaudeville from which it was borrowed. But Ghanaians dismissed the obvious racial overtones of blackface as irrelevant, and further questioning led her to believe that wearing this make-up was in fact an 'embodied performance of African American identity', undertaken in a spirit of emulation rather than contempt.

She goes on to pursue the questions of identity, modernity and performance in a series of chapters framed by a chronological history of the Concert Party through three main phases: its phase as a vaudeville style entertainment known as 'concert', 1895–1927; its development of a stylised format, originally involving three actors and therefore dubbed the 'trio' phase, 1927–45; and its post-war expansion into elaborate musical dramas performed by a greatly enlarged company known as the 'troupe', 1944–65. This is a story of colonialism 'seen from below', or rather seen from the uneasy intermediate position below the élite but above the illiterate majority. Concert Party made possible the simultaneous aspiration to, and hilarious ridiculing of, Western 'civilisation'. It made it possible to appropriate imported novelties but also to give them a local twist: 'Imported, but we have put in African culture' one Concert Party actor told Cole, making a gesture of slipping something into an envelope (p. 108). Attentively and astutely, Cole picks up on such phrases and gestures in order to disclose the changing modes of invention and styles of signification in Concert Party performances. Her discussion of the improvisatory mode by which theatrical elements are assembled and combined leads into an interpretation of the 'lady impersonators' of Concert Party – not just as a statement about gender, but rather as a way of highlighting the gap between circumscribed colonially created roles and the African people who tried to fill them. What emerges is an embodied statement about race, class and ethnicity as well as gender – that is seen in all theatrical roles, not just those of the female characters. She concludes that 'by imitating and exaggerating colonial stereotypes, Concert Party drag revealed the imitative structure of colonialism itself, as well as its contingency' (p. 129). And her last chapter, on the post-war Concert Party, is a *tour de force*, linking the new 'disjunctive, topsy-turvy style that concerts developed in the post-war years' (p. 134) with the expanding popular social imaginary of Ghana as a national and international entity.

Historians may have minor qualms about her preference for present-day testimony over archival material. This is in part necessitated by the thinness of the archival record. The present-day enactments and memories of old Concert Party practitioners do yield a far richer haul than the scanty and enigmatic newspaper reports of the first half of the twentieth century. But Cole is also suspicious of written records on principle, seeing them as imbued with the political privilege accorded them by colonial authority. She affirms that the living testimony of performers and performances in the present may offer a truer insight into the history and meaning of Concert Party. 'One could argue', she says, 'that the methodology of historical performance ethnography has much more veracity and persuasiveness than the written archive' (p. 150). She argues this point well, and one can see what she means. But presented with one indubitably valuable historical source – not a written archive but a collection of five sound recordings of complete Concert Party performances, made by the Institute of African Studies in 1961, when the 'troupe' style of Concert Party had reached its full flowering – she makes relatively little use of it. Yet, as she observes herself, this material is rich enough to support an entire book in itself. And it has a further and more important claim on our attention: however incomplete it may be as a record, it does face you with the irreducible alienness and awkwardness of the past, not yet smoothed over and edited by the subsequent operations of selective memory.

Having stated my one reservation, I now want to blow a fanfare of trumpets to welcome this book. It is a sheer delight to read – succinct, deft and light of touch. It is full of ideas and insights. And it is accompanied by a marvellous video, made by Catherine Cole and Kwame Braun. This provides a rich photographic collage to accompany the historical narrative, and also presents interviews with practitioners and extensive excerpts from present-day Concert Party performance – including a brief delightful appearance in one show by Cole herself, making a moral speech in Twi. Nothing like this has previously been available. It will be a godsend for teachers, a huge pleasure for interested readers, and an excellent accompaniment to a bright, accessible yet original and thoughtful book.

Karin Barber
Centre of West African Studies
University of Birmingham

Eckhard Breitinger and Yvette Hutchison, (eds), *History and Theatre in Africa*
Bayreuth: Bayreuth African Studies/ *South African Theatre Journal*, 2000, 191 pp.
ISBN 3-92751063-7 US$14.99

The articles, essays, reports, play text and photographs that make up this book constitute a delectable feast of impressive theatre scholarship, critical commentary on some contemporary playwrights, and documentation of significant events and trends in African theatre and performance. The feast is overcooked in some parts and a bit undercooked or even raw in others, but the ambitious scope of the whole undertaking is undeniable. From the book's title and the range of items it collects, this may be described as history's challenge to theatre and theatre's negotiation of that challenge in a continent where both history and theatre have been the object of intense intellectual and ideological controversies, making them veritable minefields for both professional practitioners and amateur enthusiasts. Because the book is a joint venture of the Bayreuth African Studies monograph series and the *South African Theatre Journal* (and indeed constitutes Volume 13, numbers 1 and 2 of the latter), the theory and practice of theatre and theatre scholarship and criticism in Southern Africa dominate the contents of the volume and are made to stand for the rest of the continent somewhat in the exploration of its ambitious topic. The editorial by Eckhard Breitinger (who is also, as everyone knows, the publisher of the Bayreuth African Studies series) bravely attempts to trim the enormity of this topic to size by drawing upon both old and new stratagems. The 'old' in this case involves breaking down this topic into the familiar division between discourses on Africa which are either Eurocentric or Africa-centred. In effect, this entails, in the pieces gathered in the book, a consistently explicit, almost predictable critique of the former and a qualified, even critical recuperation of the latter. As for the 'new' tactic deployed by

Breitinger to make the complex articulations between 'history' and 'theatre' in Africa intelligible – or even productive and empowering – his recourse here is to New Historicist ideas that are not exactly new any longer, whether in the field of Africanist historiography or in African theatre scholarship and criticism. By the light of this New Historicist theoretical grid, Breitinger conceives of history as being no less imagined, no less 'invented' than theatre. The rationale of this particular theoretical frame for the extremely varied and qualitatively uneven contents of the book seems to be a qualified progressivist view of the articulations between 'history' and 'theatre' in a continent in which neither the realities nor the portents conduce to unqualified optimism. Thus it is that in an effort to provide a grounding for this optimism, Breitinger makes pointed allusions to the recent historic transitions to democracy in Eastern Europe and South Africa. But in an apparent attempt to 'play it safe', he ends his argument by drawing attention only to those articles and essays in the book that deal with artistic engagement of especially difficult or intractable areas of recent or contemporary African history and society, such as the Truth and Reconciliation Commission in South Africa or, more generally, perplexities surrounding what 'politics' in art and culture ought to be, or mean, in post-apartheid Southern Africa and the rest of the continent.

Since the value of this book resides primarily in the range of materials it has brought together, it is perhaps useful to give a brief overview of these pieces before concluding this short review with a general commentary on the overall strengths and shortcomings of the book. There are outstanding pieces of theatre scholarship and criticism in this collection, pieces in which the general topic of the book – the articulation between history and theatre – receives, in one way or another, insightful or penetrating treatment. These are an essay by Geoffrey V. Davis on how South African dramatists have responded to the searing 'truths' which emerged from testimonies at the Truth and Reconciliation Commission; an engrossing account by Christine Matzke of folk forms of dance and their artistic appropriations in Eritrea, deftly combining feminist and New Historicist methodologies of theatre ethnography; a report by David Kerr on a theatre-for-development dramatic enactment in Botswana that probed generations and histories of ecological and social betrayal of subaltern groups and classes by the country's political and commercial élite, especially in the cattle industry; and an essay by Yvette Hutchison on the interface between myth and history in the treatment of the Moremi legend in the work of the classical Yoruba ethnohistorian, Samuel Johnson, and dramatists Duro Ladipo and Femi Osofisan. The merit of these contributions alone would make this book an indispensable item for teachers and students of African drama and theatre. But there are a few other noteworthy pieces in the book as well. Of these, I would make special mention of an interview with the late Ugandan playwright, actress and theatre scholar, Rose Mbowa, by Carol Sicherman on the use of theatre for AIDS education in Uganda, and an essay by Dennis Walder calling for 'new bearings' in African theatre criticism in the post-apartheid period through a brief, exemplary analysis of Athol Fugard's most neglected play, *Dimetos*. I know of very few other accounts of cultural and artistic work on the AIDS pandemic in Africa that display as much knowledge, insight and humanity as Rose Mbowa's observations and reflections in this interview. Dennis Walder is, of course, one of the leading authorities on the work of Athol Fugard and in this essay, he is in characteristic top form in making a compelling case for not ignoring plays like *Dimetos* that are 'non-political' but probe 'interior landscapes': such works have much to teach us in a postcolonial and post-apartheid era in which the 'political' has become infinitely more complex than the simple binaries of coloniser and colonised, oppressor and oppressed of the past. Walder's reading of *Dimetos* inexplicably leaves out aspects of the play that are, at the very least, *epiphenomenally* political – Dimetos's flight from the city as a form of individual protest against the human and social alienations of modern urbanism; and his ambiguous relationships with the villagers of the rural community to which he has fled, these being clearly marked as subaltern, 'racial' Others. But Walder is right both in his reading of the play as basically 'non-political', especially when contrasted with the world-famous 'political' plays of Fugard, and in suggesting that we will have to pay more attention to such plays in the present period.

I'm afraid I also have to report mixed feelings about some of the other pieces in this book, as well as grave misgivings about some shoddy editorial features and decisions. George Taylor's essay on anti-slavery dramas and other performances on the stage of late eighteenth-century Britain in the heyday of British abolitionism promises much but delivers little by way of a theoretical account of why most of these performances combined ardent abolitionism with openly imperialist patriotism to produce racist stereotyping of blacks that would lead later to the enduring caricatures of blackface minstrelsy; Christopher Innes's discussion of the work of the African-American playwright, Le Suzan-Lori Parks, is eloquent on her powerful dramaturgic deconstructions of the racial essentialisms and ideological absolutism of the radical or nationalist black theatre of some of Parks's predecessors, but Innes is completely blind to the self-promoting postmodernist fundamentalism of Parks's essays and interviews; and Kenneth Bain's report on the 25th Grahamstown National Arts Festival, the *premier* annual event of the South African cultural calendar, is long, very long, on sentimental musings about the role of the arts in the new millennium, but short, very short, on genuinely critical insights into this important topic.

Because there is so much valuable and noteworthy material in this book, I think most readers will readily forgive its countless awkward, and sometimes unintentionally funny typographical errors (such as when, again and again in one article, 'inferior' is substituted for 'interior', and 'infernal' for 'internal'). And I'll say that for me, it was a perversely pleasurable discovery to find that the best articles and essays in the book had the fewest such errors! Typographical pitfalls aside, it was an editorial decision unjustifiable on any count to publish Paul Oyema Onovoh's play text, *Ebubedike – a Drama in Five Acts,* in all its rawness of form and awkwardness of execution: language and dialogue that are marred by an overstrenuous and often inept attempt to sound idiomatically pastoral and folkloric; moral obtuseness in a play which is heavily moralizing; a callow and gratuitous misogyny; and, at an elementary level of playwriting, stage directions frequently out of grammatical and rhetorical accord with the text of the dramatic action. In this particular case, the myriad of misprints and typographical errors that run through many of the pieces in the book seem to find an objective correlative in the misshapen play. These are admittedly bracing words to address to a playwright who is perhaps untried and untested, but they are justified by what I take to be a basic editorial abdication. For on the evidence of this play, which is about a folk hero who successfully challenges corrupt, divisive and destabilising ethnic and regionalist politics in contemporary Nigeria, Onovoh does have talent. The play, with all its flaws, has flashes of an earthy knowledge of traditional folkways; it evinces imaginative inventiveness and demonstrates that its author has a genuine passion for social justice. With a lot of improvement in technique and craft, Onovoh will probably produce good work. It is therefore a great disservice to him – and to the readers of this volume – to have published this play text without giving sound advice to the young playwright to 'clean up' at least the most egregious of these flaws.

Because the flaws of Onovoh's play are not, in the end, permanently damaging, I think they are not only rectifiable but also forgivable. This is equally true of *History and Theatre in Africa*: despite all the typographical and editorial solecisms noted above, it is a remarkable contribution to the growing scholarship and criticism on African theatre.

Biodun Jeyifo
Cornell University

Frank Gunderson and Gregory Barz (eds), *Mashindano! Competitive Music Performance in East Africa*
Dar es Salaam: Mkuki na Nyota Publishers, 2000, 480 pp.
distributed by African Books Collective
ISBN 9976-973-82-9, £26.95/US$44.95

I should begin this review with a declaration of interest. Nearly forty years ago I began research on the Beni dance associations of eastern Africa, nearly thirty-five years ago I published *Dance and Society in Eastern Africa* (London: Heinemann Educational, 1975). At that time it was a very isolated book, making little sense in the context of the nationalist or socialist historiography of Tanzania. *Mashindano* emerges from a panel at the 1997 Society for Ethnomusicology conference which 'revisited' my book. I was invited to write a foreword to the volume which resulted and which abundantly shows that work on East African competitive dance is no longer a lonely business. The book contains no fewer than 21 chapters and makes reference to many more studies. Naturally, I was delighted to be asked to preface such an outpouring of research and, naturally, I shall continue to express my delight in this review.

Frank Gunderson in his Introduction links this outpouring to socio-economic change, particularly in Tanzania.

> Since economic liberalisation and multiparty politics have made headway in Tanzania, there has been an expansion of research activity on previously neglected issues pertaining to cultural expression. This has allowed writers to take up discussions of questions such as those posed by Ranger once again, (p.9).

The relation of dance competitions to society and economics is taken up repeatedly by contributors to the book. Some see a natural affinity between competition in the field of culture and in the field of entrepreneurship. In their chapter on Kiswahili Rap, Peter John Haas and Thomas Gesthuizen quote the rapper, Dolla Soul: 'Go ahead. To do anything you want, Tanzania is open. And the truth is not a lie in Tanzania' (p. 281). But other authors find that new possibilities of enterprise and display of wealth reduce men's interest in extravagant dance competition; or that the immiseration of the poorest makes it impossible for them to participate in contests; or that the expansion of radio and television takes away the audience for *ngoma* performances. The variety of relationships between *ngoma*, politics and economics, in short, is at least as great as in the colonial – or as in the relatively unexamined socialist – period. But academic fashions as well as 'liberalised' economies make it more possible now to use competitive dance as 'an essential decoder of Swahili' – and inland – society. (p. 53)

Many of the chapters take up directly or indirectly the question of whether competitive dance is particularly Swahili. Eight of the 21 deal with Swahili society – in Dar es Salaam, Tanga, Lamu, Zanzibar. These do not ask whether their rich analysis might be applied elsewhere but their demonstration of how *ngoma* decodes ethnicity, race, class, gender, perversity and morality takes for granted the fit between competitive dance and Swahili culture. In these chapters we are offered lengthy song texts amply illustrating the tensions between Swahili notions of dignity and respect and the alarming freedoms of song, with a particular emphasis on insults alleging homosexual or lesbian abnormality. (*Ngoma* texts would be a wonderful source for the new literature on African sexuality.)

Other chapters deal with various inland societies. Some of those which find a pre-colonial competitive dance tradition are dealing with well-known exceptional cases, as in Kezilahabi's treatment of the Bakarebe. Others achieve their effect by extending the definition of *ngoma*, as in Peter Pels's fascinating chapter on traditional, Islamic and Christian initiation rituals in the Uluguru mountains. Pels's definition of *ngoma* is that 'in all its senses it means the embodied – danced, drummed, or otherwise performed – change in the rhythm of life that metonymically connects different states of being' (p. 101). The two chapters which most systematically discuss the question of whether competitive dance is intrinsic to inland traditions or spread inland from the Swahili both deal with the shores of Lake Malawi – James Ellison on 'the Nyakusa' and Lisa Gilman on the 'Tonga' of Nkhata Bay. (I place the ethnic names in inverted commas because it seems likely that competitive dance did not so much reflect tribal identity as help to constitute it.)

Gilman's chapter addresses another big question – whether competitive dance societies are characteristic only of East Africa or whether they extend to Southern Africa as well. Gilman thinks they probably do. Like other authors in the volume she believes that Ngoni warrior groups brought military style dance with them when they came north from southern Africa. The Ngoni thus offer an alternative possible source for drill dances to the European military mode as mediated by the Swahili. She also adduces a variety of other southern African dances. I don't find these convincing. Southern African scholarship has been as much influenced by the cultural trend as East African, and there are recent studies of landscape, identity, sexuality, praise poem and so on. But I do not think it is possible to conceive a volume like this one by southern African scholars. John Janzen, who *has* written a book about *ngoma* in both East and Southern Africa, achieved this by extending its definition yet further to most kinds of healing associations (*Ngoma: Discourses of Healing in Central and Southern Africa*, Berkeley, 1992).

This splendid book, then, illuminates East Africa in general and Tanzania in particular (16 of the chapters deal with the latter). Unlike my own *Dance and Society*, it contains many song texts. Like it, though, it does not contain photographs. The performance dynamics of these dances and songs are spelt out in prose – often very evocative and vivid prose. Maybe a second edition will include a video cassette! Meanwhile this is a marvellous introduction to competitive 'music performance'. It is certainly not only a book for the specialist musicologist – its contributors include historians, anthropologists, students of literature, etcetera. Nor is it a book only for East Africanists. It is accessible to anyone interested in public dance, dialogue and drama and their relations with culture and society.

Terence Ranger
St Antony's College, Oxford

Albert Wertheim, *The Dramatic Art of Athol Fugard: From South Africa to the World*
Bloomington and Indianapolis: Indiana University Press, 2000, 288 pp.
HB ISBN 0-253-33823-9, US$45.00; PB ISBN 0-253-21504-8 US$17.95

When Athol Fugard's *The Island* appeared at the National Theatre in London last year
with its two co-creators John Kani and Winston Ntshona, the *Sunday Times*'s John Peter
exclaimed:

> Who says that such plays are dated? Apartheid is gone but history is alive, the past
> lives in the present. This play belongs with Primo Levi's *If This is a Man*,
> Solzhenitsyn's *The First Circle*, Louis Malle's *Au Revoir les Enfants* and Dorfman's
> *Death and the Maiden*: great works of art that also bear witness to the darkest nights of
> the century with the precision of a documentary.

It is astonishing to think that Albert Wertheim's book is only the third substantial study
of the work of this most prolific and important playwright, a man whose achievement
stands head and shoulders above that of most of his contemporaries. My own Macmillan
Modern Dramatists book, *Athol Fugard* (1984) was followed by Russell Vanden-
broucke's *Truths the Hand Can Touch* (1985), but since then, apart from Stephen Gray's
1984 anthology of views, reviews, interviews and critical essays for McGraw-Hill's
Southern African Literature Series, there has been nothing remotely approaching
Wertheim for scale or ambition, and he should be congratulated for having the energy,
determination and vision to offer this account of the whole range of Fugard's plays over
forty years (Fugard's latest, *Sorrows and Rejoicings*, is too recent for Wertheim's cut-off
date).

The main bibliography of Fugard studies, compiled by John Read for the National
English Literary Museum, Grahamstown, in 1991, runs to over three thousand entries,
yet hardly any critics or scholars have attempted to look at the playwright's rapidly
growing oeuvre whole. Several thesis writers have made the effort – one of whom, Jerry
Dickey, wrote an Indiana PhD on Camus's influence upon Fugard, and another,
Margarete Seidenspinner, had her *Exploring the Labyrinth: Athol Fugard's Approach to
South African Drama* published in Essen's 'Die Blaue Eule' series. And there have been
some brave attempts to come to terms with Fugard in the course of books written with
a larger agenda, such as Martin Orkin's excellent *Drama and the South African State* (1991)
and Loren Krueger's *The Drama of South Africa* (1999) – both strongly influenced by
their authors' broadly cultural-materialist, left-leaning approaches.

Not for Wertheim any such politics, however. He has been interested in the playwright for over two decades, but that interest – as earlier essays on individual plays
indicate – has been fuelled by a fundamental assumption that their art is separable from
their politics. 'It is, after all, possible to admire the playwright's art in Shakespeare's *Julius
Caesar* without rejecting that play for its anti-democratic and élitist thrust' (p. xii).
Leaving aside whether or not Shakespeare's play really is anti-democratic and élitist (that
is not how Nelson Mandela and other ANC Shakespeare enthusiasts read it on Robben
Island, nor all those of us who find in the Bard's work a more complex view of life), this
seems rather a limited way to set out to analyse the work of a playwright whose aim, as
Fugard himself has often stated, has been to bear witness to the lives of the discarded and
disinherited, to 'break the conspiracy of silence' which affected the majority of the
people of South Africa. Has Fugard failed in this self-imposed task? I do not think so –
and, fortunately for his book, Wertheim in practice allows the political thrust of many of

the plays to touch him, even at times to inform his discussion, while hammering those of us whose 'political correctness' (oh fatal cliché), he says, blinds us to the transcendental truths he claims to find.

Wertheim's method is to proceed chronologically, by means of extensive summaries: from the early Sophiatown plays *No-Good Friday* and *Nongogo*, through the 'Port Elizabeth Plays' such as *Hello and Goodbye* and *Boesman and Lena*, to the 'Acting Against Apartheid' of *Sizwe Bansi* and *The Island*; followed by chapters on *Dimetos* ('Fugard's First Problem Play'), 'Teaching and Learning' in *A Lesson from Aloes* and what he calls Fugard's 'masterpiece' (p. 136), *'Master Harold' ... and the Boys*; then there is a chapter on 'Other Problem Plays' such as *The Road to Mecca*; followed by an account of the 'eloquent record' of Fugard's 'adjustment to change' (p. 177) which begins with *My Children! My Africa!* and ends with *Valley Song*; concluding with the 'new departure' (p. 226) signalled by Fugard's much-criticised theatrical memoir, *The Captain's Tiger*. Wertheim's emphasis upon how the plays work on stage serves his view that for Fugard, theatre is a metaphor for life (p. 58), and acting the 'very essence' of being human (p. 89). His sense of the varying shape of Fugard's plays, their obsessive yet subtle articulation of relationships between individuals, is convincing, if not always compelling. He is at his best in his account of works that have been neglected or downgraded for their lack of familiar local textures and socio-political urgency, plays such as *Dimetos* and *A Place with the Pigs*, whose esoteric and parabolic overtones Wertheim effectively teases out to reveal the personal dynamic underlying their creation.

As Wertheim suggests, there may be something of the feel of Shakespeare's late romances about such plays, as there is in Fugard's most recent writing, which centres on the consciously self-questioning, nostalgic representation of the artist. But *Dimetos* is not *The Tempest*, much less *King Lear*, with which it is also compared. While intended to raise the terms of evaluation to the highest, indeed to a 'universal' level, such comparisons have the opposite effect, of diminishing the plays in such a large perspective. Surely Fugard's achievement does not require such comparisons? Wouldn't a more balanced view serve him as well – or better? Over-statement is rife: from Matisse to Milton, a whole panoply of worthies are invoked to justify dealing in detail with even such weaker plays as *A Lesson from Aloes*, which Wertheim approves of because, apparently like *'Master Harold'* and *Playland*, it shows that 'whites are possibly the greatest victims of the apartheid they have called into being' (p. 50) – a remark which indicates the dangers of trying to avoid 'politics', while in fact invoking your own.

It is surely not difficult to admit that even Fugard nods, and while Beckett and Brecht are reasonably brought into the discussion, since their influence is everywhere manifest, it is misleading to infer Shakespearean standards of depth and complexity for a playwright whose acknowledged influences could have been perhaps more usefully related (especially for the American audience of this book) to his South African context of black performance and cultural hybridity.

Not that Wertheim's acute responsiveness to many of the later plays is in doubt. His overall reading of *'Master Harold'* as a drama in which dreams and dancing struggle to overcome physical brutality and humiliation, thereby signifying 'the oscillation between hope and despair' that marks the characters, Fugard himself, and South Africa (p. 151), is nuanced and persuasive; as is his account of *Valley Song*, which he describes as Fugard's 'first proper post-apartheid play', 'deceptively simple' in being a mere two-hander with three characters, yet conveying through its 'impressive and significant' blurring of roles between white playwright and coloured character a 'fluidity' that takes us beyond the 'tragic and existential lessons' of the earlier plays, towards a 'comedic and optimistic'

vision of the new freedoms Fugard finds both in himself as an artist and in the young
people embodied in the play's naïve heroine, Veronica (pp. 212–13).

Wertheim has evidently done his research, and makes good use of such unexpected
sources as Sheila Fugard's poetry to inflect his discussion. As it happens, he is also now in
the fortunate position of having the Fugard archive's new home next door in Indiana's
Lilly Library. While he has used the holograph versions and rehearsal notes of several of
the plays to inform his discussion – pointing out, for instance, how the typescript of
Dimetos includes an illustration of the pulleys that provide the play's symbolic underpinning – his scholarship does not extend to using the best texts of all the plays. Thus he
quotes at length from the three plays printed (with errors) in *Dimetos and Two Early Plays*
(1977), rather than the two later Oxford University Press volumes for which they were
checked and collected; and he talks about *The Blood Knot* on the basis of the 1978
edition, while Fugard himself authorised substantial cuts (up to a third of the text) for
the most commonly performed version of the play, reprinted in OUP's *Port Elizabeth
Plays* (1987, 2000). Smaller errors, such as 'Middleburg' for Middelburg, 'Sophia Town'
for Sophiatown and 'Van Rendsburg' for van Rensburg, or mis-identifying Philander's
quotation from James Hutton in *Statements after an Arrest* hardly bear noting, but may
have been produced by reliance upon the wrong texts.

In short, this new book on Athol Fugard's drama is a welcome and overdue contribution to Fugard studies, although it highlights some of the problems of adopting a
rather uncritical, supposedly apolitical agenda.

Dennis Walder
Department of Literature, Open University

Alain Ricard, *Ebrahim Hussein: Swahili Theatre and Individualism*
Dar es Salaam, Mkuki na Nyota Publishers, 2000, 160 pp.
Dsitributed by African Books Collective
ISBN 9976973810, $14.95/£8.95

Nyambura Mpesha, *Mugasha: Epic of the Bahaya*
Nairobi, Kampala, Dar es Salaam, East African Educational Publishers, 2000, 77 pp.
Dsitributed by African Books Collective
ISBN 9966250646, $8.95/£4.95

When African theatre is discussed, especially outside Africa, more often than not contributions from East Africa provide limited input. The plays of Ngugi wa Thiong'o or
John Ruganda might come into the discussion as the region's representatives. Ebrahim
Hussein, one of Africa's most important playwrights and East Africa's leading one, is
little known outside the region and thus hardly informs such discussions. Alain Ricard's
Ebrahim Hussein: Swahili Literature and Individualism is, therefore, not only a welcome
contribution to African theatre studies but also brings much-needed attention to this
Tanzanian writer and poet who most outsiders might have met only through various
dissertations and theses written in English. Hussein's inaccessibility to outsiders is partly
because he writes in *Kiswahili* and partly because translation of his works has been
limited to French, Japanese, German texts (and only one in English). Ricard, however,
provides another reason when he asks, 'Why in all the French and English writings on

Tanzania is there so little interest in literature in general and Ebrahim's work in particular?' The theatre has never shared the enthusiasm shown to the other Tanzanian sectors.

The book gives us Hussein as a man, his work and environment. Ricard presents the playwright as living simply and in isolation in the middle of Dar es Salaam. We follow him and Ricard as they pass Ebrahim's familiar and sometimes historic places on the way to his favourite coffee haunts. As an observant and keen tourist, Ricard entertains the reader while providing information on Ebrahim's city through his journal entries from 1995 and 1997 visits, reproduced in the book. The book reconstructs Ebrahim's ancestral places including Kilwa where he was born and from where his religious and cultural heritage can be traced (Hussein, however, was reluctant to visit this town with the writer). Ricard patiently shades in not only Hussein's family background but also the Swahili and other popular performance traditions with which he was familiar, his academic experiences and the influence of Brecht on the writer's work. A short comparison with other East African playwrights such as Ngugi wa Thiong'o and John Ruganda contextualises Hussein's ideas on theatre and his critical reflections on notions of theatre 'based on an integrated vision of African society'(p. 30) without excluding ritual as a separate phenomenon. It is in the discussion of Hussein's oeuvre within its own cultural milieux, however, that Ricard provides his best insights into the writer's work. It is here that Ricard displays his vast literary and theatre experience, both African and European, to frame his discussion on Hussein.

Even though Ricard's analysis is informed by generalized theoretical and philosophical readings of history, culture and art, he tries to focus more on setting his presentation of Hussein's oeuvre against popular political and theoretical issues and debates on Tanzania's developmental issues, especially *Ujamaa* (socialism). Just as important are issues of identity generally and specifically what Ricard sees as a changing Swahili identity (p. 79). Ricard sees Hussein expressing the problem of multiple and divided identities in *Drums and Violins*, in the same way that Gabriel Okara expressed these issues in *Piano and Drums*. Ricard shows how Hussein moves from a simple to a more complex dramaturgy, progressively displaying deeper metaphysical sensibilities. One major factor that Ricard highlights for the first time is Hussein's use of geographical elements as important character and thematic features. Geographical symbolism is used to posit conflicts, identities and relationships through the use of water, lakes, mountains, forests, the hinterland and the coast in contrasting ensembles. Ricard argues that Hussein's complex oeuvre needs to be understood through looking at his plays as a continuum rather than individually, as most of Hussein's critics have done so far. The most important of these plays include *Kinjeketile*, which focuses on the *Maji Maji* wars and its leader (this play is so far the only one translated into English by the author); *Mashètani* (Demons); *Arusi* (Wedding); *Kwenye Ukingo wa Thim* (At the Edges of Thim); two free-verse narrative poems and two early plays. Wherever possible Ricard presents us with connecting threads in the artistic intent, form and content of these plays. Throughout, we are presented with a writer who is as comfortable with Brecht as he is with Kiswahili aesthetics and cultural idioms.

Hussein has translated one work of an Iranian writer and Ricard sees this as no accident. Hussein's choice of Samad Behrangi's *The Little Black Fish* is shown to fit Hussein's oeuvre since the text speaks of freedom and sacrifice as well as individual and collective reaping from past mistakes. His intellectual and artistic concerns, however, are shown to have been fuelled, for the most part, by African regional realities. A part of Tanzania's post-independence reality that informs Hussein's work, for example, is summarized in a 1995 poem in which Hussein laments a betrayed dream. Even though the title of the poem is *The Berlin Wall*, Ricard underlines its symbolic relevance to Tanzania. In the poem, Hussein speaks of a dreamed-of kingdom that could not materialise because it lacked solid foundations (pp. 141–2). It is a reality that Ricard sees as responsible for forcing Hussein to move from being a writer and performer who was also a political activist to a disillusioned, isolated poet. In all, Ricard succeeds in presenting Hussein as a complex man: victim, poet and writer of some of the best work to come out of Africa.

Ricard also reviews criticism of Hussein's plays, mostly by East African critics and academics. He sees this criticism as narrow and limited, and one tends to agree with him given the selected examples he cites. Ricard's dismissal of most Kiswahili criticism as presenting a misunderstanding of Hussein's work, however, may be a bit overstated and one may hope that it will generate debate. While some notions, including the vulgar Marxism embraced by some East African intellectuals from the late 1960s onwards, need to be interrogated, one cannot totally dismiss them. In the process of doing so, Ricard sometimes chooses not to engage in the complexities of East African reality generally and the Tanzanian one specifically. So much work has been done on Swahili history by both local and foreign scholars that one feels his book would have benefited from a more engaged discussion of Swahili culture, identity and performance aesthetics in a historical perspective.

Ricard shows us a Hussein who is a lone voice in a wilderness instead of a lead voice in a chorus, a voice whose virtuosity has been singular but not alone, therein finding greatness. This could be the result of certain assumptions that Ricard makes from the very beginning. This is exemplified in his postscript, where he questions Hussein's unjustified fear in leaving the country in spite of the political changes that have taken place. The issue might have been wrongly posed from the start, and the answer is therefore being looked for at the wrong place. Ricard displays a commanding knowledge of Kiswahili but the work has not come out of two translations unscathed. These, however, are issues that cannot detract from Ricard's success and achievement in bringing out this first book on the works of Ebrahim Hussein and broadening further our understanding of these works and their author. Even when ambiguous and complex, Ricard keeps our interest as we follow his analysis. Readers both familiar and unfamiliar with Hussein's work should find this book answering some questions and provoking others in many areas of art, individualism, politics and society.

Epics, wherever they have existed, have given us a glimpse into the sociopolitical, cultural and religious working of a society within a historical context. They encompass myths, legends and some events and personages whose reality is borne out by history. Because most epics have been sustained by and owe their survival to orality (before some were written down), the existence of several variations of the same epic has been the norm. The Great Lakes region of Central and Eastern Africa boasts several such epics, one of which is the epic of *Mugasha*. A familiar name in oral poetry and literature, folklore and heroic recitations, he is not only the revered deity of the waters of the rivers, lakes and seas but also a historical figure and legend told through versions which give different political meanings. For the first time the epic of *Mugasha* has been set in a play form.

In her *Mugasha: Epic of the Bahaya*, Nyambura Mpesha has combined versions of the *Mugasha* epic to create a play which for the most part follows some of the accepted exploits of this patron of fishermen and controller of the elements. Mpesha draws out a tale that is introduced by a narrator and goes on to include Mugasha's unusual and mysterious birth in exile, presented in one of the most interesting scenes of the play. We are, for the most part of the play, made to follow his journey to reclaim his kingdom and consolidate his power. Throughout, Mugasha's strength, cunning, his power over the elements and command over animate and inanimate things are highlighted as he uses them to eliminate his enemies and build the alliances he wants. The other characters are portrayed as no match for Mugasha and their opposition or victories are shown to be temporary, their end inevitable and anticipated. Mpesha's Mugasha, however, aims at reconciliation more than revenge, and thus the end is neatly tied up as all bow to Mugasha's power and his forgiveness of their past wrongs.

Adopting performance aesthetics of the region, Mpesha has incorporated Bahaya music and songs as signature tunes to events and characters. More than this, most of her characters speak in heroic recitation and poetry, with idioms of expression and imagery that make for lovely exchanges of dialogue but demand virtuosity in narrative performance skills. The play's structure is also more narrative than dramatic. Even though the writer has tried, unnecessarily, to simplify some of the events in the original versions of the epic to eliminate what she believes to be elements impossible to stage, the play presents a challenge to producers since the play's theatricality relies heavily on the presentation of Mugasha as possessing both human and superhuman attributes. Such a challenge should not intimidate: meeting it will be a tribute to Mpesha's unique contribution to African theatre.

Amandina Lihamba
Department of Fine and Performing Arts
University of Dar es Salaam

Terence Zeeman (ed.), *New Namibian Plays: Volume 1*
Windhoek: New Namibian Books, 2000, 304 pp.
ISBN 99916-31-73-9, N$69.67

A decade after formal independence in 1990, Namibia has finally witnessed the publication of the first English-language theatre texts: the collection under review and Dorian Haarhoff's *Goats, Oranges and Skeletons* (2000), also edited by Terence Zeeman. This meagre printed output, however, belies the country's actual performing arts scene which, in recent years, has made efforts to move away from imported (Western) stage commodities to a more local-style theatre.[1] 'This may be the first volume of plays *in text*', Zeeman (theatre scholar and one-time Executive Director of the National Theatre of Namibia (NTN)), asserts, 'but most of the contributors have been play *'wrights'* – *constructors and makers of plays* – for many years' (p. vii) – Boli Mootseng and Bricks Theatre Group (whose script was developed by Keamogetsi Joseph Molapong) being just two, and possibly the most long-standing, examples. Intent to put Namibia finally on the global 'African Drama' map, this collection comprises ten short plays representative of contemporary Namibian theatre. All plays were entries to the NTN's first Golden Pen Awards contest in 1998 and encompass the four award winners: *The Show Isn't Over Until...* by Vickson Tablah Hangula (Best Overall Play); *Die Stoel* (The Chair) by Kubbe Rispel (whose *The Cult* became Second Best); *Onele yo Kawe* (Place of Diamonds), a play for young people about diamond fishing and social injustice by Kay Cowley and Tanya Terblanche (Best Namibian Context); as well as Petrus Haakskeen's *Finder Keepers Losers Weepers* (Best Newcomer), a didactic dialogue between two banknotes, the Namibian hero Hendrik [Witbooi] Dollar and the South African Jan van [Riebeck] Rand. Namibian drama, this collection proves, has evidently shifted from clear-cut resistance plays in the liberation struggle to issues of internal power strife, both public and domestic, thus moving away from 'a remote, all-powerful, oppressive "*them*" to a more problematic and ambivalent "*us*" ' (p. x).

The texts can be grouped into loose thematic clusters – gender/domestic, public/political, social/communal – and as such read against each other. The somewhat misogynist, if at times acidly funny, *The Bride and the Broom* by Dawid Stone Ndjavera (a farce on the 'battle of the sexes') can be set against Maria Amakali's social comedy *Checkmate* (in which the women get their own back), or the sobering *A Moment in Our Lives* by Laurinda Olivier-Sampson (a play on domestic violence). While these plays might be called 'gender' or 'domestic' drama, Norman Job's *Mai Jekketti* (My Jacket), which falls under the latter category, makes a link to more overtly political plays by its usage of symbol and double meaning. Victor's life revolves around his obsession with the *jekketti* inherited from his father which prevents his personal growth. In Rispel's *Die Stoel*, it is a chair that turns into a powerful fetish for – and symbol of – the oppressive leadership and its final downfall. Conceived as an allegory, with stock characters such as the Leader, the Cleaner, the Tramp, *Die Stoel* relates to Namibia's present and apartheid past, but also speaks of the universal madness of power.

Power is, perhaps, the undercurrent of all of these plays, not the least in the 'real' (theatre) world where previously marginalised performers, mostly of African descent, 'must witness [a] relocation [to the centre of cultural reform] without being given the tools to negotiate terms themselves' (p. vi). *The Show Isn't Over ...*, the core and most ambitious piece of this collection, addresses this issue explicitly. Taking us into the rehearsal of a mixed-race theatre group, the play not only grapples with issues of authority beyond those within the company, it also addresses the state of the arts – or, better, the role of the arts in the state – by voicing the group's concern with the play's patent criticism of the current regime. The Director's words that they would dare to go ahead, even if '[n]obody would want to be associated with a play that is critical of the Government' (p. 36), become prophetic in the light of the actual performance history of Hangula's play. After a promising start, it was 'refused funding to enable participation in the Market Theatre Laboratory Community Festival in May 1999 on the grounds that it contained 'anti-Swapo and anti-Government propaganda'' (p. viii). Hangula's Director is right after all when he claims that 'acting is for real' (p. 20).

The intricate connection between play-acting and reality is not only expressed in Zeeman's perceptive preface (see also Zeeman article above), but also mirrored in the group of works which I tentatively want to call 'social' and 'community' drama. Boli Mootseng's *Social Avenue*, for example, attempts to reflect the 'forces of postmodernity that ravage communities worldwide' (p. 250) by depicting a community's crisis in search for a telephone. Written in seemingly fragmented scenes with extensive setting descriptions – stage directions being the wrong term – it reads more like a filmscript than a play for the stage. The issues addressed, however, correspond to those of my personal favourite, *The Horizon is Calling*, by Bricks Theatre Collective/Molapong. The only workshopped theatre text apart from *Onele yo Kawe*, it bespeaks Bricks' long-standing engagement with community mobilisation and is probably the play that draws most directly on people's experiences. Principally concerned with the desperate employment situation of high school graduates – exemplified in the protagonist Moseb, but echoed and amplified by further roles – it also touches on other issues, such as teenage pregnancy, important for 'the rising number of young people trying to make sense out of our lives' (p. 200). That the original cast acted characters with forenames corresponding to their own again suggests an overlapping of play and actual present. If, as Zeeman propounds, actors become 'agent[s] for change', and playwrights 'locator[s] of the coordinates of the stages of our lives and the encoder[s] of human action' (p. x), then perhaps it is in community plays of this kind that a great part of the country's theatrical future lies.

This collection is an important milestone in the 'wrighting' of theatre in Namibia and is profitable for scholars and practitioner alike. Zeeman aptly maps out the broader theatre geography with reference to these texts and raises questions of general theatrical importance. His prime audience, however, seems to be inside rather than outside Namibia. Neither his preface nor the blurb specify the entry guidelines for the competition; and short biographical entries on the contributors and their work might have been illuminating to newcomers to Namibian theatre, who, in all likelihood, comprise the majority of this journal's readers, including myself. It is notable that most plays are written in English – the official language since independence, though the mother tongue of few – with Afrikaans plays being made available in both the original and an English translation. Switching between the two languages is frequent, but one wonders what happened to the many other, especially African, languages spoken in Namibia. Apart from the odd phrase or two, they are conspicuous for their absence. An implicit relegation to the so-called 'traditional' performing arts – of which we learn nothing in this collection – does not seem to do justice to the country's theatrical activities. It also raises the question whether dialogue drama and long-standing performing forms are seen as rigidly separate or whether they occasionally meet. It is striking that, with the exception of *Onele yo Kawe*, none of the plays draws on more physical performance forms as witnessed, for example, in South Africa, and this calls for an explanation.

Quibbles aside, this collection has finally cleared the road for actors, academics and activists to get access to theatre in Namibia and is therefore to be commended.

NOTE

1 For further information see Terence Zeeman and Dorian Haarhoff, 'Namibia', in Don Rubin, Ousmane Diakhaté and Hansel Ndumbe Eyoh (eds), *The World Encyclopedia of Contemporary Theatre: Africa* (London: Routledge, 2001 [1997]), pp. 206–11; and Kees Epskamp, 'Playing in a Sandpit: International Popular Theatre Meeting in Namibia', *Southern African Theatre Journal*, 7, 1 (1993): 7–15.

Christine Matzke
Humboldt University, Berlin

Kofi Anyidoho and James Gibbs (eds), *FonTomFrom: Contemporary Ghanaian Literature, Theater and Film*
Special issue of *Matutu: Journal for African Culture and Society*, 5, 21–22. Amsterdam and Atlanta, GA: Editions Rodopi, 2000, 400 pp.
HB ISBN 90-420-1283-8, US$85; PB ISBN 90-420-1486-5, US$28

This special edition of the journal *Matutu*, dedicated to the arts of Ghana, takes its name from a stately Akan court dance and drum. Gracing the cover is a photograph of this ceremonial drum, enormous and spectacularly carved. In its centre, underscored with the word 'culture,' is the image of a bird looking backwards. This is the Akan *sankofa* figure which evokes the proverbial understanding that one must return to the past in order to move forward. Editor Kofi Anyidoho reads this Akan bird as a guiding metaphor of Ghana's cultural landscape. Like many of Ghana's poets, playwrights, film-makers, and journalists, the *sankofa* bird is 'reaching back into the past even as it flies sky-bound into a future of great expectations' (p. 5). So too does this volume cast a retrospective view over Ghana's national arts scene while assessing the challenges of the present.

The strengths of *FonTomFrom* are many. Simply bringing together such a wide variety of articles all focused on Ghanaian culture creates exciting cross-disciplinary connections. Topics range from literary drama, theatre history and choreography to poetry, novels, shorts stories, and journalism. There is also impressive coverage of Ghana's feature video industry, a burgeoning new area of popular culture. E. Sutherland-Addy takes stock of the whole 'Ghana film' phenomenon, while Africanus Aveh provides a useful and detailed filmography. Nearly half of the articles are focused on theatre and performance, with the majority of these dedicated to pioneer writer Efua Sutherland, who died in 1996 and to whom *FonTomFrom* is dedicated. Reprinted here is Sutherland's influential essay on the National Theatre Movement of Ghana, first published in 1965. In addition to a biographical sketch, Kofi Anyidoho offers a passion-ate, lyrical tribute to Ghana's 'Mother Courage', Madame Efua. Anne Adams works comparatively to examine Sutherland's use of ritual in relation to other African writers, while James Gibbs ensures that future scholars will understand the full range of Sutherland's oeuvre. Gibbs provides an extensive bibliography of primary materials and a checklist of secondary sources. And while much has been written by and about Sutherland, *FonTomFrom* still manages to bring us something new: a previously unpub-lished play entitled 'Children of the Man-Made Lake'.

Efua Sutherland's death, her passage to the land of the ancestors, functions in this volume as an occasion for remembering. Contributions on Sutherland form a sort of extended libation in her honour, summoning her spirit to grace the affairs of the living. For many, Sutherland's legacy towers over current endeavours, such as the National Theatre and Pan-African Historical Theatre Festival that she first envisioned. Addressing ancestor 'Auntie Efua' directly, Anyidoho pleads, 'we are doing our best to put back on the festival drama you all composed at the dawn of our nation's birth. We are doing our very best. But there are technical problems with our grand design: Your vision created so many parts for Giants. All the original cast is gone. And we are stuck with a Dwarf Brigade' (p. 84). The *sankofa* bird is looking backwards, even as it tries to move forwards.

While grand spirits of the past may loom, *FonTomFrom* provides evidence that Ghana's current generation of artists is nevertheless busily going about its work, making movies, writing novels, and creating theatre. *FonTomFrom* not only looks at the literary legacy of long-established writers such as Ayi Kwei Armah and Ama Ata Aidoo, but also includes analysis of recent poetry by Kofi Anyidoho and Kojo Laing. The volume contains nine creative writing samples, among them pieces by Abena Busia and Kwabwo Opoku-Agyeman, as well as five interviews with writers and filmmakers. What is particularly unusual for a volume devoted to the arts is *FonTomFrom's* coverage of journalism and the media. In addition to an interview with Kwaku Sakyi-Addo, the Acting Editor-in-Chief of the popular *Ghanaian Chronicle*, there are entries on book publishing, the role of print and non-print media in the development of Ghanaian writers, and copyright issues.

What emerges from this special edition of *Matutu* is a complex and multi-faceted portrait of cultural production in one African country: a reflection on contemporary Ghanaian culture written largely by Ghanaian authors (whose addresses, most helpfully, have been provided at the back of the volume). Editor Kofi Anyidoho admits that *FonTomFrom's* portrayal of Ghanaian culture is partial, at best, 'with an obvious emphasis on written literature' (p. 18). There is very little treatment of oral literature, or literature in African languages. Kwesi Yankah's contribution is an exception here: his article examines how the musician Nana Kwame Ampadu uses the sung tale as metaphor for protest discourse. Curiously absent is anything but a passing mention of the Concert Party, a type of theatre that has experienced a tremendous revival in the past six years through the National Theatre. Concert Party shows in the National Theatre series are taped by GBC and broadcast regularly throughout the country, and this programme has been one of the most avidly watched in recent times. Nor does this volume provide a clear picture of who are Ghana's up-and-coming new playwrights. Kofi Anyidoho laments to the spirit of Efua Sutherland that this generation is but a 'Dwarf Brigade'. But *who* are the dwarves? Puzzling too is the absence of any extended reflection on the meaning of *FonTomFrom*, the volume's title. Readers may find meaning indirectly, in the highly structured and formal nature of the court dance of the same name. Brave commoners may enter the dance arena only by obeying strict rules. They must dance barefoot, with their shoulders exposed, and with careful observation and deference to the drummers. This special edition of *Matutu* seems to share the ceremonial drum's formality and privileging of high culture. Yet *FonTomFrom's* coverage of contemporary Ghanaian literature, theatre and film – however partial – is dynamic and engaging. This volume will be of great interest to scholars of African literature, West African theatre and video, and anyone who writes on, travels to, or studies the country of Ghana.

Catherine Cole
University of California, Santa Barbara

Biodun Jeyifo (ed.), *Perspectives on Wole Soyinka: Freedom and Complexity*
Jackson, Mississippi: University of Mississippi Press, 2001, 264 pp
HB ISBN 1-57806-335-3, US$46.00

Biodun Jeyifo (ed.), *Conversations with Wole Soyinka*
Jackson, Mississippi: University of Mississippi Press, 2001, 256 pp
HB ISBN 1-57806-337-X, US$46.00; PB ISBN 1-57806-338-8, US$18.00

This collection of essays on Wole Soyinka is significant for a number of reasons. First, it parades the very cream of recent critical opinions on a writer about whom such distinguished commentary has never been lacking. Second, it is edited by a scholar who is one of the most respected authorities on Soyinka, a qualification nourished and sustained by decades of 'transition' through changing roles and relationships with the 1986 Nobel prize winner. Selecting essays on a writer of Soyinka's stature must be an extremely daunting task; compiling a mere fourteen essays on Wole Soyinka would be presumptuous in any editor lacking Jeyifo's credentials. James Gibbs did it – successfully – two decades earlier (twenty-eight essays in all), but that was probably because, in 1980, Soyinka was still in many ways a case of original genius waiting to be proved to the larger world. Gibbs and other earlier editors and annotators (and hagiographers!) did a lot then to lend prestige and coherence to the enormous amount of work that had gone on on Soyinka for almost two decades previously.

It is inevitable that Jeyifo's volume will invite comparison with Gibbs's *Critical Perspectives on Wole Soyinka*. The new collection features three essays – each of them a *locus classicus* in Soyinka criticism – from Gibbs's volume. Abiola Irele's 'Tradition and the Yoruba Writer', Stanley Macebuh's 'Poetics and the Mythic Imagination' and Annemarie Heywood's 'The Fox's Dance', are clearly intended as homage to earlier criticism on Soyinka. The second is by Nigeria's most accomplished rhetorician (and is one of this reviewer's favourite essays). It shares pride of place with Soyinka's own 'Neo-Tarzanism...' as a response to the initial sally by the authors of *Toward the Decolonisation of African Literature*. Nonetheless, it is a controversial judgement to prefer it in a new volume to Dan Izevbaye's 'Soyinka's Black Orpheus', which is only matched in the weight and quality of its exegesis and disciplined encyclopaedic insight into Soyinka's oeuvre by Irele's 'Tradition and the Yoruba Writer'. The case for its exclusion from Jeyifo's volume is not made (the editor does not say it is) by Soyinka's disagreement in his interview with John Agetua with the paper's claims on the switch from the Dionysian to the Orphean motif in the works of Soyinka's post-incarceration period. Niyi Osundare's 'Wole Soyinka and the Atunda Ideal' is a welcome example of an essay that *theorizes* Soyinka on the writer's own terms.

Jeyifo's preferences may point to a narrow collective of 'names' and associates, but this need not distress anyone. The challenge to put together 'a special collection' of 'truly insightful, landmark essays' on Soyinka will continue to inspire editors and compilers for decades to come. The thunder may have been stolen from Jeyifo's attempt in this regard by Adewale Maja-Pearce's *Wole Soyinka: an Appraisal* (1994) which, if taken along with Gibbs's *Critical Perspectives*, pushes the count to six out of the fourteen essays in the new collection. It is curious that no editorial mention is made of these two earlier compilers, just as there is no attention to essays that address continuities in Soyinka criticism, especially in the contributions written in the post-Gibbs phase. The title of the editor's introduction has a soundbite on postcolonial discourse (and there is Kwame Anthony Appiah's essay to show for it, not to mention the inimitable Wilson Harris). But the larger question is simply that postcolonial theory has not found a ready handmaiden in Soyinka for some of the cut-and-dried binary oppositions upheld by that school of criticism. The point came up for some attention at the 2001 conference on Soyinka at the University of Toronto. It would have been interesting to see essays in this new collection that consciously try to make the transition from the 'old', monocular Soyinka criticism to the postcolonial and 'global' view.

Brian Crow's essay, 'Soyinka and his Radical Critics' surveys the bumpy terrain of the great debates of the 1970s and the 1980s between Soyinka and Nigerian 'leftist' critics led by Jeyifo himself. Crow's summaries lean quite heavily on Jeyifo's flagstaff positions and lend an impression of elegance and overall coherence to the tradition of radical criticism in Nigeria, but that is false. It is easy to exaggerate the claims of Nigerian Marxist literary criticism, especially in relation to Soyinka's post-civil war career. Too often the integrity of intellectual positions was marred by coterie scholarship, reductionism, *carte blanche* endorsements of positions and figures whose standpoints even at the best of times only added to the force of numbers. The editor prefers to include his own brilliant and wide-ranging introduction to the important collection of essays by Soyinka, *Art, Dialogue and Outrage* (1988), which he also edited. If he wanted he could have chosen either of two major statements on the dramatist from his own original volume, *The Truthful Lie: Essays in a Sociology of Nigerian Drama* (1985). In addition to its forensic merits, the introduction to *Art, Dialogue and Outrage* courts a different, more conciliatory language in engaging with Soyinka's career; its rhetorical frame of mind moves on to something close to its perfection in the new, laid-back, dulcet-toned introduction to the edited collection under review. But neither introduction really *documents* the combative and acerbic Jeyifo of the Nigerian leftist tradition.

There are several jewels in the crown of the collection. Three of those attempt comparative studies of Soyinka and other major figures. Wilson Harris's 'The Complexity of Freedom' reads *The Road* against *Heart of Darkness*. Philip Brockbank's 'Blood and Wine: Tragic Ritual from Aeschylus to Soyinka' and Joachim Fiebach's 'Wole Soyinka and Heine Muller' follow a similar pattern. Brockbank may be familiar for his edition of *Coriolanus*, with an introduction that must rank as one of the finest; Fiebach will awe many by the firm control of his materialist reading of Soyinka. The two contributions illustrate that a strong essay will very often grow from a thorough grounding in the *verities* of a literary tradition, so that even its departures and rebellions do not always come tainted with the blood of precursors. Ato Quayson's contribution is in this sense an excursus on the matter of Irele's essay, just as his book from which the contribution derives is largely a study of tradition and the Yoruba writer. 'Wole Soyinka and the Living Dramatist' is both a homage to a mentor and an advertisement for savvy and style by Femi Osofisan, who deserves a lot more attention as a master of expository prose.

Soyinka is one of those writers whose dual location as writer–critic helps in illuminating several aspects of the creative process. An interview with the dramatist also almost invariably comes with the additional input from his activist role in the politics of Nigeria. *Conversations with Wole Soyinka*, Jeyifo's companion volume to *Perspectives...*, is both a triumph and something of a let down in this regard. On the one hand some of the more recent interviews document Soyinka's travails with the different Nigerian governments. In a country where one political outrage tends to drag the next in tow, it is so easy to forget or downplay the historic location of individuals and figures on the Nigerian political landscape whose voices and moral dissent have always made a difference. The several interviews touch on politics, commitment and the relationship between 'art, dialogue and outrage', and help to document the particular encounters of the best known of Nigeria's small but unique breed of political activists (Gani Fawehinmi and the late Tai Solarin being the notable others). They also bookmark the restlessness of a mind in motion and in stress. Soyinka's shuttle in the loom of Nigerian life weaves art and politics into one near-seamless web.

On the other hand few of the 'literary' interviews seem to elicit enough from the writer, because they seem to be preoccupied with questions which have been making the rounds since the 1960s. Jeyifo's (along with the evergreen Agetua's) is arguably the best because the most pointed and sophisticated, but it wouldn't have hurt the book's project to conduct a special session with the writer at which the quality of the editor's short interview with Soyinka might have been permitted an extended run. Several of the interviews were probably conducted after the writer had just concluded a public engagement (a lecture, a public appearance or an airport arrival). Cornering a busy person for significant utterances will always incur predictable deficits, and few of the interviews scratch the surface of what might be got in the quality of literary opinion from a distinguished mind.

Typos litter both books and the reviewer's copy of the first is missing 32 pages. Osofisan, Osundare and Quayson had to be read from their original sources. But this detracts nothing from Jeyifo's commanding presence in his introductions, rich in privileged information and insight, which confidently nudge into rarefied zones of critical perception a long way from the ideological contestations of the Nigerian leftist phase.

Titi Adepitan
Department of English
University of British Columbia

Brief reviews and books received

From the **African Books Collective**
The following books may all be obtained directly from the African Books Collective at Unit 13, Kings Meadow, Ferry Hinksey Rd, Oxford OX2 0DP, UK

J.P. Clark, *All For Oil*, Lagos: Malthouse Press, 2000, 68 pp., ISBN 978 023 132 3, £4.95/$8.95.
This is Clark's first internationally published play since the 1983 *Bikoroa Plays* (an historical trilogy that deserves more attention than it has been given) and was performed at various venues in Nigeria in 2000 under the direction of Dapo Adelugba. The oil of the title is both the palm oil that brought traders (and colonialism) to Nigeria and the oil that today pollutes the lands of the Niger Delta. Clark's clever play, centred round generations of his own family, is an historical and contemporary parable about destructive forces.

Pierre Meunier, *The Comedy of Marriages*, 1999, 108 pp., ISBN 978 029 076 1, £4.95/$8.95, and *Zumji and Uchenna*, 1999, 45 pp., ISBN 978 029 069 9, £3.95/$6.95, both published by Spectrum Books, Ibadan. Two simple lively plays, the first a rumbustious comedy concerning lecherous old men in pursuit of young girls, the second a melodramatic love story showing the destructiveness of tribalism.

Tess Osonye Onwueme, *Then She Said It*, San Francisco and Lagos: African Heritage Press, 2002, 116 pp., ISBN 096 288 642 4, £8.95/$14.95. Another epic play from the prolific pen of Africa's leading woman playwright. This is an allegorical drama concerning the plight of the poor and the persecuted in their fight against the forces of multinational capitalism and a corrupt state. The fictional setting, 'Hungeria', is a thin disguise. The play has been staged in Nigeria: the critic of the Lagos *Guardian* observes that 'were it to be staged during the military era, the playwright, cast and crew would have successfully booked themselves a place in some detention camps that dotted the length and breadth of this country'.

Ola Rotimi, *Akassa You Mi*, Port Harcourt: Onyoma Research Publications and University of Port Harcourt Press, 2001, 134 pp., ISBN 978 232 115 X, £7.95/$13.95. This fine historical drama is a fitting tribute to the huge theatrical talent of the late – and greatly missed – Ola Rotimi. The play had its premiere in 1977 and has existed since then in memory and various reworked manuscripts, culminating in a final version in

1995 which forms the published text. Rotimi's historical dramas have ingeniously and informatively 'revised' many events in precolonial and colonial Nigeria, and *Akassa You Mi*, dealing with events in 1895 when the Nembe people attacked premises of the Royal Niger Company at Akassa, again challenges the official record and brings to life the courage and frustration of people whose culture is being undermined. As ever, Rotimi creates a drama that is theatrically exciting and widely relevant, bringing to the anonymity of history the real experience of the human beings involved. In a letter to the present reviewer in 1996, Rotimi wrote 'it talks to the condition of [Nigeria] TODAY'. The publishers are to be thanked for bringing out this play now; it is a reminder of the power of one of Africa's greatest dramatic artists. When will an international publisher bring out a collection of Rotimi's plays? It is high time.

Mary E. Modupe Kolawole (ed.), *Zulu Sofola: Her Life and Works*, Ibadan: Caltop Publications, 1999, 95pp., ISBN 978 331 879 9, £6.95/$11.95. A collection of nine essays dealing with the life and work of the late Nigerian playwright, described as 'a foremother of African creative writing'.

Other books received

Plays

Ade-Yemi Ajibade, *Parcel Post/Behind the Mountain*, 2001, 147 pp., ISBN 978 2659 89 4, no price, and *Fingers Only/A Man Named Mokai*, 2001,142 pp., ISBN 978 2659 88 6, no price, both published by Y-Books, Ibadan. These are lively and effective plays. *Parcel Post* is a witty domestic comedy set among Nigerian expatriates in London, distinguished by good dialogue, an energetic narrative and convincing characterisation – thematically wise and observant without being profound. *Behind the Mountain* (written for the University of Ibadan Travelling Theatre and therefore having a didactic as well as an entertainment role) tells the story of a young man bound into a medicine/healing cult who is frustrated by poverty in the city and attempts to establish himself back in his own community but who falls prey to the temptation of corruption. *Fingers Only* is set in Nigeria during the 1939–45 war and is a splendid and quite complex comedy about a group of vagabonds who use their tricksters' skills to steal a living. A short and very 'playable' play, this illustrates Ajibade's confident craftsmanship and sound theatrical instinct. *A Man Named Mokai* is a powerful commentary on the brutality of Nigeria's military coups and the activities of evangelistic movements, mixing satire with social commentary. Four good plays by an assured playwright.

Philip Begho, *Power of Lions*, Lagos: Monarch Books, 2001, 98 pp., ISBN 978 32224 1 4, no price. A re-creation of the biblical story of Daniel in the Lions' Den.

Femi Euba, *The Gulf*, Ikeja: Longman Nigeria, 1991, 76pp., ISBN 978 139 638 5, no price. This play by the distinguished Nigerian actor is a work of considerable storytelling skill and power. A young investigative reporter tries to solve the mystery of the destruction of a passenger bus on one of Nigeria's dangerous roads and meets an African-American woman searching for her culture. Metaphorically the play explores their roots and relationship.

A. B. Odaga, *Something For Nothing*, Kisumu: Lake Publishers, 2001, 60 pp., ISBN 9966 847 86 3, no price. A campaigning play centred on the plight of women facing decadence and corruption, from a playwright who is Chair of the Gender and Development Centre in Kisumu, Western Kenya.

Femi Osofisan, *Restless Breed*, 2002, 134 pp., ISBN 978 36136 0 X, no price, and *Seasons of Wrath*, 2002, 144 pp., ISBN 978 36136 1 8, no price, both published by Opon Ifa Readers, Ibadan. Two collections of short plays by *African Theatre*'s co-editor, the distinguished Nigerian playwright. *Restless Breed* contains *A Restless Run of Locusts*, *The Oriki of a Grasshopper*, *No More the Wasted Breed* and *Birthdays are not for Dying*, and *Seasons of Wrath* contains *Altine's Wrath*, *The Engagement*, *The Inspector and the Hero*, *Flood!* and *Fires Burn and Die Hard*. These are amongst the most popular plays of this prolific playwright and are greatly to be welcomed in these accessible editions.

Play collections

Biodun Jeyifo (ed.), *Modern African Drama*, New York: W.W. Norton and Co., 2002, 646 pp., ISBN 0 393 97529 0 (paperback), no price. This volume in the Norton Critical Editions is of great value to teachers, students and the general reader. The renowned critic Biodun Jeyifo offers eight plays from the African theatre, ranging from Tewfik al-Hakim's *Fate of a Cockroach* (Egypt) to Osofisan's *Esu and the Vagabond Minstrels* (Nigeria), with other plays from South Africa, Algeria, Ethiopia, Kenya, Ghana and Nigeria. Jeyifo prefaces the plays with a brief but informative contextualising essay and footlights them with a brilliant selection of critical essays on both general and specific topics from a range of the best of critics – amongst them Frantz Fanon, Wole Soyinka, Joachim Fiebach and David Kerr. Each play has its own set of authoritative and stimulating accompanying critical comments, and the volume concludes with a chronology of African drama and a helpful bibliography. This is a thoughtfully selected and edited 'reader' and is likely to be widely adopted for teaching purposes as well as being an excellent stand-alone source of play texts and reference.

Helen Gilbert (ed.), *Postcolonial Plays: an Anthology*, London: Routledge, 2001, 469 pp., ISBN 0 414 16449 4 (paperback), £18.99. As its title implies, this collection is concerned with more than Africa, but includes plays by Maponya, Jane Taylor (*Ubu and the Truth Commission*), Soyinka, Osofisan, and Aidoo, each play prefaced by a brief critical introduction and bibliography. The collection is especially interesting in bringing together, and allowing comparison to be made between, plays from many parts of the anglophone postcolonial world, including the West Indies, Canada, India, South East Asia, Australasia and – perceptively – Northern Ireland.

Criticism

Austin Asagba (ed.), *Cross Currents in African Theatre*, Benin: Osasu Publishers, 2001, 306 pp., ISBN 978 2979 10 4, no price. The essays collected here are mainly concerned with West African – and predominantly Nigerian – theatre and were presented at a conference on 'The Political Imperative in African Dramaturgy and Theatre Practice' at the University of Benin in 1990. This is lively and varied material, with some established critics (Femi Osofisan, Ahmed Yerima, Dele Layiwola and others) as well as many fresh and welcome voices. The collection shows the vigour of the debate concerning the role and function of theatre in Africa, and the enthusiasm of many younger scholars to challenge their elders!

Duro Oni and Sunday Enessi Ododo (eds), *Larger Than His Frame: Critical Studies and Reflections on Olu Obafemi,* Lagos: Centre for Black and African Arts and Civilization, 2000, 350 pp., ISBN 978 039 024 3, no price. These essays are gathered together to honour Olu Obafemi's fiftieth birthday. All of them discuss aspects of Obafemi's creative and critical work, reminding us of the ingenuity and richness of his playwriting and his bravery in speaking out, through his plays and his teaching, against the oppressive forces that have dominated so many of his adult years in Nigeria. Obafemi's plays deserve to be much better known than they are outside Nigeria: within Nigeria the respect and affection in which he is held is manifest in this excellent collection.

Femi Osofisan, *Literature and the Pressures of Freedom,* 2001, 198 pp., ISBN 978 33259 7 3, no price, and *Insidious Treasons: Drama in a Postcolonial State,* 2001, 256 pp., ISBN 978 33259 6 5, no price, both published by Opon Ifa Publishers, Ibadan. We know our colleague Femi Osofisan not only as a playwright, but also as a lively and provocative critic. These two volumes bring together lectures and addresses – and the odd song – given at a range of international venues. There is no better commentator on contemporary Nigerian theatre, its personalities, politics and practice.

Ahmed Yerima and Ayo Akinwale (eds), *Theatre and Democracy in Nigeria,* Ibadan: Kraft Books, 2002, 258 pp., ISBN 978 039 053 7, no price. These 23 essays were gathered from the convention of the Society of Nigerian Theatre Artists (SONTA) held in Ilorin in 2000. The title of the collection reminds us of the crucial role theatre plays in Nigeria, and elsewhere in Africa, in challenging oppression and corruption, often at great cost to the theatre practitioners themselves.(Can you imagine a collection with 'Great Britain' rather than Nigeria in its title?) The collection may be variable but the debate is always relevant and lively.

Miscellaneous

Ulli Beier, *The Hunter Thinks the Monkey is Not Wise,* Bayreuth: Bayreuth African Studies 59, 2001, 230 pp., ISBN 3 927510 71 8, DM 44.95/€ 21.99. This is a selection of Beier's essays carefully edited and introduced by Wole Ogundele. There is only one specifically on theatre – a wonderful memoir of E. K. Ogunmola, but the collection remains a delight and, as ever with Beier, an education on the Yoruba world.

Akin Euba, *Chaka: an Opera in Two Chants.* CD from The Music Research Institute, PO Box 70362, Point Richmond, CA 94807-0362, USA, 1995. Akin Euba's opera, from Senghor's epic poem, is a wonderful work. Euba describes his music as 'not entirely African, not entirely Western, but a marriage of the two'. This is a powerful, lyrical and entirely engaging work that the composer has been developing in various forms for several decades. It is highly recommended as a fine example of serious musical theatre.

Theatre Research International, 27, 3 (October 2002), IFTR/Cambridge University Press, is devoted to theatre and performance in South Africa.

Anglophonia: French Journal of English Studies (2000), ISBN 2 85816 505 X. This volume, entitled *Seuils/Thresholds*, brings together papers presented at the first conference on Anglophone African Literature to be held at the University of Toulouse-Le Mirail (February 1999). The conference coincided with the award to Niyi Osundare of an honorary doctorate by the university, and some of the essays focus on his work. Other papers include Wole Soyinka on 'Exile', Biodun Jeyifo on 'Colonialism and Modernity', Chris Dunton on *Moonshine Solidarity* by Tunde Lakoju, Anne Fuchs on 'South African Storytelling and Drama', Kacke Götrick on 'Rituality and Liminality' in *The Road* and *Death and the King's Horseman*, Geoff V. Davis on 'Innovation and Reorientation in Post-Apartheid South African Drama', and Richard Samin on Zakes Mda's *Ways of Dying*. Abiola Irele's 'Second Language Literatures: an African Perspective' provides a fitting introduction to the volume.

Martin Banham

Index

AFRICAN LITERATURE TODAY
James Currey Publishers & Africa World Press

After more than 30 years Eldred Durosimi Jones has retired from the editorship of *African Literature Today*. The announcement that Ernest N. Emenyonu has taken on the editorship has been widely welcomed:

'A very good omen for African Literature' – Wole Soyinka

'It is a most appropriate and logical development, and a very happy event for African literature.' – Chinua Achebe

'African Literature Today *is part of the tradition from the Alan Hill, Keith Sambrook & James Currey days...Eldred performed wonders for African literature & literary scholarship with it...I cannot think of a better successor to him than Ernest Emenyonu...the time has come for us to do a Nigerian edition.'* – Aigboje Higo, Heinemann Nigeria

Editor: Ernest N. Emenyonu
Assistant Editor: Patricia T. Emenyonu
Associate Editors: Simon Gikandi, Francis Imbuga, Nnadozie Inyama, Emmanuel Ngara, Charles Nnolim, Ato Quayson, Nana Wilson-Tagoe
Reviews Editor: James Gibbs

IN PRODUCTION
ALT 24 *New Women's Writing in African Literature*

CONTRIBUTIONS ARE INVITED FOR FORTHCOMING TITLES

ALT 25 *New Directions in African Literature*
ALT 26 *War in African Literature*
ALT 27 *New Novels in African Literature*

Articles should not exceed 5,000 words and should be submitted double-spaced on hard copy and disk to:
Ernest N. Emenyonu, Department of Africana Studies
University of Michigan-Flint
303 East Kearsley Street, Flint, MI 48502, USA
email: eernest@umflint.edu

Books for review and review material to:
James Gibbs, 8 Victoria Square, Bristol BS8 4ET
email: james.gibbs@uwe.ac.uk

BACKLIST TITLES ALSO AVAILABLE
ALT 15 Women in African Literature Today
ALT 16 Oral & Written Poetry in African Literature Today
ALT 17 The Question of Language in African Literature Today
ALT 18 Orature in African Literature Today
ALT 19 Critical Theory & African Literature Today
ALT 20 New Trends & Generations in African Literature
ALT 21 Childhood in African Literature
ALT 22 Exile & African Literature
ALT 23 South & Southern African Literature

James Currey Publishers 73 Botley Rd, Oxford OX2 0BS, UK   www.jamescurrey.co.uk

Africa World Press PO Box 1892, Trenton, NJ 08607, USA   www.africanworld.com